THE GUYS-ONLY GUIDE™ TO

GETTING OVER DIVORCE

and on with LIFE, SEX, and RELATIONSHIPS

SAM J. BUSER • GLENN F. STERNES

Bayou Publishing

HOUSTON, TX

Editing: Jennifer Schaffer & Erica Forster
Back Cover Copywritng: Susan Kendrick—Susan Kendrick Writing
Cover Design: George Foster—Foster & Associates
Printing: Green Button, Inc.
Author Photographs: Stacy Bratton Photography & Sandy Wilson Photography

Printed in the United States of America
First Edition 10 9 8 7 6 5 4 3 2 1

Cataloging-in-Publication Data Available

Published by Bayou Publishing
2524 Nottingham • Houston, TX 77005-1412
713-526-4558 • http://www.bayoupublishing.com

ADVANCED READER COPY

Uncorrected Galley

CONTENTS

DEDICATION

I (SJB) would like to dedicate this book to two men that I wished could have read it. First, I think of my father, who didn't have a clue about how to do either marriage or divorce. Perhaps, he would have found this book useful. Secondly, and more painfully for me, I dedicate this book to my brother, Joe, who went through three agonizing divorces and was on the verge of a fourth at the time of his death. My brother, like our father, never quite figured out how to live comfortably in marriage, to find the right woman, or to divorce with dignity and hope for the future. This book might have helped him. He was also a writer, and I know that he would be pleased for me with this book's publication. I have often wished for his counsel when stuck searching for a phrase. As I write this, I am looking at a picture of him working at his desk on one of his own publications. Thanks, Joe.

Sam J. Buser, Ph.D.

In the writing of this book, I (GFS) would like to honor my three families. My father, Dr. Frank C. Sternes, taught me that the world can be safe and trusting, and that learning is a good thing. My mother, Lillian Korecky Sternes, taught me kindness and compassion. Both taught me the love of music and travel, and we spent one summer in Europe together while I was in high school. They were killed in a plane crash, together with my maternal grandmother, less than a year later.

My second family was my mother's sister, Adeline Korecky, who took over after my parents' deaths—only later did I understand her sacrifice. When I was in college, she married George C. La Bree. From "Auntie" I learned a sense of fair play and assertiveness, and from George, I learned how important an easygoing nature was when dealing with step-children.

My third family consists of my wife, Yvonne, and children, Matt, Katie, and Krista. From them I learned about giving love and moving away from being self-centered. While some times as a husband and parent, I may be reminded of the Biblical phrase "long-suffering", they may remind me that my work as a husband, father and step-father is not yet completed, and that I am still in the learning-role. I give my love to them all.

Glenn F. Sternes, Ph.D.

ACKNOWLEDGMENTS

The authors would like to acknowledge the help of numerous people who enabled us to complete this work. First, we want to thank our families who gave us encouragement and were tolerant of the many hours that we devoted to producing this book. Secondly, we want to thank Dr. Victor Loos of Bayou Publishing for his patience and assistance in producing the finished work. We also want to thank family attorneys Judy and Jim Dougherty for their help in understanding the legal challenges faced by men who go through a divorce. They have been steadfast friends and a constant source of compassionate guidance to the men we have referred to them for assistance in times of figurative and literal trial. We would like to thank Dr. George Dempsey who made an interesting presentation at the Texas Psychological Association on how to write a book in just 28 days. George's enthusiasm about the writing process inspired us to give it a try. Just as he predicted, 28 days (make that 28 months) later our book was published. Glenn and I began as acquaintances after that seminar with an idea about a book. Through the months we have become close friends, a nice bonus. Furthermore, we are very indebted to the many men whom we have been privileged to serve through our work as psychologists. The practice of psychology is always an interactive process whereby both the psychologist and the client are changed. We are grateful for the many things we have learned from these men. Finally, we want to acknowledge the "bees" from the men's retreat at Esalen Institute in January 2008. Their zeal in making suggestions for our book was vital as we sough to bring this project to "blossom."

M

Is this book for me?

So she told you she wanted a divorce. Of course you had heard that a million times. But this time, she really meant it. Maybe you're one of those guys who came home to find her gone already. Perhaps, you found an empty house with only a "Dear John" letter lying on the bed—if you still had a bed. Or maybe while you were at the office some stranger handed you some papers to notify you that you had been "served."

Or maybe, *you* were the one who decided the marriage had to end. Perhaps you reluctantly came to the conclusion that you just couldn't live with her anymore.

Either way, the questions pop up: "What happens now? What should I do? Is there any chance she'll change her mind? Would I want her back? Should I start dating? Can I find another woman, and would she be a better wife? Will I ever be happy again...and, oh yeah, what about my kids?" There are so many questions.

This book is for men who are in the process of going through or recovering from a divorce. Whether she moved out today, you just left the courtroom after the final hearing, or you have been divorced awhile and are already dating, this book will help you make the decisions and do the things that will make life after divorce better. Sure, you could do this without help, but you might avoid a few potholes if you are willing to hear some suggestions. We have been with hundreds of men going through divorce, just like you. We know the kinds of questions you may be having, and we know how guys usually get themselves into trouble around divorce.

This book is arranged in a question and answer format reflecting the most important questions men ask about divorce and recovery as well as the questions they *should* ask. Think of the book as the kind of advice that a psychologist would give you about coping with a divorce. Of course, the book does not substitute for actually seeing a psychologist in person, but it will give you the benefit of over 50 years of accumulated wisdom from two psychologists. If you do decide to consult with a psychologist, the book will steer you toward the issues that will be most important for you to address.

Although we touch on some of the legal aspects of divorce, our attorney colleagues are more the experts in this area. Our focus here is on the psychological aspects of divorce and recovery. Long after the legal proceedings are over, you will continue to deal with the psychological experience of divorce. It will affect your self-esteem, your connection with your children, and your next romantic relationship.

Feel free to read the book cover to cover, or you may choose to read just those sections of the book that are the most relevant to you right now. Later, you may want to read additional sections of the book as your situation evolves. The Q &A format is designed so you can jump in anywhere that best fits.

The book is designed so that it will be simple for you to find the sections that are of most interest to you. The first section of the book concerns the divorce process itself. In the second section we focus on how to get your head together immediately after the divorce. The third section focuses on beginning to date once more. We discuss what you need to consider as you become sexual again in the fourth section, while in the final section of the book we discuss developing a new relationship that may lead to marriage. The book also contains an annotated bibliography with our comments and recommendations about some of our favorite resources.

So, sit down, get comfortable, and learn a few tips from a couple of fellows who have been there with your brothers.

GOING THROUGH DIVORCE

"I don't know why it is called heartbreak. It feels like every other part of my body is broken, too."

—*Unknown*

CHAPTER 1

"It's better to have loved and lost than to have lived with a psycho the rest of your life."

—(seen on a tee shirt)

IS IT REALLY OVER?

I came home at about the usual time. When I walked in, I knew something was wrong...things were missing. My gut started to ache. Then I saw a letter left on the table. Oh, no, not a "Dear John" letter. It can't be. She's gone! I don't want to believe it. I can't believe it!! I read the letter again in disbelief. There was a knot in the pit of my stomach. It just can't be. She's left, and I never saw it coming. — (Martin, 34 year old chemical engineer)

When a marriage ends, most of the time, it is the woman who makes that decision. Constance Ahrons,[1] a leading authority on divorce, reports that between two-thirds and three-quarters of divorces are initiated by women. So the majority of this chapter addresses how guys respond when the woman leaves the marriage. However, sometimes it is the husband who decides the marriage is over. So we also include answers for many of the questions that men ask when they have decided to go.

Before a woman leaves a relationship, especially a marriage, she usually makes a lot of complaints about why she is unhappy. If the complaints fall on deaf ears, the woman will usually intensify her complaint, perhaps with a different twist. If she concludes that it does no good to complain to her man, she may eventually give up the complaining, but that doesn't mean she's satisfied.[2] It means she has given up trying. For most women, it takes years before they are truly convinced that nothing is going to change.

Q: How was I to know she was ready to leave?

A: Many guys are surprised when their woman leaves, despite the fact that she may have been threatening to leave for years. Maybe guys get a false sense of security from endless threats. It's like the story about the little boy who cried "wolf" too often. After awhile the villagers stopped believing him. Maybe you stopped believing your wife's threats, as well. Or maybe you knew she was mad or unhappy; you just didn't know she was *that unhappy*. Remember that, in general, women are less likely than you to express their feelings directly, especially when they know it will cause a conflict with you. If the two of you have tried discussing problems before to no avail, then she's probably not going to tell you that she's fed up enough to leave.

> *George came home from work one day to find his house empty, his kids gone, and a note on the fireplace mantle stating, "I've filed for divorce." Stunned, he walked outside only to be confronted by a sheriff's deputy who asked his name. The deputy then officially served him with papers indicating that his wife was suing him for divorce. "I never saw it coming," he told the psychologist as he paced the consultation room.*
>
> *"Didn't you know she was angry?" asked one of the group members. "Well, I knew she was mad, but I didn't know she was THAT mad," he replied. George then went on to describe detailed complaints that she had made for years—all of which he had essentially ignored. The only surprise, really, was that she had waited so long to leave him. He got lulled into a false sense of security because she had not left him before. Sometimes, the handwriting on the wall is quite clear, if we could just see it..*

Q: Why wasn't she honest with me about leaving?

A: If your wife left you, and you had no clue it was coming, it may have been because she was afraid of your reactions. If there has been a history of violence between the two of you, she wisely chose not to tell you of her plans. Or maybe you never touched her, but at some point, you threatened to harm her or make her life difficult if she tried to leave. In an argument, you may have used "You'll never see the kids again," or "I won't let you have a penny" or even "I'll never let you leave." Even if "all you did" was put your fist through the wall a couple of times when you were angry, you may have scared her sufficiently that she was unwilling to be honest with you when she made her decision to go. If any of these scenarios fit, your wife may have been smart not to tell you. You might say that you never "really" would have done any of those things, but how was she supposed to know that? The best you can do now is to not do anything else she would *experience* as threatening.

Q: If she was so unhappy, why did she wait so long to leave?

A: Women are generally reluctant to leave relationships, even bad ones. They tend to stick it out in an effort to make it work. Women stay in unsatisfactory relationships for a number of reasons:

Love. "I still love him. He's like two different people."

Children. "Our children are better off with a father. I couldn't raise them as well by myself."

Economics. "My standard of living—and that of the kids—will go way down if I leave him."

Religious Beliefs. "Marriage is a solemn commitment. Divorce is against my religious beliefs."

Pressure from Family and Friends. "They tell me it is my duty to stay with him. They keep urging me to stick it out, promising it will get better."

Family History. "People in our family never divorce."

Culture. "Divorce goes against our cultural values."

Work Reasons. "I would have to go back to work. I don't have job skills."

Isolation. "I have no place to go."

Fear of Failure. "I don't want to feel that I failed at marriage."

Q: Is the woman always right?

A: Please note that we are not saying that the woman is always right. Rather, we are saying that when she becomes convinced that it does no good to complain to her man, the relationship enters a dangerous phase. At this point, a seemingly minor—even innocuous—event can precipitate her moving out. One wife we know left her husband immediately after she overheard him say something negative about her to their child. They had argued repeated over the years to the point of major conflicts, but she remained in the marriage. However after overhearing this one conversation, she suddenly packed her bags. Was it really the man's remark that ended the marriage? No, his wife had given up on getting him to address her complaints, and this simple overheard conversation was just the proverbial straw that broke the camel's back.

Q: I've been thinking about leaving her. How honest should I be?

A: Unless your wife is likely to be violent, suicidal, take the kids and hide their whereabouts, or burn the house down, be totally candid with her. Of course, we are not saying that you should use threats of divorce to indicate how angry you are with her. Only tell her that you are planning to divorce if that is what you are going to do. By being honest with her about your intent to divorce, you begin the transition in a more healthy way. As Robin Green[3] put it, "The best way to lend dignity and respect to the end of your marriage is to be as honest with your spouse as he or she will allow you to be."

Q: I left her, but what if I'm having second thoughts?

A: It is not uncommon for men (and women) to decide to leave a marriage and then later to have second thoughts. After all, she may seem like an impossible person right now, but a few years ago you thought you wanted to spend the rest of your life with her. Is she really all that different from the person you first chose to marry? While it is true that you learned more about her after you married, it is also true that you have built some history with her.

If you are having some second thoughts, give yourself more time before you take further actions. If you have hired an attorney, ask the attorney to put matters "on pause" while you contemplate what you want to do. We don't recommend that you dismiss your previous concerns about the marriage—just take some extra time to evaluate. Don't completely cancel legal proceedings until you have greater clarity about what you want. You may want some alone time to think. You also may want to meet with your wife to discuss what she is willing to do (e.g., make certain concessions, go to marital counseling, join Alcoholics Anonymous).

One benefit from having seriously contemplated divorce *and acted upon it* (for example, by moving out or hiring an attorney) is that your partner knows that you are serious about ending the marriage. You may have threatened to divorce or leave before to little effect. Such threats lose their impact unless it becomes clear that you are willing to go through with the action. Now, however, it is more evident that you are willing to end the marriage. This may give her greater reason to reconsider her position.

If you've reached such a point in your relationship, you may be well off to seek a competent marital counselor. A marriage counselor can help mediate your disputes and disagreements. Having an experienced third party to listen to both sides can be invaluable at this juncture.

If you are reconsidering your decision to leave the marriage, you might want to check out Dr. Phil's book *Relationship Rescue*.[4] It offers a pretty good, no-nonsense, man-friendly approach to reconnecting with your partner.

Q: I had an affair, and I'm hot for my new love. Should I leave the marriage and not look back?

A: The first thing that you should know is that the odds are heavily against going from an affair with someone to a long-term, lasting relationship with that same person. One reason is that both parties know the other has already had an affair. They cheated once, and are both capable of deception. So they each lack trust in the other's fidelity. We have seen men who gave up their careers, their children, their homes—everything—to pursue a woman. Most of those men eventually come back to see us or our colleagues for more counseling because they have jumped from the frying pan into the fire. Affairs are not good solutions for a failing marriage. They only make matters worse. If you are in the midst of an affair, we recommend that you, at least temporarily, put the affair on hold, and resolve what you are doing about the marriage. If the marriage cannot be salvaged, then it is best for you and all concerned to end the marriage rather than to carry on a double life.

Q: Should I offer to go to marriage counseling?

A: Perhaps your partner said that you should go to a therapist or that the two of you should see a marriage counselor. You probably blew the idea off. Most guys ignore or even ridicule their partner's request for marriage counseling, perhaps convincing her even further that nothing is going to change.

> Jerry was asked by his wife to go to marital counseling. His response? "If you don't like the marriage, why don't you go to counseling? You've got the problem." He reported to us that the next time he saw her in person was three months after their divorce was final. If she suggests marital counseling, just say "yes."

If you are interested in reconciliation, we recommend that you take the initiative and suggest marital counseling yourself. Your partner's response is likely to be that it's too late—you should have agreed to it before. Tell her she is right. Confess you made a mistake and urge her to reconsider. Sometimes, if she does not really want to leave you, she will accede to your wishes. If so, don't assume that the battle is over. She may only be going to counseling now as a way of reducing her guilt about leaving you. On the other hand, she may be holding onto a shred of hope about the relationship. She will need to see that you are sincere in your willingness to change things in the marriage. This is *not* the time to point out where she is at fault. It is a time to recognize and acknowledge *your* contribution to the marital problems. If marital counseling continues, there will be time later to address your complaints about the relationship.

You may be skeptical that you can get any kind of benefit from marital counseling. However, in his survey of married men, Neil Chethik[5] found that two-thirds of the guys who had gone to a marriage counselor believed that it had been helpful. At this point, if you are interested in keeping the marriage, you have little to lose.

"She said, 'I'll go if you go,' and I said, 'I'll go if you go,' and here we are."

Q: What should I be feeling?

A: If your woman leaves you, you are likely to feel a variety of emotions. Initially, you may feel devastated or overwhelmed. "How could she do this?" You may feel shocked or surprised. "I never thought she would really do it!" You may feel angry, sensing that she has betrayed you. Or you may feel desperate to get her back, saying to yourself, "I'm glad she's gone" yet in the middle of the night saying "I wish she were here."

Men sometimes wonder if they are feeling what they are *supposed to be feeling*. There are no rules here. What you are feeling is what *you* are supposed to be feeling. Somebody else might feel differently, but that man is not you. Whatever your emotions, they are likely to be intense.

The majority of the men we work with initially seem to be in a state of shock. Even if their wives have been threatening to leave for years, they cannot believe it is really happening. After all, they reason, if she has gotten mad but never left before, or if she always comes back after a few days, why should anyone expect that this would be any different?

Q: How can I stop the pain?

A: *Wait a moment!* Who says you should stop the pain? Of course, no one wants to experience pain, but the only people who don't experience pain are dead people. Pain is a natural response to losing the woman in your life. If you aren't feeling any pain, then you probably didn't care too much about her.

Maybe you're feeling anger and outrage more than pain. This is one of the favorite ways we men have of not experiencing pain. Divorce doesn't hurt so much if we are "pissed off" at her. Covering the pain with hostility is a major reason why so many divorces end with huge animosity. It is also the source of a steady stream of nasty jokes about the "ex." That kind of anger, though, will often come back to haunt you. It makes it harder to let go of the marriage if you are dwelling on how she wronged you. It can interfere with your next relationship, and it can harm the kids since it makes it more difficult to function as parents after the divorce.

A lot of men try to deaden their feelings about divorce by hitting the bottle, smoking that "whacky tabaccy," or working even harder. We don't recommend any of these. Sooner or later you have to feel the pain of the loss. You can postpone the pain, but you will eventually have to deal with it. If you postpone the feeling of pain, it will generally hurt even more later. This will be especially true if you make a few bad decisions while seeking to avoid your pain (e.g., getting remarried too soon; getting a DUI).

The best strategy is to "belly up" to the pain. Yeah, the situation sucks, but you will get through it. Rather than working on bad habits to avoid the pain, try doing those things that are good for you that you have been putting off: lose that extra weight; join the gym; develop that hobby.

Other men focus on improving their ability to relax by learning about relaxation techniques, taking a martial arts class, or trying hypnosis.

Oh, and by the way, just about the time that you think you are over the pain, it will probably sneak back in and smack you again. Something unexpected may remind you of your partner or of some special time that you had together, bringing back the pain. Over time, though, the pain will generally lessen, especially if you are making the right decisions about your life.

Q: Can friends help?

A: Friends can help, but they can also harm. Your friends don't want to see you hurting. Their advice is usually an attempt to protect you. They are likely to take your side, to see how you were wronged by your wife: "I can't believe that you put up with her so long," or "I always knew this would happen." Such comments may feel good in some ways, but the advice is unlikely to lead to reconciliation.

We're not saying that you shouldn't associate with your friends. Just be aware that their well-intentioned advice is biased and may even impede your hopes to get back together with your wife. You might tell your friends that you appreciate their concern, but what you need most right now is support—not suggestions, solutions, or sarcasm.

Q: What about help from the family?

A: Even more than your friends, your family is apt to take your side. You may find yourself asking for their sympathy. Your family may become enraged at your partner for how she has treated you. If the two of you ever get back together, it can be awkward. Your family may continue to resent or distrust her even after you and she have let "bygones be bygones," which can set the stage for more problems between the two of you.

We're not saying to keep things secret from your family, but rather to be careful about what you say. A good strategy is to let the family know what is happening and also to ask them not to take sides. Indicate that she has grievances about the marriage just like you do. Explain that you are unsure if things can be worked out. If it is true, tell them that you hope to reconcile, and you don't want to do anything that might jeopardize that possibility.

*Q: Is there **anything** that can help?*

A: This is not the time to become more isolated. If you are religious, this is a good time to become more involved with your church or synagogue. More generally, reach out to your friends and associates without asking them to be on "your side." Tell them that this is a rough time for you and you would like to play golf this weekend, or go to the movies, or have a barbecue. You don't need them to fix this thing for you. They can't, and you both know it. It can help a lot, though, just to be around people who still *want* to be around you.

Q: Should I want her back? Should I just let her go?

A: Some relationships should just end. Be honest about your relationship with her. Was it really unhealthy and unhappy, and you just couldn't admit it? Were you secretly hoping it would end, but now you are having regrets? Do you believe that a bad relationship is better than no relationship at all? Are you more worried about being alone than about being unhappy? Have you been putting up with stuff that you would tell others never to tolerate?

> *Steven was always reacting to problems in his marriage with outrageous anger directed at his wife. His anger was disproportionate to whatever the problems were. When asked about the source of his anger, he ruefully admitted that since he didn't value the marriage so much, he played "marital roulette," seeing if his anger would cause HER to end the relationship.*
>
> *He told members of the men's group: "If YOU want out of the relationship, take the necessary actions to leave rather than making her miserable in hopes of avoiding making the decision yourself."*

Sometimes, a guy will do anything to get his woman back, but the price can be too high. Ask yourself if the relationship is really worth saving, or is this the time to let it go? No one but you can really answer that question, but it is vital that you consider it.

Q: What about her annoying habits?

A: Every person has annoying habits—including you! A person who has no annoying habits is one that you do not know well. In every relationship you have to put up with the annoying habits of the other person, and, of course, they have to put up with yours.

We don't think that relationships are made or broken on the basis of annoying habits. They come with the territory. It is best to recognize that they are inevitable features of every relationship. If you get back together with her, she will still have annoying behaviors.

Q: Can we get over "big" problems?

A: Annoying habits are like hangnails. They are painful, common, but seldom life-threatening. "Big" problems are like fractures. They limit our freedom and mobility and can even threaten our lives if left untreated. By big problems we mean things like affairs, alcoholism, irresponsible spending, and the like. In and of themselves, big problems do not usually lead to divorce. Divorce is more likely the outcome when the big problems recur or when the couple is unable to talk about the big problem.

If there is a big problem in your relationship (e.g., an affair by either party), it will have to be addressed for reconciliation to have any meaning. That means that the two of you will have to talk about it …a lot! Usually, marital counseling is necessary in these situations. Invariably, the person who committed the transgression (e.g., the person who had an affair) wants to talk about it less, while the other partner wants to talk about it more. It's like a roller coaster ride with many ups and downs, and you will want to get off before the ride is over. All you can really do is sit down and hang on. The ride will eventually end.

Q: If we do get back together, can this happen again?

A: You know there are no guarantees. Of course, it can happen again. One of the inevitable risks of being in a relationship is that you may be hurt. You can try to fix what was wrong in the relationship, but that doesn't mean it will ever be bulletproof. The best you can do is to try to establish more meaningful conversation and better relationship habits to prevent a recurrence.

Q: If we were to get back together, could we trust each other again?

A: This is one of the most common questions people have about reconciliation. Everyone agrees that it takes time to rebuild trust, but it takes more than the mere passage of time.

Trust can grow only when there is no repetition of the problem. If either of you promises to be different, you have to be consistently different. If you soon revert to your old ways, no trust can develop. Trust can be broken in an instant, but it can only be rebuilt over time.

> *Bob and Sara got back together after a separation with repeated promises by Bob that he would be in better control of his anger. Sara, although reluctant to try again, did not really want a divorce. Eventually she allowed him to come back to the home with his commitment to be less hot-tempered.*

They were anxious about how it would work out. Initially, Bob was careful to manage his temper, and things went pretty well. After a matter of a few weeks, though, he became irritated about some minor matter. Although his expression of anger this time was not extreme, it reminded Sara of all of his previous incidents of outrageous anger, and she began to rethink her willingness to reconcile. Trust requires consistency.

Trust requires changes of behavior, not just changes of words. All of us believe what we see more than what we hear. Whatever changes are needed or demanded will have to be seen.

If your wife has lacked trust in you, and you want to reconcile, make obvious and visible efforts to address her concerns. For example, if she complained that you never wanted to spend time with her, commit to having a weekly date with her, and most importantly, let nothing prevent you from keeping that date. If she was unhappy about your treatment of the children, enroll in a parenting class. Take actions that unmistakably signify your desire to be different.

If, on the other hand, it is you who lacks trust in her, demand that she engage in the behaviors that will signify a change of heart to you. Don't settle for promises. One strategy that can be helpful is to ask for her to make behavioral changes and then to contact you after she has maintained those changes for a period of time, say, six months.

Another impediment to rebuilding trust is constantly threatening to leave again. Such threats make the other person unwilling to make the commitments necessary to revitalize a relationship. There should be a moratorium on such threats while the two of you explore reconciliation. You both should agree that neither threatens to leave during this time.

For many couples this is hard to do for two reasons: (1)They have a bad habit of making such threats; (2) Such threats are an effective way of getting the partner's attention.

Nonetheless, you both must stop making threats to leave if you want to give reconciliation a fighting chance. Of course, stopping threats does not mean the other person can't leave, but it removes the threat as a weapon to get your way.

A better way to handle this issue is to agree to have periodic meetings to discuss the state of the relationship. These should be scheduled and put on the calendar. Initially, the meetings probably should be held weekly. Later, if you are successful, monthly meetings might suffice. Even happily married couples should adopt a habit of discussing their satisfaction with the relationship on at least a yearly basis.

Furthermore, in order to rebuild trust, both of you must act in a trustworthy manner in all things. If a person is willing to be dishonest in a small thing, there is no reason to expect they would be honest over a big matter. Little "white lies," minor indiscretions, and failures to fully disclose information are behaviors that doom reconciliation.

Q: What about dating?

A: You are a precocious one! Even if you feel certain that the marriage is over, now is not the time to think about new relationships. Some men immediately seek the company of another woman as a way of salving their wounds. They feel hurt by the loss of their woman and look for reassurance in the arms of another. Maybe friends will offer to "set you up" since you are "free" or "single." They may be well meaning, but it is way too early to consider this. We strongly advise you to avoid this short-term tonic. It is likely to make dealing with the divorce far more complicated. It could even be used against you in court. If you have children, you will further confuse and perhaps alienate them. The time to think about new relationships is when you are completely disentangled from your old one. [See Section III on Dating Again (pp. 171-240) for further guidance.]

CHAPTER 2

"Better a tooth out than always aching."
—*Thomas Fuller*

CAN *I* GET HER BACK?

If your wife has left you, you may feel desperate to get her back. It may seem that your life is over unless she relents and comes back to you. This puts you in the supplicant role and often makes matters worse. The guy with these feelings typically will say to her (and to us) that he will "do anything to get her back." Be careful! You might commit to doing something that you really can't or won't do. Nothing is more likely to lead to the final demise of the relationship than to promise something that does not happen or does not continue to happen in the future. As they say in the business world, "Under-promise and over-deliver."

Many men in this situation go into "Super Wooing Mode." We think that half of all flower shops exist because of men who are trying to prove to their departed lovers that they should come home. A better time to buy flowers is when you are happy with your woman, and you want her to know it. Ditto for candy, jewelry, and fur coats. Good ideas for some occasions—not this one.

Our advice is simple, though not easy to follow: *If you don't know how to fix it, at least don't make it worse.* For example, if you don't know anything about automotive mechanics, you probably shouldn't disassemble your ailing Volvo's engine. When your woman leaves you, wait for direction from her before trying to make things better. If, for example, she says the dreaded "I need space," give it to her. Tell her that you will wait for her to tell you how and when she wants to communicate. This will probably be hard for you because you will be giving up control, but let's face it...you don't have control if she's moved out!

Q: What can I do to get her back?

A: Consider the list of "Do's" and "Don'ts" on pages 34-35 along with some "Be-Careful's."

Remember that your friends and family are automatically on your side. They don't want to see you in pain, and they are biased. Often their advice is too one-sided to be helpful. Furthermore, if you do get back together with her, the relationship between her and them can be strained or even broken by what you say to them now about her. Imagine going to a holiday dinner with her at your parents' home after you told them how she treated you so badly during your separation. "Bad mouthing" your woman now can lead to serious future problems if you do reconcile.

Q: What if there is another man?

A: Most guys seem to think that if a woman leaves them, there must be another man. In our experience, this is not usually the case. Sometimes there is another guy, but most of the time there is not. Maybe we guys are just too egotistical. We can't picture how a woman could leave us. So if she did, it must be for another man.

Many men query and cajole their estranged partner to determine if she is seeing or sleeping with another man. Even if she denies it, many men remain suspicious. Some men even hire a private investigator to follow their woman and perhaps catch her in another man's embrace. To our way of thinking, this is a big waste of time and money. If she is having an affair, it will probably come out sooner or later. It almost always does. You won't have to spend money to find out. If she's not having an affair, she will probably find out that you had her investigated, and she will be mad and even more convinced that she should leave you.

> *Javier was convinced his wife was having an affair. So convinced was he, that he hired a private investigator to follow her around. The detective trailed her about, videotaping her every move—just like a TV reality show. One day the frazzled husband brought the tape into his individual therapy session to demonstrate his wife's guilt. When we reviewed the video, it showed his wife, a business woman, apparently having lunch with a male associate at a prominent restaurant. The wife, appropriately attired in a business suit, remained a respectful distance from her companion throughout the meal. There was no physical touch between them. Although their dialogue could not be heard, it seemed likely that they were discussing sales figures, not bedroom techniques. At the conclusion of the meal, they both stood up and walked away cordially. Javier, however, declared that as his wife left, she had kissed the other man. Thinking that perhaps we had somehow missed this pivotal moment, we replayed that portion of the tape numerous times, even in slow motion, but we never found what this man so adamantly exclaimed he "saw" on the tape. Sometimes our fears make us see what we think is there.*

Let's pretend for a moment that your woman *is* having an affair. How does that change things? Not as much as you might think. Despite what it feels like, you are not really in competition with anyone else. The only competition is between the old marriage in which she was unhappy and the possible new one where she might be happier. If she chooses to leave you for another man, it's like a trip to fantasy land. Affairs and marriages are like apples and oranges. They are really very different kinds of relationships. You don't raise children, pay taxes, or attend family events with your affair partner. Affairs are driven by secrecy, sexual attraction, and dishonesty. Marriages, at least good ones, are based on openness, sacrifice, and sharing. Given enough time, many people, males and females, realize the distinction between affairs and marriages and will reconsider their leaving. However, if you have had her tracked, embarrassed, or persecuted in an effort to force her to

Do's

THINGS TO DO IF YOU WANT HER BACK

- ❏ When you communicate with her, tell her directly that you want to work it out.

- ❏ Talk with friends or family so that you are not isolated.

- ❏ Ask friends and family not to give you advice, but rather just to be supportive.

- ❏ Consider seeing a counselor, minister, or rabbi for a neutral second opinion. Sometimes, you just need to talk and blurt out everything. If so, it may be better to talk with a counselor, psychologist, or religious leader than with friends or family.

- ❏ Keep regular contacts with your children through visitation and phone calls.

- ❏ Offer to see a marriage counselor with her if she feels that would be helpful.

- ❏ Agree that changes are needed in the relationship for it to be viable.

- ❏ Acknowledge that she has legitimate complaints, and you want to address them.

- ❏ Focus on developing healthy habits such as exercise, losing weight, and eating a healthy diet.

- ❏ If you are religious, get more involved with your faith.

Don'ts

THINGS TO NOT DO IF YOU WANT HER BACK

- ❏ Don't beg, plead, or cry. She doesn't want a wuss.

❏ Don't bug her with multiple e-mails, phone calls, or notes.

❏ Don't show up at her place of business to talk to her.

❏ Don't hire a private investigator to follow her.

❏ Don't increase your use of alcohol, tobacco, or other substances.

❏ Don't become a workaholic.

❏ Don't complain about her to your family and friends.

❏ Don't speak ill of her to the children.

❏ Don't spend lots of money on her to prove that you love her.

❏ Don't start another relationship to make her jealous or to consider your options.

❏ Don't be angry during your interactions with her.

❏ Don't ask her if she is seeing another man.

❏ Don't cruise by her place to see if she's home or if there's another car in the driveway.

DANGEROUS COMMENTS TO AVOID

Be careful of what your friends and family tell you. They often give loads of well-meaning advice such as:

❏ "You ought to show up at her place and tell her you love her."

❏ "I wouldn't take that from her."

❏ "She'll come running back to you...wait and see."

❏ "I can't believe you've stayed as long as you have."

❏ "She's just trying to get your money."

❏ "She must have someone else."

get rid of the other person, she will probably do what you would do: get mad, get stubborn, and persist in the affair.

Q: What if she hires a private investigator?

A: Unless you are trying to hide something, her decision to hire a private investigator does not really mean much. Go about your business as usual. If, on the other hand, you have been less than honest with her (e.g., you have someone else on the side), it will probably be discovered. Consider whether it would be better to bring the secret out in the open yourself rather than to have her spring the information on you in some dramatic way. Clearly, the best course of action is to make decisions that will not come back to haunt you later. If you have made those sorts of errors, though, you must expect that the detective will find out about them and that the information will be used against you. Do what you can to lessen the blow by managing how the information will be revealed.

Q: What about wearing my ring?

A: Wearing a wedding ring is an important symbol of commitment in marriage. If you decide to stop wearing your ring, your wife may see this as an admission that the relationship is over. It also may be interpreted as "open season" for a new relationship. If you don't want the marriage to end, we recommend that you continue wearing the ring. On the other hand, if your wife takes off her ring, don't necessarily see this as the end. It is an important symbolic act, but it will also be an important symbol if she decides later to put it back on.

> *Riva and Estefan made a habit of dramatically removing their rings whenever they had a big fight. It was sort of a trump card that was used to indicate when one of them was particularly upset. Unfortunately, Estefan used this strategy once too often. Riva reciprocated by taking her own ring off, but she declined to put her ring back on after the fight finally ended. He realized that she was coming closer to ending the marriage—something he did not want, but he had failed to see that his own "symbolic" threat might precipitate her "real" action.*

Q: How long should I wait before giving up on the marriage?

A: We men tend to be impatient creatures. We want this matter to be resolved—and resolved quickly. Why? Because we want to reduce our anxiety.

> *In the therapy office, George told us he would do anything to get his wife back. A week later he told us he was driving down the street and told himself, "Aw, f---- it" and filed for divorce.*

During the separation try becoming a scientist. Collect data about the likelihood that the two of you can get back together, plus data that you would stay together if you did, and if you would be happier together than apart. You'll get plenty of opportunities to collect that data during the separation. Would you be willing to stay in the limbo state of separation for five years? Of course the answer is no. Do you have to decide in the next ten minutes? Again, the answer is no. So, you already have set the parameters. You'll need more than ten minutes and less than five years to figure it out. Like with pornography, it's hard to define, but you know it when you see it. You'll know when you know it's time to give up. There's no reason to hurry. This is not a fast food restaurant. Give yourself time to collect the data, and then pay attention to the data you collect. You'll see indications of whether it is possible to reconcile. Divorce, like marriage, should be approached slowly and cautiously.

> *Some time ago a man in crisis came to our office for consultation. He was very upset because his wife had just discovered his long-term affair. Not only had Mark had an affair that had lasted literally for decades, he had fathered children by the other woman. He also had generously provided for her financially. Not surprisingly, his wife filed for divorce. They went through many twists and turns in their legal proceedings, but after months of wrangling, they met in court for the final decree. Just before the judge was about to lower his gavel, his wife proposed that they try to reconcile. After all, she said, she still loved him, and she believed—despite all of his infidelity—that he still loved her. They cancelled the divorce proceedings. You never really know when it's over.*

GUIDELINES FOR SEPARATION

Make it a real separation. Don't just move into the spare bedroom thinking she might change her mind. Trying to live in the same house while "separated" is like trying to take a shower without changing clothes. It's awkward and probably will lead to further conflict, decreasing the likelihood of you working it out with her.

Don't move in with the parents. Look, you're both grown people! Face this like adults. If you move in with your parents—or hers, it's hard to feel and act grown-up. This is a time to be perceived as an adult, not as a child by your mate. In addition, if you are with your parents and the two of you get back together, you will make the relationship between you, your parents and your partner much more difficult.

Caution: The major reason guys give for moving in with parents is to save money. This is penny wise and dollar foolish. A divorce costs much more, both in money and in heartache, than renting an apartment for a while. If you are truly short on cash, consider moving in with a friend.

Separate for at least 90 days. Many couples separate for only a few days or a week or two. That's generally not long enough for the two of you to figure out what divorce is really like.

Don't become Mr. Handyman for her. During separation, many women call their husbands every time they run out of gas or the sinks get clogged. Oh no! This is not the time to be the mechanic, plumber, or roadside support man. Part of what she needs to experience is that she will be without your assistance post divorce. Help her experience this by politely telling her "no" when she calls at 2 a.m. to tell you the toilet is overflowing. Direct her to the Yellow Pages listing for "Home Repairs," not "Suckers."

Make rules about dating. It is important to be clear about dating. Make no assumptions. Whatever the rules are, they should apply to both parties. Most couples agree that there will be no dating during the separation, and this is generally the best course if the two of you are considering reconciliation. If your partner is already involved in an affair, though, she is unlikely to agree to this. If dating is permitted during the separation, then agree to rules about sex. Again, the best course of action is no dating and no sex, but partners will not always consent to this.

Tell the kids you are separating. It is best to do this together as parents. If you have more than one child, it is usually preferable to meet with all of them at the same time. The children need to be told that there will be a separation because Mommy and Daddy are not getting along. (This may not be a surprise to them!) Don't blame yourself or your partner. Keep the explanation general. It is OK to appear sad. After all, this *is* sad. That lets them express sadness if they want to do so.

Contact with the kids should be as normal as possible. The kids, of course, are not to blame for the problems in the marriage. Be sure that you stay involved in their lives. Do whatever it takes to see them and participate in their activities.

Don't seek to interact with your spouse when you are seeing the children. When you are with the kids, focus on them. If you use your time with the kids as a ploy to interact more with your estranged partner, then (1) your spouse will hate you for the manipulation and (2) the kids will be angry with you for using them.

Q: Does separation mean divorce is inevitable?

A: Maybe she has suggested that the two of you separate for awhile. Or perhaps she has made the dreaded "I just need some space" request. Most guys hear those statements as a prelude to the end. They often figure that the next step is divorce. That's sometimes true, but in our experience, couples often get back together after a separation. The best separations amount to a "trial divorce" answering the question, "Is this really what we want?"

We recommend that couples follow certain guidelines for separation (see pages 38-39). The guidelines are intended to help the couple rethink their positions, to learn more about what divorce will mean before committing to it, and to facilitate a transition to a divorced life if that becomes inevitable.

Q: How do I tell others about the separation?

A: Your question suggests that you may feel some shame about the separation. Maybe you feel that you failed somehow if you are separated from your wife. You might be tempted to blame the whole thing on her, but there are no innocent bystanders in divorce. Like it or not, you have something to do with what has happened. That does not mean, though, that you have done something that warrants embarrassment. Furthermore, as we have noted, separation does not necessarily lead to divorce.

You don't need to announce from the rooftops that you are separated, but you shouldn't treat it as a state secret either. It makes sense to tell your closest friends and family about the separation soon after it occurs. In that way, they can offer their support and concern. You don't want to wait a long time to tell people and hear them say, "Why didn't you tell me?" or "Why didn't you trust me?"

With people who are less close, tell them if the matter is relevant. For example, if you are missing work because of the separation, let your boss and/or fellow employees know what has been happening to you. Most people will have compassion for you, and they generally won't judge you harshly. Be careful not to get into the particulars of what has happened. Keep your comments general (i.e., "My wife and I are separated"). Don't succumb to the temptation to explain your side of the story even if they invite you to do so. If you do, you will find it increasingly awkward if they want more "juicy" details in the future. It will be especially difficult if you and your wife reconcile.

Q: What are the chances we might remarry someday?

A: Occasionally, you hear stories about couples who divorce and later get back together, sometimes with another marriage in between! It does happen, but not very often. Sometimes, in retrospect, couples realize how much "good" was in their relationship. After experiencing life without you, your ex-wife might decide she made a mistake. Certainly, though, you should not keep a light in the window hoping that she will return. If you still have the wish to get back together with her, you want to be more careful about how you handle the divorce. You don't want to punish her in the divorce process if you are hoping she will view you sympathetically in the future.

However, remember that the odds are against you working this out. Furthermore, second marriages end in divorce more often than do first marriages.

Q: What if I decide I don't want her back?

A: Quite often, men change their minds—even those who initially said they would do anything to get her back. Perhaps, it becomes clear that your woman is not coming back. Maybe she had an affair, and you can't forgive her for it. You might even realize that, after all, it is better for the marriage to end. This may be a time when you feel more sad and depressed, or just plain "crappy."

Guys sometimes respond to this by getting drunk, getting laid, or getting wasted in some other way in an attempt to relieve the pain they are feeling. It is not recommended. Sadness and emotional pain are the natural response to loss. For example, if you lost your arm, you would experience pain, and later suffer the psychological effects of being without your limb. There would be a period of adjustment as you learn to face the world with only one arm. You might feel sorry for yourself for a while, thinking that you got a bum deal, that life is unfair. You might even wonder how on earth you will make it. Chances are, though, that you would eventually adjust to the loss and live a nice life. You probably would not continue to feel handicapped, but rather, you would figure out how to make the best of an unfortunate situation. You might even someday feel fortunate that you still have one good arm. Going through the loss of a relationship is a lot like that, too. You will feel badly initially. There is no way around it, short of chemically numbing yourself or working yourself to death. If you do those, however, you will probably make a bad situation worse—turning lemons into rotten lemons.

"No heroic measures."

THINGS TO DO WHEN YOU SEPARATE[1]

Obviously, if you are rushing out the door to escape a beating or protect your children, forget about the following list. If, on the other hand, your situation allows you the time to think and plan, consider this "checklist".

1) Copy documents. Copy machines are plentiful and cheap. Paying a lawyer to obtain financial records is very expensive and time consuming. If you do not have needed information after the divorce is filed and/or your spouse becomes angry, you may be required to pay your lawyer to help you get information that your spouse refuses to turn over. If your spouse will control the records after separation, make copies before you separate. Things to copy include:

❑ Recent paycheck and check stubs

❑ Tax returns

❑ Real estate instruments, deeds, and deeds of trust, if possible

❑ Loan documents, promissory notes, financing statements, etc.

❑ Financial statements

❑ Certificates of deposits, savings passbooks

❑ Stocks, bonds, statements from stockbrokers

❑ Bank statements, checks, deposit slips on all accounts

❑ Checks or stubs showing income from trust, oil and gas production, sale of property, dividends

❑ Employee benefit plans, retirement, profit sharing, pensions

❏ Titles to cars, trailers, boats, motorcycles, airplanes

❏ Statement of charge accounts, credit card accounts, house payments, payment books, and other records of debts

❏ Insurance policies

❏ Documents evidencing ownership interest in corporations, partnerships, trust, or businesses of any kind

❏ Correspondence or emails related to businesses or personal matters

❏ Any other items that seem to be related to the finances or marriage

2) *Protect keepsakes, heirlooms, collector's items, photographs.* Consider your spouse's personality. If it is likely that small items of relatively large economic or sentimental value may be damaged or hidden, take appropriate steps to protect these items. Photographs, scrapbooks, letters from parents and friends, special gifts from loved ones, and family treasures are all irreplaceable and , perhaps, priceless. Additionally, most of these items are small and easy to carry. If you're the one leaving, it's about a thousand times cheaper to move them to your parents' house than it is to pay a lawyer to go to court and get them for you. If there's only one copy of children's photographs or other items that are meaningful to both you and your spouse, consider getting duplicates made so that both of you can have one of everything. Not only is this the decent thing to do, it will save the cost of fighting over these objects and the cost of one or the other of you being angry over something special being lost.

3) *Ascertain whether or not any real estate is held only in your spouse's name.* If such realty is community property, or if payments for improvements have been

made from community funds, these facts need to be promptly related to your lawyer. Upon the filing of divorce proceedings, your lawyer will probably file a *lis pendens* notice to prevent your spouse from selling the property without your knowledge.

4) Do some thinking about joint bank accounts. If possible, talk to your lawyer about this subject in advance. Circumstances vary so much that it is difficult to make hard and fast rules about this part of the transition from joint finances to individual accounts. Obviously, if your spouse is financially irresponsible, you have no choice. You must immediately establish your own separate account.

If, on the other hand, your spouse is supporting you by continuing to deposit large sums in a joint account from which you pay joint bills and draw your living expenses, you may be hurting your own pocketbook to enter discussions about separate accounts. In deciding whether to 'raid' the joint checking account, consider the following:

> a. If you are responsible for the day-to-day care of small children, you must have the funds to get them through the coming days. If it is likely that your spouse will cut you and the children off from your sole source of income, take the necessary funds to get you and the children through the coming days until a temporary order requiring him or her to pay temporary support can be entered, and the first payment can be received. This means every penny in the account, if necessary.

> *b.* If you are suffering physical abuse or threats of physical abuse from your spouse, use whatever money you can get your hands on to get away. Rent an apartment, buy a plane ticket, hire a lawyer, etc. Money is not as important as your neck.

c. Try not to cause your spouse to write hot checks. If possible, notify your spouse that the funds are gone, before the spouse writes the checks.

d. If the funds in the account are not necessary for your survival, consider taking only half. If your spouse cannot be trusted with half the proceeds, and you must remove it all, be prepared to account for every penny.

5) If you have young children, schools and day care centers should be notified that one of the parents has a new address and phone number. As much information as possible should be given about the whereabouts of both parents. Since you are no longer living together, your child may have a needless wait of several hours if an accident or emergency keeps the one parent away and the school or day care center does not know how to reach the other parent to pick up the child. If the "other" parent is not accountable, this is definitely the time to get grandparents, uncles, aunts, friends, or other trustworthy adults "plugged in" so that they can be reached in emergencies or when there is just a plain old mix-up.

6) Check your insurance coverage.

a. Make sure that both you and your spouse have your names on the automobile insurance policy. Most standard Texas automobile policies cover the "named insured and members of household." Hence, a single name on the policy means that the other person is not covered when separation occurs. If your name is the single name on the policy, you are still not protected. Since your property could be taken to satisfy your spouse's torts, you must protect your spouse in order to protect yourself.

b. If your homeowner's insurance provides coverage for personal property, such as furniture, appliances, clothing, jewelry, etc. it is likely that this coverage will not protect the property taken by a spouse to a new residence.

c. If your spouse is the named beneficiary on your insurance, neither separation nor divorce will keep your spouse from receiving the payment upon your death.; If this is not your desire, you must change the beneficiary. This may not be possible until after divorce.

7) *Protect your credit.* You are responsible for charges made by your spouse on joint credit accounts, whether or not you have knowledge that the charge is being made. Neither separation nor divorce will change this. If you desire to limit your liability in the future, you must notify each creditor that you will not pay for debts incurred by your spouse.

8) *Consider changing your will.* Your separation does not affect your spouse's right to inherit from you. When you divorce, any provisions in your will providing for your spouse to receive property from you will be disregarded. But, this is only when your divorce becomes final. Until then, your will is unchanged by law. Also, if you do not have a will, your spouse, by virtue of being the surviving parent, will probably gain control of any property that your minor children inherit from you.

9) *Establish separate credit.* If all of your joint credit accounts are carried in your spouse's name, you may not have the credit history necessary to obtain credit in your own name. The Equal Credit Opportunity Act gives you the right to have credit information in your own name from accounts used or held jointly with your spouse. Changing the credit history to your name does not guarantee that you will be able to get credit in your own name since other factors such as your income may also be considered; however, it might help .

CHAPTER 3

"It is a wise father that knows his own child."
—William Shakespeare,
The Merchant of Venice

WHAT ABOUT THE KIDS?

For most people, dealing with the children around the time of divorce is the most difficult aspect of the whole process. In this chapter, we discuss the initial problems in dealing with the children at the time of divorce. In a later chapter, we will address post-divorce parenting.

Q: How do I tell the kids about the separation?

A: Lots of parents "freak out" at this point in the process. We don't blame you. It is tough sledding to break the news to the kids, but it has to be done.

Children need to be told about the divorce as soon as it is certain that it will occur. It is a bad idea, though, to tell the kids what *might* happen (e.g., "Mommy and I might divorce"). Such statements just tend to raise children's anxieties and are hard to retract later. In addition, these kinds of statements will inflame the other partner. Parents should make up their minds and then tell the kids.

Here are recommendations for how you tell the children about the divorce:

RECOMMENDATIONS FOR TALKING WITH KIDS ABOUT DIVORCE

❑ It is best if both parents participate, rather than one parent explaining the situation.

❑ Try not to be overly emotional, but if you shed some tears, it is not the end of the world and is certainly understandable.

❑ Don't blame the other parent or try to explain your side of the story.

❑ Keep your explanation simple and use age-appropirate language.

❑ If the kids don't show a lot of emotion, don't assume things will be fine.

❑ If the kids do show a lot of emotion, reassure them that things will work out over time.

❑ If the kids have no comments or questions, don't try to over-talk the issue. There will be time in the future to handle questions or concerns

All kids tend to pretty much have the same questions in this situation. Here are some of the typical questions with recommended answers:

Q&A FOR TALKING WITH KIDS ABOUT DIVORCE

Are you going to divorce?

We haven't decided that yet. We are going to separate for a while and then decide.

or

Yes, we have decided to divorce.

Will we have to move?

No. You are going to continue living here for now. If Mommy and Daddy divorce that might change, but, for now, you will continue living here.

Will I have to change schools?

No. You will continue to go to the same school, at least for now.

Will I still see you?

Yes. I will continue to see you very often.

Don't you love Mommy/Daddy anymore?

Sometimes even when people love each other, they don't get along too well. Have you ever gotten mad at a friend and didn't want to play with them?

Will you divorce me?

No. A parent will never divorce a child.

Of course, we don't want children to feel responsible for the parents' marital problems. Most parents reassure the kids that they are not to blame, and then heave a big sigh of relief when the kids say they understand. However, you are not out of the woods yet.

It is one thing for the kids to parrot back that it's not their fault, yet quite another for them to be guilt free. Kids often do blame themselves at a deeper level. This sort of feeling is expressed through more subtle behaviors and statements. Kids commonly try to change some of their behavior in the hopes that their parents will reunite. This implies that they are somehow responsible in the first place for their parents' separation.

Typically, kids want their parents to get back together. Sometimes they will scheme how to accomplish this. Remember the Disney movie, *The Parent Trap*? In the movie, twin daughters who were separated by their parents' divorce, conjure elaborate plans intended to bring their parents back together. In the movie this is done with hilarious antics and is predictably a successful Hollywood story. In real life, however, such efforts usually are embarrassing or messy. If you see hints of this from your kids, reassure them that you know what they want, but it is not their job to fix their parents or their parents' marriage.

Q: What are the signs that my kids are having trouble?

A: Reactions of divorce among children may be sudden and obvious, or more pernicious and long-term. Negative reactions may occur in the child's behavior, in school performance, or in their emotional state. Typical problem reactions include:

- ❑ *Depression* (sadness, crying, low energy, withdrawal from others, decreased or increased appetite)

- ❑ *Anger* (temper tantrums, breaking things, difficulties in getting along with others, greater irritability, increased aggressiveness in play, accusations towards parents)

- ❑ *Anxiety* (nightmares, hyperactivity, nervousness, difficulty sleeping)

- ❑ *Shame* (avoiding talking about the divorce, not telling others about the divorce)

- ❑ *Dependency* ("clinging", avoidance of school, fear of separation)

- ❑ *Regression to earlier behavior* (requests for the bottle, needs for extra reassurance at bedtime, reemergence of bedwetting or thumb sucking)

- ❑ *Physical Complaints* (stomachache, headache, vague illnesses)

- ❑ *School Problems* (drop in grades, failure to complete work, lack of concentration, lack of interest, missing school)

- ☐ *"Parentified Behavior"* (acting like a "little man" or "little mommy," attempts to parent younger siblings)

- ☐ *Behavior Problems* (violation of family rules, oppositional attitude, getting into trouble with authority figures, substance abuse, lying, stealing)

- ☐ *Denial of Problems* (statements that the divorce doesn't bother them or that it doesn't affect them)

- ☐ *Attempts to Reunite Parents* (asking ex-spouses to hold hands, attempts to "entertain" the parents, schemes to get parents together, misbehavior in order to draw attention of the parents)

- ☐ *Self-destructive Thoughts* (frequent accidents, cutting with sharp objects, running away from home, vague comments about being gone)

The ways in which these behaviors are expressed vary according to the age of the child, but there is considerable uniformity in experience. Most kids will manifest some of these symptoms. For that matter, most adults will experience some of them as well.

Q: Does every child have problems with divorce?

A: Lots of people, maybe most, proudly tell us that their kids are not having problems with the divorce. "Junior is fine. I explained to him that it wasn't his fault, and he said he understood that. Then he went back to playing with his child prodigy toys." Nice picture, but often inaccurate.

We're not saying that every kid will wind up at the therapist's office because of their parents' divorce; however, the divorce is often much more traumatic to the kids than the parents want to admit.

The best psychological research on the subject[1] indicates that most children do not become maladjusted as a result of divorce; however, children from divorced families are more likely to have emotional problems than children from intact, married families. Children from divorce, for example, are more likely to suffer from financial insecurity, academic underachievement, substance abuse, unemployment as young adults, and divorce in their own marriages. *Marital conflict* is actually a better predictor of childhood adjustment than the divorce itself. It appears that the *financial issues* faced by children as the result of divorce are the main cause of many of the negative consequences associated with divorce. Most children are resilient. However, divorce is incredibly painful even for those who emerge as "psychologically hardy."[2]

As parents, we don't want to feel that we have harmed our children, so we tend to overlook or underestimate problems that they have as a consequence of the divorce. Sometimes, we blame those problems on the ex-spouse rather than acknowledging them as an after-effect of the divorce itself. Even if there has been a high level of conflict between parents, the kids may not see divorce as a logical way to reduce the fighting in the family, even though parents see it as the only realistic option.

Furthermore, children are not always clear about how the divorce is affecting them. Indeed, many times they don't really know. They can't necessarily sit you down and say, "Gee, I'm feeling depressed about the two of you divorcing." They also may pick up on your feeling when you're hoping they will say they are OK, and then say exactly that.

Our experience as psychotherapists is that adults usually describe the divorce of their parents as a pivotal moment in their lives. In some cases, the adults remember divorce as a good thing. This is especially the case if the parents were fighting a lot. For others, divorce was important—but much less positive. Some remember divorce as one of the worst events of their lives. However your kids will remember it, the point is that they *will* remember it.

Children generally expect both parents to be there for them forever. The notion that one parent is leaving—regardless of the justification or rationalization—feels like a betrayal of the most basic security the child expects. It is relatively rare, even in highly abusive families, for children to want their parents to divorce, and even more unusual for children to not desire contact with one of the parents.

If given a choice, kids almost *always* prefer their parents to work out their marital difficulties. Kids begin with the dream (prayer?) that their parents will stop fighting/arguing. Eventually, if the conflict persists, children accept that their parents will continue to fight, but they still wish that it would stop. In some cases, the kids may feel relief when their parents divorce because they think that at least the fighting will end, too.

> *We were asked to consult in a facility with abused children. A 7-year-old boy had been stabbed and practically disemboweled by his parents. He had been removed from the home and sent to a "safe house," yet his continuing question was, "When can I be with my parents again?" Children naturally want to be with their parents.*

Regardless of what kids say at the time of the divorce, they may express regret about their parents' conflict and divorce years later. It is common for even adult offspring to become depressed or disillusioned when their parents divorce.

Most divorces are preceded by considerable—frequently open—conflict between the parents. Sometimes these parents reassure the children that although the parents argue, they will still stay together. In other situations, the kids themselves become used to the level of conflict but assume that it does not portend the parents' divorce. The parents usually divorce, despite what they say or what the children observe, and the kids may still feel blindsided and shocked.

Q: How about if we didn't fight much? How will our kids respond?

A: Parents often feel that the kids will be less negatively affected by a divorce if they have not witnessed their parents fighting. There is some logic to this because the level of conflict present in the family is a key determinant of the degree of negative impact on the child. There is a lot of research that indicates the more children are exposed to the parents' conflict, the more negatively they are affected.[3]

However, if you and your spouse did not openly fight, your children may be even more surprised by the divorce. They may react in shock and immediately display problems as a result of your announcement. We are not advocating that parents fight more openly, but we are pointing out that kids who do not perceive their parents' conflict may still need special attention. We recommend that you ask all kids, but especially kids in this situation, if they were surprised about the announcement (i.e., that their parents are separating/divorcing). If the kids indicate that they are surprised, you might point out that you have deliberately tried to shield them from the conflict in an effort to protect them from it.

Of course, maybe you were surprised as well. You might be as shocked as the kids—maybe even more so. It is appropriate to say that to the kids. For example, "I am just as surprised as you are by your mother's decision, but we will get through this together." Be careful not to use this moment to "bash" the other parent.

Q: What if we fought a lot?

A: It should be no surprise that it is not good for kids to witness parental fighting. Indeed, it has been shown in some research that the major negative effects of divorce stem from the level of parental conflict, not from the change in the family structure (i.e., the divorce itself).[4]

Generally speaking, most people would agree that the best arrangement for raising children is a family of two parents who love each other. Next best would probably be two parents who remain involved in the children's lives, although divorced, but with a low level of conflict. An even less healthy scenario for children is a couple who stays together "for the kids" or other reasons but continues with open, never-ending altercations. A couple who stays together with relatively little conflict yet without much love either, is probably less negative for the children, but still not optimal. In this kind of marriage, children have little picture of what marriage and love are supposed to be like. Thus, they are less well prepared for adult relationships later in their lives. If you want your children to have happy marriages, it helps for them to see one.

Without question, the worst arrangement for children is to have parents who conflict, divorce, and *then continue to fight after the divorce*. These parents frequently appear on the family court dockets—often multiple times, fighting over what may ultimately be trivial issues. If you "enjoyed" your divorce, just think about how much you could "enjoy" going back to court several times fighting with your ex-wife over who pays for the *bar mitzvah* or who gets to have your son for Halloween. Hardly "family fun, "but such continued conflict does provide a valued retirement plan for family attorneys.

Continued litigation after divorce, of course, drains financial resources for the family. Ultimately, that money comes from the children because otherwise it would be available for their first car, for their college needs, or for an inheritance. In addition, children find continued litigation emotionally draining. Most kids love both parents. They don't want you to fight.

Worse yet is when kids feel dragged into their parents' conflicts. This is actually common, especially in families that continue to battle in litigation after divorce. Lawyers, judges, and even juries often ask the children to render preferences and opinions on their parents. The kids are ultimately put in the position of having to choose between parents, a terrible position for children to experience.

All parents solemnly state that they don't want to put their child in the middle of a marital conflict. However, in practice, many parents don't seem to know what that really entails. Parents often rationalize their reasons for pursuing legal remedies for disputes with ex-spouses. These continuing legal battles are generally more deleterious than helpful.

> *Stephanie and Richard, a divorced couple of 10 years, went back to court multiple times, frequently for minor grievances. For instance, Richard failed to return the child's laundry after a weekend visitation, and a hearing followed. The parents were sufficiently financially successful so that they could repeat this process over and over. When asked about the wisdom of their actions, the parents protested that they were only concerned about the child's welfare. Don't use the court to deal with minor problems.*

We are not saying that you should never go back to court to redress grievances. Rather, we are advising you that going back to court should be a rare event and a last resort. If the children are genuinely being endangered by the actions of your spouse, and your spouse steadfastly refuses to cooperate with you in the matter, then court action may be necessary. In our experience, though, most of these matters do not rise to this level of imperative.

We have seen people go back to court alleging that their ex-spouse is endangering the children by being irresponsible in one way or another. Yet when the couple was married, the partner did the same sort of things without any objection from the other parent. Remember that after divorce you have less influence over your ex-spouse than you did when you were married. This may seem basic, but we often see parents who complain about their ex not listening to them about how to deal with the kids. Typical complaints are that the other parent is too lenient or doesn't put the kids to bed on time, etc. One of the costs of divorce is that you will have less control on what the other parent says or does. If you think your spouse didn't listen to you *before*, just wait until *after* the divorce is finalized to find out how little influence you have then.

Q: *Do children take sides in divorce?*

A: Although not always the case, quite often children do take sides in divorce. They may identify more with one parent or the other and may castigate the other parent as essentially the one at fault in the relationship. Sometimes, the child will feel sympathy for the parent who has left the home concluding that they have been "driven away" by the other parent. Other kids may resent the parent who has left, feeling the parent has abandoned or rejected them. The "leaving" parent may be idealized, or alternatively, demonized. Children of 12 years or under will have a more difficult time with any sense of neutrality. They tend to think more in black and white, concrete terms. People are either good guys or bad guys in their eyes, and they tend to categorize their parents in such ways as well.

> *Gerald felt a degree of smug satisfaction when the kids blamed their mother for the divorce rather than him. They openly sided with their father, preferring him in all things over the mother. Gerald experienced some vindication from the children's behavior, and essentially permitted and even encouraged their reaction.*

Unfortunately, he did not see how this presaged the children's future problems with depression and self-esteem as a result of losing connection with their mother who had been extensively involved in rearing them throughout their lives. Encourage the children to feel close to both parents.

Q: If I had an affair, will it hurt my chances of being with the kids?

A: We have seen some parents who seek to "get the goods" about their spouse's affair with the intent of using this as leverage with the judge who makes decisions about the children. In most areas of the country, though, the parents' record of sexual infidelity has little or nothing to do with decisions about child custody and visitation. While having an affair is generally not going to result in the judge awarding a "Good Conduct Badge," most jurisdictions don't use this kind of information to make decisions about the children. Maybe the best way to understand this is to recognize that marital infidelity is more about the partner than about the children.

Q: What might make the court decide to limit my time with the children?

A: The major reason that contact between parents and their children is sometimes limited is if the court fears that the child might be at risk when with the parent. If, for example, a parent has been abusive towards the child, the court, quite understandably, might act to limit access to the child.

The court is especially concerned when there is evidence that there has been harm to the child. On the other hand, even when there has been violence between the marital partners, it does not necessarily mean that there is a risk posed to the child. Of course, we are not trying to excuse marital violence; we are just noting that the courts recognize there are differences between getting into a fight with your spouse and harming a child.

In some situations, the courts may order a psychological evaluation to determine if a parent poses a risk to the child. If you are ordered to participate in such an evaluation, we recommend that you cooperate fully with the examining psychologist or other professional. This person has considerable influence with the court, and the report that the professional renders can be crucial.

The psychologist appointed by the court may be asked to determine if you (or your spouse) have a problem managing your anger. If so, you might be required to complete an anger management course as a condition for having more access to your child.

Similarly, you could be asked to complete a substance abuse evaluation. Often, this will include a drug screening (either urine or hair analysis) to determine if you have been using illegal substances. If your spouse knows that you have a habit of drinking too much, have a history of DUI's, or sometimes use drugs, this type of evaluation is more common. The reasoning here, of course, is that you might put the child at risk if you are under the influence of drugs or alcohol while the child is with you. If an evaluation determines that you do have a substance abuse problem, restrictions may be placed on your time with the children. You might be required to complete some sort of substance abuse treatment before having unrestricted time with the kids. You also might be ordered not to use any alcohol or drugs during your times with the children.

Frequently, men object to such limits being placed on them, especially if similar limits are not placed on their ex-wives. However, if the court believes that both you and your ex-wife have similar problems, both parties are usually given the same rules to follow.

Q: My wife and I do not agree about custody of the children. I heard that sometimes a psychologist decides where the children will live. How does that work?

A: When the parents cannot agree on where the children will live, the courts sometimes appoint a psychologist or other mental health professional to render an expert opinion on the matter. It is certainly better if you and your wife can come to some sort of agreement on this issue, but if you are unable to do so, the courts are usually reluctant to decide without the input of a professional.

During the evaluation you and your wife will meet, separately, usually on multiple occasions, with the evaluator. During these meetings you will have the opportunity to explain your side of the story, and you will be asked questions that have been raised as the result of the professional's interactions with your spouse. If there are allegations that there has been physical violence between you, for example, you will be able to describe what happened from your perspective. In addition, you will be asked numerous questions about such topics as discipline methods, child rearing techniques, and your ability to provide financially for the children.

Usually, you will also have some joint sessions with your children. The purpose of these joint meetings is to give the professional a view of how you interact with the kids. Naturally, your wife will also have joint meetings with the children. In addition, you and your wife will probably complete several paper and pencil psychological measures that evaluate such things as personality, attitudes, and use of substances. Often, you are also given the opportunity to have others (e.g. neighbors, family members, friends) render their opinions as to your parenting skills, ability to manage your temper, and the like.

Eventually, the professional prepares a report for the court with recommendations regarding placement of the child, visitation procedures, and other child-related details. Although the court does not have to follow the recommendations of the professional, typically the judge does.

Please note that if you are ordered to participate in such an evaluation, it is quite different than most other situations where you consult with a mental health professional. Typically speaking, mental health professionals scrupulously guard your privacy, but when you are ordered to complete an evaluation for the court, there is no confidentiality. Indeed, you should expect that anything you say can and will be revealed to not only the court but to your soon-to-be ex-wife and her attorney as well. We are not saying to be dishonest or less than candid during the evaluation. In fact, that would be a very bad idea since it is likely that the mental health professional will recognize your deceit, and this would probably weigh heavily against you in the subsequent report. However, you should be clear that there is no confidentiality in this situation.

Q: How does a psychologist determine if I am a good parent?

A: We have often met men who object to the findings in their divorce case made by a psychologist or other mental health professional. "How do they know enough after spending only a few hours with me and my child?" they ask.

The professionals who take on this kind of work are usually seasoned clinicians with extensive experience and additional training on rendering expert opinions to the court. They usually employ sophisticated psychological measures that have been well researched as part of their evaluation. In addition, they have seen many other families in similar circumstances, and they are highly trained in such areas as child development and family dynamics. If the court begins to feel that the professional's opinions are not well grounded, the court will soon begin to refer elsewhere. You may not like the results of the evaluation. In fact, it is our experience that everyone objects to some parts of the evaluation, but it is the method that courts usually prefer in obtaining an expert, outside opinion on these sensitive issues.

CHAPTER 4

"It was all love on my side, and all good comradeship on hers.
When we parted she was a free woman, but I could never
again be a free man."
—*Sir Arthur Conan Doyle,*
The Adventure of Abbey Grangee

THE LEGAL ANGLE

Lawyers tell us that even good businessmen frequently make bad business decisions when it comes to divorce. Marriage is always one part romance (about the "heart") and one part business (about the "head"). Divorce is not a good time to forget this duality.

When it becomes clear that a divorce is going to occur, many men (women, too) just want to get it over with as soon as possible. Sometimes, a man takes that position out of guilt. Maybe he had an affair, feels guilty, and therefore wants to end the marriage as quickly as possible with little fuss. Or maybe the guy chose to end the marriage, knows it will hurt others, and feels badly about the decision. These kinds of feelings may make you want to proceed rapidly so as not to prolong the agony. This rush to end things can lead to bad decision-making. As it is said, "Act in haste, regret in leisure."

Although it may be slower to let the process unfold through many steps, you will be less likely to feel poorly about your decisions in the future. We recommend that you heed the advice of your attorney as you go through the divorce in order to obtain a fair and equitable settlement.

AN EXAMPLE OF THE TRADITIONAL DIVORCE PROCESS[1] (AT LEAST IN TEXAS):

Petition the court for a decree of divorce. Hire a family attorney to represent you.

This lawyer then files a motion for the dissolution of marriage with the intake section of the county clerk's office. The clerk's office then determines which court will hear the case, calls the court clerk and sets the preliminary hearing date.

The spouse is then notified and "served" with divorce papers with notification of date and place of the preliminary hearing. She then hires her own family attorney. The two attorneys determine the issues of the divorce, asking for "discovery" (information).

At this time, motions may be filed for temporary restraining orders to prevent the other side from making major changes with regard to child custody, visitation, occupation of the home, and sale or transfer of community property. If so merited, the judge may choose to appoint a third attorney (known as an *ad litem* or *amicus* attorney) to represent the legal interests of minor children (paid for by both parties).

In a preliminary hearing, temporary orders are issued regarding child custody and support, temporary spousal support, and other issues needing attention.

Shortly after this hearing, either attorney or party requests a trial date from the court coordinator. If no mediation has been successful, an "impasse" is declared, and a trial takes places as scheduled, with the adversarial system in full swing. The judge will make sure that the rules are followed in cross examination, but this will not prevent emotional damage as every aspect of your married life is open to discussion and aggressive questioning. The judge will then either render a verdict and give final orders to the dissolution of the marriage, or adjourn the proceedings and set a later date to reconvene and issue final orders.

In Harris County (Houston), Texas, this process (before mediation was allowed) took an average of 59 months before getting ready for trial. Also, temporary orders often tended to be the final and permanent orders. Note that if, during any phase of this process, the petitioner failed to appear or did not respond or comply, then a motion can be submitted by the respondent to the court for a dismissal. And, if either side failed to comply with any of the court's preliminary or final orders, the other side can file a contempt motion, which the judge can decide without a jury trial. The offending party can then be sentenced to the county jail for a period of up to 179 days.

(modified by permission from Peter Sperling (2003))

Q: I think divorce is probably the best idea, but how can I afford it?

A: We frequently encounter men who express this sentiment. Sometimes they are referring to the high cost of divorce itself, while at other times they are talking about how much it will cost them in terms of their retirement plan, equity in the house, investments or child support.

First of all, even poor folks divorce. It may be expensive at some level, but there are ways to make it more affordable. In many locales, there are free or low cost legal services available through either the local bar association or some sort of other professional group. In our area (Harris County, Texas), the Houston Volunteer Lawyers Program will provide free legal representation in divorces as long as the total annual household income does not exceed a certain amount.[2] Another way to reduce the cost of the divorce is to represent yourself in the proceedings. Although this will undoubtedly reduce your expenses, you should pay attention to our caveats about this idea described in the next section. If you have no children and little property, representing yourself is less risky.

In some cases, you may be able to get an attorney to review your documents and give you advice without charge. For example, you may have a friend or relative who is an attorney who can do that for you, or that might be a service of your local lawyer's associations.

Another possibility to make divorce affordable would be to see if there are any attorneys in your area who are willing to work for a reduced fee. If you cannot get a reduced fee, you may still be able to structure your payments to the attorney so as to reduce the impact of the costs.

Now let's talk about the cost of divorce in terms of the long-term consequences to your bank accounts resulting from the division of property. (We discuss child support and alimony later in the book). While it is true that you and wife will have to split your joint assets, you also stand to benefit if she, too, has been contributing to a retirement account or similar investment. Whichever person has earned less is likely to benefit more, but, on the other hand, that person is also likely to be earning less in the future as well. So the burden is likely to even out over time. The guys that seem to have the most trouble with this are the ones whose wives were either not working outside the home or earning very little. No one likes to give up part of their hard-earned wealth, but that's the law. Most of us don't like to give so much to the government for taxes, either, but it is what we have to do. Likewise, you don't necessarily have to agree with the family law code, but we all have to abide by it. The best thing for you to do is to focus on your future earnings, not your past.

Q: Do I have to use an attorney to get a divorce?

A: The short answer to this question is "no." You don't have to use an attorney. Some people do what is referred to as a "kitchen table settlement" (more formally known as an uncontested divorce). Essentially, the two parties come to an agreement about settlement of assets, liabilities, and the children. They then draw up a document outlining their agreements. There are numerous on-line services (e.g. (LegalZoom.com; Divorcewriter.com; CompleteCase.com) available to help you do this. The couple then seeks to have this agreement sanctioned by a family court. The specifics of this vary from jurisdiction to jurisdiction. The cost of the on-line divorce assistance programs can be quite low ($150—$250 as of this writing). The ones we have listed are generally affiliated with the Better Business Bureau, and some have been featured on news stories on CNN, MS-NBC, and the like. They also offer guarantees that their divorce agreement will meet the test of the courts in your state. However, to use these services you and your wife have to agree on a lot of issues beforehand. That is often a problem since if you and she were in such ready agreement you probably wouldn't be divorcing.

The long answer to this question introduces another question: "Why in the world would you do this?" Most people indicate that want to avoid using an attorney because of one of more of the following reasons:

- ❏ To save money.

- ❏ Because they don't trust lawyers.

- ❏ They believe they are smart enough to do legal papers themselves.

Let's look at these reasons a little more deeply.

Of course, it is cheaper not to hire an attorney. That would be true in *any* legal situation. An attorney is expensive, but it can be a lot more expensive to undo what you have agreed to in court or other proceeding without legal advice. Most of us use an attorney when a lot of money is involved (e.g. to buy a house or business) or when the implications because of the proceedings are grave (e.g. when we are accused of a crime). In a divorce, probably half or more of your estate is at risk. In addition, the consequences of this legal agreement to you and your children will probably affect the rest of your life. In our opinion, it is penny wise and dollar foolish to do a divorce without an attorney.

A lot of people don't trust attorneys. They see them as "bottom feeders" that make their money off other people's pain and misery and don't contribute to society themselves. Others rant about "sue happy" lawyers who look for any provocation to seek damages. Of course, these negative opinions tend to vanish when we ourselves feel the need for legal protection or when we feel we have been wronged.

Some see family lawyers, in particular, as encouraging divorce in order to make a buck or as villains who are willing to do or say anything to win for their client. As in any profession, there are bad lawyers, but it would be unwise to "throw the baby out with the bath water."

The key is for you to find an attorney whom *you* trust. Select your legal counsel carefully. Make sure that the attorney works for you and not the other way around. Your attorney should be advising you as to how best to accomplish your objectives, but you should remain the decision-maker. If your attorney recommends options that are unacceptable to you, make your position known. If necessary, change lawyers! One of the most common complaints we hear about lawyers is that they are not responsive to phone calls from their clients. We recommend that you get a clear understanding from your attorney about how to communicate with him/her.

- ❏ What is their policy about returning phone calls or e-mails?

- ❏ Should you pre-arrange phone conference times?

- ❏ What should you expect in the way of communication with them?

Keep in mind that you will probably be charged for all of these communications, including those "brief" phone calls.

For those of you smart enough to do legal papers without an attorney—Bravo! But remember this is not an IQ test. This is your life and your money. This is probably your first or second divorce, but a family attorney has done hundreds of divorces. They know the questions to ask and the details to consider. (They know the judges, too.) Of course, if your divorce is relatively simple, you may be more able to manage the matter without outside counsel. However, many people start the divorce process thinking that it will be simple only to have it become much more complex as it unfolds.

You might have heard the adage "A lawyer who represents himself has a fool for a client." Consider its meaning before deciding that you don't need a lawyer.

Q: Can my wife and I use just one attorney?

A: You're not the only man with this question. In fact, we run into this idea quite often. Of course, it will be cheaper if you use one attorney. However, ethically an attorney can only represent one side of a case. That means that one attorney either represents you or your wife—not both. If the attorney represents you, that may be in your favor initially, but it may set in motion a future conflict if she later grows dissatisfied with the settlement. If, on the other hand, the attorney represents your wife, how comfortable will you be that you were fairly treated?

Q: How do I pick a good attorney?

A: Picking a good attorney is a very important step in ending a marriage. People typically get recommendations for an attorney from friends and family. The trick, though, is not just finding an attorney who can get you a divorce, but finding one who will represent your interests and concerns well. If you are concerned about being fair to your soon-to-be ex-wife, you probably don't want the attorney who advises you how to take most advantage of the situation. If you fear your ex will seek to limit your contact with the children, you want an attorney who values your role as a father.

There are probably times to hire the "bulldog" lawyer who will seek to get the most for you regardless of what it does to the other side. For the most part, though, this is a mistake, especially if you have children. Usually what happens then is that you set up future conflicts with your ex. We recommend that you select an attorney who prefers *negotiation* to *litigation*. If negotiation is not possible, though, you want to have confidence that your attorney can represent you well. You do not want to fear that you will be at a disadvantage because of the lawyer you hired. You need someone who can protect your rights without going so far as to impede your relationships with her and the children after the divorce.

In metropolitan areas, there are specialists who practice "family law." In rural settings, lawyers may be more generalists. It is helpful, though, if your attorney is familiar with the local family courts and the judge that will decide your case. For that reason, you are usually better off hiring a local attorney rather than bringing in a high-powered expert from out-of-town.

In any case, interview your attorney as if he or she is applying for a job to work for you. In fact, that is exactly what the lawyer is doing. Make sure *your* prospective lawyer understands your goals in the divorce (e.g., joint custody, fair settlement of the debts, possible reconciliation). A good attorney tries to understand where you are in the process, rather than advising you where you ought to be. Maybe you are only contemplating divorce. Maybe you have filed twice before and withdrawn the petition. You might have had an affair and are afraid about how that will affect the divorce. Perhaps you hope that if you file for divorce, she will realize you are serious about your dissatisfaction and will change her behavior. Ask how your attorney would proceed in accomplishing your goals. If your goals are unrealistic, your attorney should tell you so.

During your initial meeting notice how your prospective attorney listens to you. If the attorney is not listening well during this interview, he or she probably won't start listening better later. Look for an attorney that takes a "team approach." Explain what you want. See if the attorney can articulate a plan to accomplish *your* goals. On the other hand, is your attorney willing to respectfully disagree with you when necessary? You don't need a "yes man" (or "yes woman"). You need an expert who can work with you to accomplish your goals.

The cheapest attorney is not always the best deal. Nor is it better necessarily to have a high-priced attorney. If your wife has hired the most feared family lawyer in town, though, you probably don't want to select someone in their first year out of law school.

HOW TO SELECT AN ATTORNEY

Many men do not have a relative who is an attorney, so they wonder whom to use in conducting their divorce proceedings. Even if you do have such a relative, this may not be the best idea. Word of mouth, whether from friends or family, may not fit three major considerations in selecting a divorce attorney: *compatibility*, *experience*, and *income*. *Compatibility* means that he or she has the right "chemistry" for you—not for your family, or your friend. *Experience* refers to getting someone who is a full-time family lawyer, not a jack-of-all trades. *Income* means getting an attorney that serves your income sector of the community. Just like you wouldn't buy a Cadillac if you only needed a Chevy to get around, you wouldn't get a "high-priced attorney" if you only needed an attorney who specialized in middle-income bracket clients.

Some people look in the Yellow Pages or local phone book to find an attorney, but this is not a good method as you are selecting based on chance, not information. Even if you contact a lawyer-referral service, you are choosing from among those attorneys who have signed up to be referred. Sperling (2003)[3] recommends that a family attorney be selected based upon: the number of cases disposed of annually, the number of new cases opened annually, and an Efficiency Factor (EF), which he calculates as the least amount of activity to close cases. A higher EF means that the attorney requires less activity to close cases, thus saving money for their clients and the courts. The attorneys should be interviewed personally, and they should give you a ballpark figure on costs to complete the divorce process, both for traditional and the mediation methods. The lawyer should give you a free 20-minute session in which to do this. If not, look for another attorney.

Q: What should I discuss with my wife before hiring an attorney?

A: Although we recommend that you hire an attorney, we also think it is a good idea for you and your wife to try to work out the framework of an agreement on your own. Most couples try to do this, but if the level of animosity and anger is too high, it simply can't be done. If you believe that a productive discussion is possible, we recommend that you begin by assuring her that you want to create a settlement that you *both* will feel is fair. Rather than posturing as a negotiating ploy (i.e., asking for more than you want), indicate what you want plainly. Think also about what her biggest concerns are likely to be:

❑ Where will the kids live?

❑ How much alimony/spousal support will you provide?

❑ Will she have to go back to work?

Your goal should be to reduce rather than to increase her anxieties, which would benefit all parties. She will be more likely to see you as trustworthy and reasonable, making negotiations easier.[4]

There are usually four areas that need to be discussed:

❑ Children (*Where will the children live and what are the visitation arrangements?*)

❑ Financial Support (*Who pays child and/or spousal support, and how much?*)

❑ Assets (*Who gets what?*)

❑ Liabilities (*Who owes what?*)

Here are our suggestions in dealing with these areas:

Children. If you believe that the kids will be better off living primarily with your ex-spouse, don't try to make "points" by threatening to "take" the kids. Instead, acknowledge that you believe that the kids should live with her and that you want to have ample time to be with them as well.

If, on the other hand, you believe that the children should live primarily with you, understand that this may be very threatening to her. In today's world fathers generally have equal rights to the children. In many states, joint custody is the rule rather than the exception. Even so, children more commonly reside with their mothers post-divorce. If your soon-to-be-ex-partner agrees that it would be better for "Junior" to live with you, then there is no problem, but if she wants to have the child with her, then this can lead to a bitter conflict. Encourage her to consider that it is better for the two of you to make this important decision together rather than to turn it over to the court or to outside experts.

We do not suggest that you ask the children where they want to live. Doing so puts extraordinary pressure on them. However, if the two of you cannot resolve the issue, the children may be asked exactly that by the court or appointed experts. As parents, you know them best, and you should be the ones to make that decision.

Both of you should consider what the child has typically experienced. Which of the parents, for example, does most of the childcare? Who takes the child to the doctor? Who attends the school conferences? If you are not the parent who customarily has done these things, you could possibly begin now, but it will be another transition and adaptation the child will have to make.

The work and travel schedules of the two parents are other areas of consideration. If one of you travels a great deal, it may be less realistic for the children to reside with that parent. If your soon-to-be ex-wife is returning to work, she may be less sure of her schedule, while you may be able to make reasonable guesses.

If you are accustomed to putting the kids down at night or waking up with them in the morning, you may find it very difficult to accept that you will no longer be able to do this every day. It may be part of the cost that you have to pay when the marriage ends. It may be lousy, but you will have to make the best of it. Instead of lamenting that loss, plan on how to be a more involved father post-divorce.

We will talk more about visitation arrangements in Chapter 6, but for now, suffice it to say that we recommend that both of you be intensively and extensively involved in the children's lives. The children will do best when they feel loved and cared about by both of you, and they will not feel loved by you unless you are a frequent part of their lives.

Financial Support. The issue of financial support includes both *child support* and *alimony* (or spousal support as it is sometimes called). After all, they both come out of the same wallet.

Typically, since most children reside primarily with the mother, the father is the one who will pay child support. If the children reside with you, though, your ex might be required to pay child support. Most fathers say they are willing to pay child support, but they may balk at the amount. State laws publish guidelines that stipulate the minimal amounts of child support a parent has to pay. Frequently, dads look to these guidelines and with the support of their attorneys seek to pay minimal child support. They don't want to provide a "lavish post-divorce lifestyle" to their ex. Remember, though, that if the children are living with their mother, the amount of child support you provide will directly affect the children's standard of living as well. This is especially true if your ex has limited ability to earn an income.

Our advice is for you and your wife to be realistic about both the income you can expect to generate and the expenses you both will encounter. We have included a budget table from Marrgulies (2004) that we think can be most useful in this process. We recommend that you and your partner (soon-to-be ex) make copies of this form and complete the following exercise.

1. Create a joint budget, filling in the blanks of the form based on the actual expenses you have encountered as a family over the last three months. You will note that the form includes the major expenses that most families have as well as some blanks for additional items unique to your situation. If you use a financial management program such as Quicken (Intuit) or Microsoft Money (Microsoft), this is an easy task because it categorizes the various expenses. If you don't use such a program, go through your checkbook, debit card receipts, and financial papers to get a realistic picture on how much you are spending. We admit that creating a budget can be rather time-consuming, but the goal is to get realistic about money. Always a good idea!!

   2. You (and your partner) should then each repeat the process on your own, creating separate budgets based on the amounts of money you expect to spend now that you will be living apart. Include in your estimated expenses the child and spousal support that you expect to be paid. Note that some expenses will go up, some will go down, and some will be unchanged. For example, if the kids are with you about 40% of time, you will have to pay for the groceries you need for yourself as well as the groceries you will need to feed them when they are with you. Similarly, both you and she will have housing expenses, but they may be determined, in part, on the need for both of you to provide bedrooms for the children. Some expenses might change for one of you but remain unchanged for the other. For example, your partner's gasoline expenses might not change, but yours might go up because you have to drive across town to pick them up multiple times a month.

   In doing this process, it is important to be realistic. Don't "pad" your anticipated expenses. Try to get a real feel of the costs both of you will encounter. Of course, these are only estimates, but they should be based on your experience from Step 1 (i.e., from the expenses that the family has actually encountered recently). We think that this step is especially important for men because they often underestimate the expenses associated with running a household and raising kids. This step will help you become more prepared for the expenses you will encounter and more able to realistically negotiate the child support.

   3. Both of you should then complete the sections of the separate budgets concerning anticipated income. Base these estimates on past history as well as on realistic projections. Include in your estimates of income the child support that will be paid. Don't overestimate what

BUDGET FORM[5]		
MONTHLY EXPENSES		
SCHEDULE A: SHELTER		
Tenant		
Rent		
Heat		
Utilities		
Tenant insurance		
Homeowner		
Mortgage		
Real estate taxes		
Homeowners insurance		
Heat		
Utilities		
Other		
Tenant or Homeowner		
Telephone		
Cable TV		
Other		
Total Shelter Costs		
SCHEDULE B: TRANSPORTATION		
Auto payment		
Auto insurance		
Maintenance		
Fuel		
Commuting expenses		
Total Transportation Expense		

Sample Budget Form adapted from Margolies by permission[5]

SCHDULE C: PERSONAL EXPENSES		
Food at hoome and household supplies		
Restaurants		
Nonprescription drugs / cosmetics.		
Clothing		
Hair care		
Entertainment, sports & hobbies		
Gifts & contributions		
Newspapers & periodicals		
Life insurance		
Medical insurance		
Unreimbursed medical & dental		
Psychotherapy/ counseling		
Prescription drugs		
Payments to nonchild dependents		
Prior family child support		
Adult educational expense		
Monthly debt service		
Domestic help		
Orthodontics		
Children's private school costs		
Day care expense		
Children's lessons		
Children's tutoring		
Summer camp		
Babysitting		
Other		
Total Personal Expenses		
Total Budget (Schedules A + B + C)		

one of you can earn. If your wife has been out of the work force for a while, consider how this will affect her earning potential as well as her ability to even find a job. Maybe she can earn a good salary, but it might take her a while to "ramp up." She may need to return to school or to retrain in order to attain an adequate income level. Rather than seeing this as a "scam" to get you to support her, we recommend you see this as a "win-win" proposition. If she is more able to support herself financially, she will have less dependence on you in the future, and the children will get a better lifestyle.

If there are questions about your ex-spouse's ability to work or which career field she should pursue, we recommend that the two of you agree to contract with a skilled career counselor with the goal of getting recommendations for her career direction. This type of counseling is generally short in duration and is solution-focused. Rather than agreeing to an open-ended counseling experience, we recommend that you contract for a limited number of sessions, say three or four. The cost would be split between the two of you. The contract should specify that if she chose to continue the counseling, she would bear the full expense of additional sessions.

It is in your best interest for her to be successfully employed. Of course, if you are the one who is returning to work or needs further career direction, these same rules should apply for you.

4. Now compare the income side with the expense side for both of you and answer these questions:

- ❏ Will the child and spousal support be adequate for the lifestyles you both want for your children? If not, can they be adjusted?

- ❏ Will the amounts of planned child and spousal support be too burdensome for the parent paying the support, given the anticipated income and expenses?

- ❏ What are the difficult choices the two of you will have to make in order to meet your budget goals (e.g., selling the house, getting a higher paying job)?

We stress the importance of making these financial decisions during the ending of the marriage in a business-like way. Put your businessman's hat on, not your emotional one.

Assets. Generally speaking, what was yours before the marriage will be yours after the marriage. Likewise, what was hers before will be hers afterwards. There are some exceptions such as when something you owned before (e.g., a house) was improved (e.g., remodeled) with money earned during the marriage. These are technical issues that vary with the law from state to state. The point we want to make is that you and your soon-to-be ex should discuss what would be the preferred way of dealing with these assets. Don't try to lay claims to her family heirlooms as a way of getting back at her or simply because you always liked that antique bureau. That can make the negotiating process much more difficult and nasty. Of course, the same rules should apply to her.

Liabilities. We recommend that you handle liabilities in more or less the same way as assets. Discuss the indebtedness you share and what parts, if any, are individual debts. If you just had to buy that new Corvette, maybe that should be your liability. If the credit card bills are largely hers, maybe she should shoulder the majority of that debt. The main thing is to try to create an atmosphere of fairness so that the divorce process can be as smooth as possible, especially if children are involved, since you will need to maintain a more functional relationship post-divorce for their sake.

I've heard about mediation. How does this differ from divorce court?

A: When many of us think of "divorce court" we picture a scene out of *Law and Order* or *Perry Mason*. Actually, most divorces nowadays are settled out of court in some kind of "alternative dispute resolution."

Simple Mediation. No attorneys are used except to review the agreements before they are formally submitted to the judge in the family court. Simple mediation is more appropriate when there are no children and few assets or liabilities. It can be done in one to two sessions with a mediator.

Formal Mediation. An agreement is eventually reached between the two parties with the help of their respective attorneys. The judge eventually reviews the agreement to ensure that it meets the standards of the law, and then signs off. Actual court proceedings, especially those involving juries, only occur in very contentious cases. This is not the scenario that you want. It is the most expensive way to go and generally results in more legal wrangling in the future. Furthermore, if you have children, the kids are more apt to become involved in the divorce suit, much to their detriment.

"Just another of our many disagreements. He wants a no-fault divorce, whereas I would prefer to have the bastard crucified."

Formal mediation is often used to resolve the differences outside of court. The intent of mediation is to avoid the trauma and the expense of the couple going to court to settle their differences. Furthermore, it is generally believed that mediation empowers couples to make the important decisions regarding the ending of their marriage rather than leaving those decisions to a judge or jury. In mediation, a neutral third party is either appointed or agreed to by the two sides to strike an agreement between the parties. Many mediators—though not all—are themselves attorneys. Others are psychotherapists or other kinds of professionals. Mediators typically go through a training program to equip them with the necessary skills. They may also employ other kinds of professionals (e.g., accountants) to provide them with additional expertise or information pertinent to the divorce (e.g., tax liability, assets).

At a formal mediation, you will be represented and accompanied by your attorney. Your spouse will be similarly represented. Just like in a business deal, each side will present their wants and "demands." The mediator will attempt to bring the two sides to an agreement. Sometimes the mediation is done "face to face" with all the parties in a single room. In other situations, the setup is more like "shuttle diplomacy." In this arrangement, the mediator shuttles between two rooms bringing proposals from the other side seeking to negotiate a deal.

Mediation often appears to proceed very slowly, especially at the start. It takes time for the mediator to help the parties come to basic terms with each other, to ascertain how they view the circumstances surrounding the ending of the marriage, and to determine how well they will work together through the divorce process. It is also slow because there is an emphasis (necessarily) on the feelings that need to be expressed and processed prior to working on agreements dealing with the sensitive issues of children and property. Experience has shown that once these feelings are out in the open, the parties can come to a quicker (and better) accord. If the couple has children, a good mediator may ask that the parties open their wallets and put pictures of their children on the table before them, to remind the often-warring parties that the negotiation should not be adversarial between the two (soon-to-be) ex-spouses. Rather, it should be focused on establishing a partnership in rearing the children post-divorce. The marriage will soon be over, but cooperation will be needed with the two parties working together to make the best plans for the children's education, living arrangements, and quality of life post-divorce.

The actual mediation can sometimes be a difficult experience. Quite often, the negotiations go on for hours, sometimes into the wee hours of the night, especially when the two sides are far apart or are struggling around a key issue. Sometimes when tired from a long struggle, couples agree to something that they later regret. If the two parties don't ultimately sign the agreement, the whole process may be rendered null and void when your spouse changes her mind about what she verbally agreed to do. Remember, too, that the mediator's job is to obtain an agreement, not to make sure that you are fairly treated. Your attorney has the role of watching out for your interests. Mediation is not cheap, either. After all, there will be two attorneys as well as the mediator present—all of whom usually charge by the hour. Even so, the expense of mediation is much less than the cost of a trial in family court.

If it appears we are being negative about mediation, our apologies. We actually think that there is merit to mediation, particularly in contrast to settling a divorce in court. However, many of our clients have expressed dissatisfaction—even dismay—about the mediation process, expecting it to feel more balanced and less stressful. Our commentary is intended to help you be more realistic in your expectations.

> *In an effort to save money, Bruce repeatedly tried to personally negotiate a divorce settlement with his wife, which constantly fell flat. Recognizing that he was making little progress, he suggested mediation. Bruce, his wife Robin, their mutual attorneys, and a third attorney who served as the mediator met in an effort to end the impasse and to avoid an even more costly court battle. The mediation was set for 9 AM, and Bruce expected that after a few hours the mediator would be able to hammer out an agreement between the two sides. However, at 2 AM, the two sides were still struggling over every provision. Eventually, after many, many hours of "negotiation", a deal was struck. However, his wife refused to sign the document that evening, saying she needed to sleep on it. As you might guess, by the next day she decided not to sign at all, rendering all of their discussions pointless. Eventually, another mediation day was scheduled. After lengthy deliberations, a document was finally agreed upon. It was virtually identical to the*

first. Mediation is not always a civil affair; keep your expectations humble.

Q: What is a collaborative divorce?

A: Let's face it. No matter how you do it, divorce is a corrosive process. It is no fun hearing your wife's attorney accusing you of deception while they also ask for more child support. Whether it is in court or in a mediator's office, hearing such accusations is guaranteed to be stressful. Your self-esteem can surely take a tumble during divorce proceedings, just at the time when you may already be feeling like a failure because your marriage is ending.

Collaborative divorce is a new legal trend intended to make divorce less negative.[6] It is based on different assumptions than the adversarial forms of divorce we have been discussing. In collaborative divorce, each side is represented by an attorney who agrees to practice a collaborative model. Essentially, it is a non-adversarial procedure. Rather than trying to win for his or her client, the collaborative attorney is committed to seeking a fair settlement for all parties. In collaborative divorce the two attorneys share more openly with each other about their client's position in an effort to be above board and equitable. Outside experts, such as psychotherapists for the children or tax accountants, may be employed to render expert opinions on the deliberations. Rather than using a third-party neutral mediator, there is more direct negotiation between the two parties with attorneys guiding and advising the process.

There is usually a series of joint meetings with both parties and their attorneys discussing their concerns openly. Sometimes, the outside experts attend these meetings. For example, your child's therapist might attend a meeting to give an opinion as to where your child should live.

Sometimes, though, it is impossible for the two parties to come to an agreement. If it is necessary for the parties to go to court, the collaborative lawyers typically withdraw from the case. This is to ensure that the lawyer is motivated to settle the case through the collaborative process rather than to seek resolution in court.

The real bonus in the collaborative process is that it is the least toxic to the couple. It typically feels more humane and less "legalistic." It also gives maximum emphasis to the wishes of the couple, which is especially helpful for couples who have children as it tends to cause less animosity post-divorce.

Collaborative divorce is more expensive than the use of a single attorney; however, it is less expensive than a courtroom battle and less traumatic for most people than mediation. It is best suited for couples who are willing to negotiate, those who are not seeking to damage their former partner, and for those committed to work out the best arrangement for the children, even if it is not necessarily what they want. Collaboration will *not* work if you and your spouse are in such dispute that you cannot stand the sight of each other. We recommend the collaborative process when possible because it is less damaging to all parties.

Q: Should I go to counseling during a divorce?

A: A lot of people feel reluctant to go to counseling while going through divorce. Although this is inarguably one of the most stressful times in a person's life, these people reason that it is somehow a bad time to seek outside counsel or support, or that it may be used against them.

If this is not the right time to talk to a counselor, when would be the right time? It does not make you a "wuss" to ask for help and support. We're not saying that everyone will have a mental breakdown when going through a divorce, but virtually everyone will have difficult moments. A counselor can provide both emotional support and an outside perspective that can be both reassuring and insightful.

You're right. We're counselors ourselves. You would expect us to say something like that—tooting our own horns, so to speak. However, we've seen lots of people going through the divorce process, and we know from their feedback that it helped to have a concerned listener who had experience in such situations "on their team" as they went through the divorce.

You may feel that you have friends in whom you prefer to confide. "Why do I need a counselor if I have friends? I can tell them anything. I don't want to get advice from a stranger that doesn't even know me!" The advantage of seeing a counselor is that counselors have been through a lot of divorces with others. We counselors know how people generally react, what will usually work, and what doesn't work. We also know the court system, which can be an intimidating place to negotiate. Furthermore, we can be more objective than your friends. We're not going to just take your side or fuel you with comments like "You shouldn't have to take that stuff from her."

Another fear men sometimes offer for not going to see a counselor is that it might be used against them in court. The reasoning here is that going to see a counselor implies that you might be mentally ill or somehow inadequate as a parent. That stereotype is antiquated. If anything, courts usually view going to counseling as a positive step towards self-responsibility, not a negative admission or an indictment of inadequacy. If you truly have a "mental illness," the court would look favorably upon your seeking help. On the other hand, very few people who go to counseling have what would be accurately diagnosed as a mental illness. Rather, they are part of the "worried well" who make up the vast majority of clients who seek counseling or psychotherapy. Sure, they might feel some depression or anxiety at times, but this should be distinguished from those few people who have severe mental illnesses such as schizophrenia, bipolar (manic/depressive) illness, or severe major depression. Most judges look favorably upon those who seek help. After all, the judges have their hands full with petitioners who are locked into combat over such matters as child custody, precisely because they have ignored the advice or counsel of mental health professionals.

Frequently, people going through a divorce will say that they don't have enough time to address their emotional needs. They argue that they are so busy taking care of the legal, financial, and child problems, they can't afford the luxury of taking care of their "mere" emotional concerns. Essentially, they are saying that emotional health is not all that important, especially in comparison to these other themes. If you don't take your emotional health seriously during a divorce, however, you are much more likely to make bad decisions during the process. Those bad decisions can cost you a lot of money as you may fight over inconsequential matters. They also make you less able to help your children as they deal with the divorce. The amount of time and money you spend in counseling is usually relatively small compared to the overall time and money needed to bring about a divorce. In addition, you are less likely to make costly mistakes in going through the process.

We men are well-known for our reluctance to go to counseling. In part, this is because as men we have been socialized to:

❏ Avoid being dependent on others. *("I can handle this myself.")*

❏ Not acknowledge our losses and pain. *("I hate her for what she did to me.")*

❏ Hide vulnerability and apparent weakness. *("I have it all under control.")*

❏ Emphasize doing something over experiencing our feelings. *("What's the point if you can't do anything about it?")*

Psychologists Fred Rabinowitz and Sam Cochran in their book *Deepening Psychotherapy with Men* (2002)[7] note that we men are most likely to externalize our psychological distress through action, distraction, and/or compulsive acting out. Consequently, men are more likely than women to get in trouble because of substance abuse, anger, violence, antisocial behavior, or difficulties in social relationships. If you are having trouble in any of these areas, we suggest that you give counseling a shot. If you are not experiencing any of those problems, you might still want to consider counseling because going through a divorce, even when it is necessary, always brings up issues of loss. Probably all men (and women) have some feelings of rejection, defeat, and discouragement as a result of the divorce. Those feelings, whether openly admitted or not, are often the source of problems post-divorce if they are not adequately addressed as you go through the process.

However, it has been noted that psychotherapy or counseling, at least as it is often practiced, doesn't necessarily fit well with the sensibilities and needs of men.[8] It probably would not surprise you that perhaps three-fourths of all counseling clients are women. This has been true throughout the history of counseling as a profession. One of the negative consequences of this is that most counselors are far more familiar and comfortable in working with women than with men. Furthermore, the models and techniques that they employ were largely developed to help women. For these reasons, if you are thinking about going to counseling, we think that it is important to find a professional who is skilled in working with men. (Note: This does not necessarily mean that you should see a male counselor since female counselors may be very skilled in helping men, too.)

Most men prefer counselors who:

❏ Are active more than passive

❏ Give direct feedback

❏ Offer practical advice or direction

❏ Collaborate rather than act as the expert

❏ Offer tools for overcoming problems

❏ Don't have an anti-male attitude

If the above criteria make sense to you, ask the potential counselor about his/her style of work and see if it is congruent with this list. In addition, find out about the counselor's previous experience in seeing men. A telling question is to ask about his/her view of the differences in working with men and women in counseling. If the answer is "not much," you may want to keep looking. Finally, in some larger communities you may be able to find a psychologist or other mental health professional who specializes in seeing men.

Q: What exactly is community property?

A: Some states are described as *"community property"* states. Although the legal definitions of community property vary somewhat from state to state, in general, "community property is all property acquired after the marriage, except property that one spouse is given, inherits, or recovers from personal injuries."[9]

A few examples:

- ❑ The money Aunt Minnie left you is *not* community property.

- ❑ The income you earned from your job *is* community property.

- ❑ The golf clubs given to you by your brother is *not* community property.

- ❑ The interest you earned on your savings account *is* community property.

- ❑ The judgment you received for the injuries you sustained in an accident at work is *not* community property.

- ❑ The recovery for loss of earnings due to the injuries *is* community property.

- ❑ The money you made while gambling *is* community property.

"Separate property" is the term used to describe the property owned by a married person that is not community property. Your attorney will clarify any questions that you may have regarding what is separate property and what is community property.

Community property is considered to be owned by both parties, so at the time of divorce it is divided between them. Although the community property may be divided evenly, the court is not required to do so. In contrast, separate property is retained fully by one party (i.e., it is not divided). Indeed, the court must award separate property to the spouse who owns it.

Q: How should I negotiate during divorce?

A: In a good business negotiation, both parties feel positive about the ultimate deal. Neither side feels disadvantaged. Both sides think they got what they most needed. Perhaps it is rather optimistic, but we feel that the same kinds of goals should be established for negotiations during divorce.

"Negotiations are going to be tougher than I thought. Your wife is being backed by Syria."

Speaking of goals, get as clear as you can about *your* goals during the divorce. Clarifying your own goals is important regardless of who filed for the divorce. Perhaps you don't want the divorce at all. If so, then your goal might be reconciliation, but remember the divorce might just happen anyway.

> Bernard stated firmly in a joint counseling session with his wife, Theresa, "Divorce isn't an option." He should have added the caveat "...for me." Despite this sincere declaration, his wife divorced him anyway.

Remember your partner doesn't have to agree with you about the divorce. It takes two people to stay married, but only one to divorce.

If she wants the divorce, and you don't, you better come up with some other goals in case she prevails and you get divorced in spite of your desires. You need a backup position. What will your goals be if you *do* divorce? For some people, the goal might be to recover from the divorce as quickly as possible. For others, it might be to have equal say in raising the kids. Yet others are more focused on the financial impact of the divorce (e.g., on their retirement funds).

Today, a common goal for men going through divorce is to have more time with their children and more opportunities for maintaining a relationship with them post-divorce. Some men give up on their goals regarding the children too quickly, believing that they can't prevail with the courts. In many jurisdictions, though, fathers are perceived to have every bit as much right to the children as do mothers. In fact, the presumption that mothers have more rights to children than do fathers is a relatively recent phenomenon largely observed in the 20th century. In centuries past, the children were considered the natural "property" and responsibility of the father, not the mother. Now in the 21st century, fathers and mothers are generally seen to have equal rights to the children.

The courts don't like to make the decision as to where the children will live. They prefer the parents to make the decision themselves. The courts feel (and we agree) that the parents are in the best position to decide what is best for their kids. It is commonplace for the courts to award "joint custody" to the parents, meaning they both have equal rights in decision-making. However, the real sticking point is often where the child *will actually live*. As we previously suggested, it is in the best interests of all parties for you and your wife to come to an agreed decision about where the children will live. This is often the most painful and difficult issue in divorce. Sometimes, a mediator or a counselor can help you resolve this dilemma. At other times, when the couple is too contentious, a psychologist or other professional is appointed to recommend to the court where the child should live, whether joint custody is feasible, how visitation should be handled, and/or similar concerns regarding the children.

Most of us don't make good business decisions when we get too emotionally involved in the process. Remember how hard it is to get a good price from a car salesman after you have "fallen in love" with that red convertible? Your attorney can really be helpful here. When you are emotionally over-involved in the divorce, your attorney can remind you of your goals as you begin "foaming at the mouth" because of what your wife said, wrote, or hinted.

It will be useful for you to keep in mind your wife's major goals in the process. If, for example, she is worried about having to go back to work, she will perhaps fight more around issues that impact her ability to make a good living. If you can support her in the goals that are most critical for her, she may be more willing to make concessions in other areas. For the most part, we think it is best to appeal to the "kinder side" of your spouse. When you do, she is more apt to be generous in return.

Of course, you may feel that no matter what you do, she (and/or her attorney) will try to "screw you." Sometimes that's true. No matter how nice you are the other side will be out to get whatever they can. You may wonder why you should make any concessions feeling that they'll just come back to bite you later. We recommend that you at least start with the hope that the process will be civil and fair. If that hope proves ill founded, then, sure, don't stick your head in the sand when you are getting pounded. Keep in mind, though, that if you expect the worst from people, that's what you will usually get. Get counsel from your attorney about whether or not what she is wanting is really unusual or unreasonable. Most importantly, think of this in the long term, especially if you have kids. This is not the last negotiation with her. It's one of the first. Separate the emotional elements as best you can from your business judgment.

Then there are those men who attempt to appease their partners by giving up too much too readily. Sometimes this is out of guilt, but often it is in the hopes that the other side will then be "nice." Remember the historical example of the English Prime Minister Neville Chamberlain attempting to appease the Nazis in Czechoslovakia. If your wife acts like a "storm trooper" this strategy will not only fail, it will be a disaster, but most wives are not quite so draconian. Here again, heed the advice of your attorney if you are told you are being too gracious or generous. Seek to be fair, not self-sacrificing or selfless.

As people go through a divorce, they vacillate in their emotional reactions. Sometimes they will feel angry and want to punish their spouses. At other times, they will seem almost indifferent to the process, putting the whole matter seemingly "on the back burner." At other moments, they may become focused on how wonderful "single life" will be: wine, women/men, and song. At yet other times, they will be focused on the burdens inherent in divorce: raising kids alone, going back to work, moving out of the family home. Don't be surprised when your spouse (or you) seems to be in a very different mood than when you last talked about a matter. Of course, your respective moods will have a lot to do with how successfully you have been able to talk about things. Don't expect to make progress if one or both of you is too angry to talk without yelling. That's a lot like the story of teaching pigs to sing…it's frustrating to you and annoying to the pigs.

Q: Can filing for divorce bring us back together?

A: As couples come close to the precipice of divorce, they often get frightened. Do I really want to go through with this? The consequences frequently become more real to the couple as they negotiate the terms of the divorce. Sometimes, they plunge back into the relationship in order to avoid dealing with those consequences. Quite often, they become sexual again hoping to rekindle the old fires or to forget the pain of what was wrong. This is not necessarily bad, but it is not necessarily good either. After you get your clothes back on, the problems that led you to contemplate divorce will still be there. If the two of you are really considering getting back together, this is a great time to seek joint counseling. You both may now be more motivated to fix the problems in the relationship as you have realistically considered the alternative (i.e., divorce).

Family lawyers tell us that women, more often than men, go to an attorney with the hope that this will prompt their partner to change. They don't necessarily want the divorce, but they *do* want him to be different. For these women, going to an attorney or filing for divorce is a "shot across the bow." It may be a final effort to get their husbands to heed their concerns. If you think that this is the situation with your wife, and *you* want to save the marriage, this is your chance to tell her that things will be different. Of course, if you don't follow up those words with real actions, then you may only postpone your divorce. Our advice is not to make vague promises or to make commitments that you know you cannot keep. If you want to reconcile, the two of you need to become as clear as possible about what has to change and how will she (and you) know if it happens. Again, this effort is much more likely to pay off if you engage the services of a good marital counselor. One of our favorite techniques to make this change commitment more successful is to postpone the divorce action for a specific period of time, say six months, and then decide if enough progress has been made to justify staying in the marriage.

> *Annie filed for divorce after her husband blew up one too many times. Fortunately for him, what she really wanted was for him to do something about his anger. When he began to go to anger management classes, she became more hopeful that he was sincere about making a change. Later, the couple started marital counseling, and he was relieved to see that there were some things his wife needed to learn, too. She subsequently withdrew the divorce action.*

Q: I'm in my dream house. Do I have to give it up?

A: The question of who gets the house is often a tricky one in divorce, especially if the house has a lot of history for the family or if it is your "dream house".

If kids are involved, an important question to address is where they will be living. Ideally, you want them to continue living in the same home. Staying in the same house allows the kids to continue in the same schools and to have their same friends. It provides an element of continuity for them. Their lives will be disrupted enough by not living with both parents.

Sometimes, however, it will not be possible for the children to remain in the home. When the parents have to sell the home because one or both cannot afford the payments on their own, financial reality takes precedence over continuity. If finances are the primary motive for selling, there may be creative alternatives (e.g., refinancing can prevent loss of the house).

If you are trying to stay in the home yourself, be realistic about the decision. Can you really afford the payments without the financial contributions from your spouse? Would you really want to stay in a place that big? Do you need all that space? Will you be haunted by memories when you walk in the bedroom? The living room?

For couples with more than one house, similar issues arise. For example, which house do you get: the one in the city or the one at the lake? The lake house might be great for the weekends, but it might make for a long commute during the week. Again, be realistic about your lifestyle and about what is most important to you.

As to the dream house you may lose, build or buy another. You don't want your original dream home to become your nightmare house. Create a new dream home.

Q: What about my other prized possessions?

A: When it becomes evident to men that divorce is likely, they often begin to think of the loss of prized possessions. For some of us it is the shiny red sports car ("She never liked to drive it anyway"). For others, the boat ("My boat...I need my boat!"). We have also seen both men and women who in their anger took perverse pleasure out of depriving the former partner of some personal treasure (e.g., half of her collection of rare dolls or his baseball cards).

We would discourage you from using the divorce to take petty revenge on your spouse. She might take another tack, but we recommend that you take the moral high ground so at the end of the day you will still have your self-respect. If she is asking for your prized possessions, try to negotiate the matter with her. Usually, there is something else that she wants, and she is using your possession as a bargaining chip. Of course, what she wants you to concede may make the price too high. In that case, remind yourself that it is only "stuff," and as the late comedian George Carlin told us, you probably already have more "stuff" than you need. Besides, you can still get more "stuff."

If you have children, think about the impact on them. It might be nice to have the sports car, but you might really need the mini-van, especially if you have the children a lot of the time. And that leather furniture or the formal dining table may be less useful post divorce.

Phil participated regularly in a men's counseling group during his divorce. He tried to get the court to award him his wife's heirloom china. It wasn't that he really fancied it; he lived in a mobile home!! What he wanted was to punish his wife. The group was divided:

those who said, "Go for it! Make that woman pay!" ; and those who said, "Don't do it. We've been down that road. It's like drinking poison for you."

In the final settlement he didn't get the china, but he did manage to make his ex-wife stiffen her position on other matters, costing him in the long run. Furthermore, he looked bad to his kids who, naturally, learned about the whole mess.

"You don't know a woman until you've met her in court."
—Norman Mailer

THE FIRST PHASE AFTER DIVORCE: GETTING YOUR HEAD BACK TOGETHER

CHAPTER 5

_____

"My toughest fight was with my first wife."
—*Muhammad Ali*

GAMES AND SERIOUS STUFF

In this chapter, we discuss issues that are often troublesome post-divorce. Some of these problems may be started by actions of your ex-wife, but others are the result of decisions you have made, or simply contemplated. Our goal in the chapter is to steer you away from common problems.

Q: My friends tell me I'm obsessed with getting even with my ex-wife. Is this normal?

A: If you're so angry at your ex-wife that you can't think of much else, we commend you on acknowledging your obsession. You are probably right. You are not going to be able to make much progress on making a future until you can let go of some of that feeling towards the ex.

Sometimes letting go of anger is made more difficult by remembering what happened during the divorce process. You may wonder how she could have thought of some of the things she did, or said some of the things she said. We have seen many men struggle for a long time over comments from the wife such as "I haven't loved you in ____ years" or "You were always too controlling." Consider the fact that people often make extreme statements during a divorce to justify their decision to leave the marriage. Later, in retrospect, people frequently regret having made such comments or even forget having made them at all. Many people come to realize that their ex wasn't nearly so bad, and may even have fond memories.

Men may also be bothered by what the wife's attorney said or did during legal proceedings. Remember that attorneys are apt to say provocative things in an effort to advantage their client (in this case your ex-wife). Try not to take these comments personally. Remember what happens after a tough football game: After beating on each other for 60 minutes, the players congratulate each other on a well-fought game.

If you find it impossible to let go of your anger towards your ex, you may need to talk with a psychologist or psychotherapist. For most of us, though, those angry feelings recede with time. Get busy in some new projects: the trip you postponed, the business idea you put on hold, or getting down to "catching weight" (i.e., making yourself more attractive).

Q: What can I do about my sense of failure?

A: Most people who go through a divorce experience some sense of failure. After all, when we marry, we usually expect that the relationship will last for the rest of our lives. Indeed, most wedding ceremonies say something about "til death do we part," not "til divorce do we part." On the other hand, divorce is a common phenomenon. Michelle Weiner-Davis (2001) notes in her book *The Divorce Remedy* that more than one million people divorce each year, and it is well-established that at least 40% of marriages end in divorce.[1] So if you conclude that you have failed, welcome to the club. It's a big club, so don't be too hard on yourself.

Men often tell us that the divorce means that they "wasted" ten, fifteen, or more years on a marriage that didn't or couldn't work. By that sort of reckoning we are all constant failures since life is always a series of trials and errors, learning from our experiences, and moving from one stepping stone to the next. We don't think that the "wasted time" framework is a fair way to evaluate your marriage. In fact, it is a downright depressing way to look at things. We would recommend that you take a more balanced view.

Consider the positive moments and experiences that you had together, rather than focusing only on the negatives. It might even be useful for you to take out a piece of paper and write down the benefits that you received from this marriage. You really don't need to write down the negatives; you are already very familiar with them. In doing this exercise, most people, if they are parents, begin by thinking about their children. They frequently return too quickly, however, to recounting—in exquisite and agonizing detail—their losses. Don't underestimate how much you have gained from your marriage: not only the children, but also the times that you did enjoy with your wife. Marriages, even those that end in divorce, have good moments. In addition, while married, other important moments have occurred for you. You may have progressed in your career, you might have traveled together, and don't forget the time at the party when you both dressed up as Elvis. It is better to see divorce as an important transition to a new phase of your life than as a failure.

Q: How can I get over my guilt about the marriage ending?

A: For some of us, guilt, and perhaps even shame, are primary emotions after divorce. If you feel that you were the "cause" of the divorce, this kind of guilt is more likely. However, divorce is never the product of just one person, no matter what the circumstances. We are not trying to let you "off the hook" here. You are accountable for your part in the marriage ending. You have at least some responsibility in the outcome. If you made some obvious errors (e.g., you had an affair or hid money from her), then your role in the outcome may be pretty clear. On the other hand, even if she made some blatant mistakes, you still have something to do with it. Indeed, you picked her.

Guilt sometimes gets a bad reputation. After all, it is not a pleasant emotion to experience. However, guilt is nature's way of telling us, "Don't keep making the same mistake." Use feelings of guilt to remind you of how you want to act differently in the future. Try to get clear about your role in the end of the marriage and come up with some lessons that you have learned from the marriage. If the lesson you learned was "don't marry a 'b...'," then you probably haven't looked deep enough. On the other hand, if you are concluding that everything is your fault, then you are absorbing too much of the blame.

Q: Am I a sinner because I went through a divorce?

A: Of course, we are psychologists, not clerics. We really can't answer this question for you completely, but it may be a vital one for you to ask. If you struggle with the role of sin in divorce, then spend some time with a trusted religious leader of your faith and ask for some spiritual guidance. For some of us, that can be very painful, but it can also provide you some relief as you discuss your situation and the choices that are congruent with your religious tradition. Even if you are not actively religious, or even if you consider the question quaint or trivial, you may find that the divorce experience sends you on a spiritual search. It is important to find a comfortable religious community in which you can ask these questions and conduct this exploration.

Q: Should I throw a party for my divorce?

A: It has become somewhat fashionable these days for people to throw a party to "celebrate" a divorce. Merchandisers are even getting in on the act, printing "divorce cards" and special balloons commemorating the occasion. A "divorce celebration" should not be confused with a wake or similar event held when a beloved person dies. A wake is about honoring the life of a deceased person, while a "divorce party" is more like crapping on the person who is gone. Imagine how you will feel if you learn that she and her friends hold a party to rejoice getting rid of you. Such events really "kick sand in the face" of the other person, and they can be a source of continuing animosity if your ex finds out about it. So tell your friends to skip the cake or the keg party.

There is another reason why this kind of "make happy" event is inappropriate. Many of us try to avoid painful experiences by pretending that they are cheery ones. Most of us would agree that divorce is fundamentally not a happy time. Even when divorce is clearly the right decision to make, it also marks the end of some of the dreams about your life. It really is OK to experience some pain here. If you do, you are being more realistic about what has happened. We think that this will help you in facing your future and you will be less likely to lead to a delayed, increasingly negative reaction (e.g., depression) later.

Immediately after your divorce you may wish to take some time to both reflect on the end of the marriage and to recuperate. It might be a good idea to spend a few days, either with close friends or by yourself, at a place or setting where you can relax, unwind, and de-compress.

Q: If you're not advocating "divorce parties," is there such a thing as a "divorce ceremony?"

A: While relatively uncommon, some couples do have a ceremony to commemorate the ending of their marriage. We have never personally dealt with a couple who has held this kind of ceremony, probably because couples who can agree to that sort of process may be less in need of counseling as they go through their divorce. Divorce ceremonies often parallel marriage ceremonies in that clergy may preside over the event as a way of addressing religious beliefs about the dissolution of the marriage. In addition, friends and family may be invited to attend as witnesses. The children, just as in many marriage ceremonies, may also be given a role to play. The couple may exchange vows releasing the other from their role as spouse and seeking to maintain a friendship for the future. Guidelines on how to conduct a divorce ceremony are available, along with detailed accounting of some couples' experiences along the way.[2]

We are not necessarily recommending that you start calling the caterer with a divorce ceremony in mind. The real goal is to somehow diminish the anger that is common post-divorce. If a ceremony helps you do this, great!

Q: What other things could I do to symbolize the end of my marriage?

A: Most people do something to signify their changed status when they go through a divorce. Women, for example, often revert to using the name they had before marriage. Of course, both men and women may change their address. Some men do obvious things like removing pictures of her from the house or throwing out drawers of makeup. Others may make more subtle changes like deciding to stop making the bed in the morning. We are not suggesting that on the night of your divorce you have a big night on the town with wine, women, and song, but you might want to give some thought about a ritual, activity, or event that would be a way of signifying what has happened. For example, we have known guys who, on the day the divorce was final, burned their old love letters or who smoked a cigar on the patio (something he never did around "her"). It is a good idea to think about some sort of ritual before "D-day" arrives. We are more in favor of ideas that denote that divorce is a significant change rather than ones that say "I'm glad you're gone."

Q: How should I express my anger?

A: Women often say that men aren't into their feelings. "They only have eight colors in their crayon box, and seven of them involve sex." Actually, men *are* into their feelings, and we have them just as intensely as do women—after all, we have the same nervous systems. Indeed, research indicates that men's and women's emotional experience is essentially similar.[3]

Many men, however, have not learned to *associate their feelings with words*, particularly when the feelings are intense or sudden. Psychologist Ron Levant (1995) has labeled this phenomenon "normative male alexythymia," which translates to mean that it is typical for men to have no words to describe their feelings. It is not an unusual condition. Rather *normative male alexythymia* is labeled "normative" precisely because it is normal for most men. (Turns out this is the case for many women, too). But as men we're not off the hook. We need to be able to use our language to express our emotions more fully. Fortunately, this skill can be improved.

Think of a child who has a parent whose anger goes from one extreme to another. Sometimes—perhaps most of the time—the parent seems to show little, if any, anger. However, the next moment the parent may display extreme rage. Wisely, the child learns to avoid the parent who is enraged. Such a child grows up with a very black and white conception of anger, perceiving such feelings as operating like a light switch—either totally on, or totally off.

A healthier way to think about anger, though, is to conceive of it as more like a rheostat in which the light is controlled by the dimmer-switch. Children, who grow up with parents in the "rheostat-type" home see their parents with varying shades of anger. Sometimes, the parent is mildly "ticked-off," at other times annoyed, occasionally petulant, angry, or maybe even just plain mad! These children learn cues and clues to recognize diverse emotional states and behave differently according to what type of anger is being expressed. They also develop a wider repertoire of behaviors to express their own feelings of anger. Furthermore, they learn that one can care for (and love) another person while still being angry with him or her. These children perceive that anger in a relationship reflects disappointment that something is wrong and needs to be fixed so the relationship can once again be close. They don't view anger as signaling danger or the end of the relationship.

Don't hide from your feelings, including anger. Use them in constructive ways. For instance, learn about all the shades of anger. Understand that the opposite of love is not anger, but indifference. Often the presence of "healthy" anger shows the presence of love.

> With the Jackson family expression of anger had developed into a family tradition. C.J., a middle-aged man, had been a hell raiser in his youth. He still raged about life's injustices, but focused most of it on his wife. His verbal intimidations of her were periodically marked by physical abuse. His wife, Cindy, gradually groomed their son to be her protector. Following the example set by his father and the encouragement of his mother, he, too, became a "tough" guy as an adolescent. When the father threatened the mother, she called upon the teenager to defend her. Jason was only too glad to prove to his father who was the "baddest" in the house. Unfortunately, Jason also took to intimidating others as a way of getting what he wanted. He eventually was arrested for holding up a convenience store with a shotgun.

Q: Should I get back at her for what she has done?

A: It is true that there are women who seek to damage their ex-husbands. We have known men who were stalked, spied upon, and sent threatening messages. We have known others who have endured public scenes at work, or have had he family SUV crashed into by the ex-lover. It is usually best to ignore such actions. Don't respond to e-mails or phone messages designed to upset you. If you respond in any way, it usually encourages more of the same behavior. Most of the time, if you don't respond, your ex-partner will eventually give up that tactic.

Some men also play very clever games to "get even." We have seen men who sabotage the careers of their ex partners, spread malicious rumors about them, or try to get them in trouble with the law for real or imagined infractions. We strongly admonish you not to engage in such behavior. Maybe your ex has done bad things, but don't appoint yourself the avenging angel to set her straight. It's time to move on with your life. Try to figure out the best course for you rather than seeking to hurt her. As long as you are seeking revenge or justice, you are not over the divorce. Furthermore, your resentment and retaliatory urges are like poison, toxic to your psychological well-being in more ways than you can know.

Q: But what if she's playing games with the kids? What do I do?

Parenting post-divorce is tricky and doesn't look the same as parenting while married. And if co-parenting when married is a challenge, try co-parenting when unmarried. Conflicts between the parents frequently emerge around such matters as times for picking up and dropping off the kids, when summer visitation periods start, who will be with the children if the custodial parent goes out of town or gets sick, rescheduling planned events, etc. In general, we would recommend that you go slowly in reacting to such conflicts. Remember, you have limited power in the situation. You don't want to "go to the mat" over minor matters. Try to accommodate your ex-partner's needs and requests when possible. You may feel that she is being unfair at times (and maybe she is), but the best way to get her cooperation is to expect her to be reasonable when you ask for considerations. As they say "you attract more bees with honey than with vinegar." Don't give in to the temptation to speak ill of her to the kids when you are having difficulty negotiating with her. Often, the conflicts between you and your former partner lessen as you become accustomed to the new routine. It can be surprising how well both parents and children adjust over time, sometimes even after a very rocky beginning.

Communication by e-mail or voicemail is often a good way to make arrangements regarding the children. Try to make your communications matter-of-fact. Avoid sarcasm, accusations, threats, and snide remarks. Like Joe Friday "stick to the facts."

Direct phone calls to your ex should be limited. They are often difficult because they are more likely to bring up a lot of painful memories and emotions. Make sure that you call at a reasonable time of day. If she asks you not to call at a certain time because she is working, putting the kids to bed, or whatever, honor her wishes. Don't put yourself in the position of being accused of "harassing" her. If you leave her a voicemail, make sure it will sound OK if played in court someday. Remember that many people who have gone through a divorce record their conversations with the ex-spouse. Of course, if you and your ex have good communications, then these precautions may not be necessary.

If your ex uses these communications as a way of attacking you, try to ignore the barbs and deal with the facts. If these communications are very upsetting, consider using a "screener": a person who listens to the voicemail message or reads the e-mail for you and then communicates what you really need to know.

In most situations, after the divorce is settled and time passes, the conflict abates. Don't assume if your divorce is off to a rocky start that it will always be so difficult.

One event that often serves to dissipate the animosity is when your ex develops a new romantic relationship. When that happens, her attention is usually focused more on the new person than on continuing to fight with you.

On the other hand, if you begin a new relationship, she may feel some jealousy and renewed anger towards you. This may be especially true if she herself has not begun a new relationship.

Q: What about "Parent Alienation Syndrome"?

A: In some cases, parents try to deliberately poison the relationship between a child and the "other" parent. This may be done overtly and directly or through more subtle hints and suggestions. Less direct approaches suggest that the other parent doesn't really care for the child, is not paying child support, or is in some other way harming the child or the "good" parent.

Often divorced parents believe that when a child misbehaves, particularly after coming from the other parent's home, it is the result of alienation efforts on the part of the other parent or because the other parent is a bad influence on the child. The child's misbehavior in this situation, though, is frequently the result of instability and concomitant anxiety for the child arising from going from one household to the other. The child is going through a readjustment each time he or she switches from one home/parent to the other. For many children it is like reminding themselves of the divorce multiple times a week. If you have ever felt disoriented during a trip when you have switched hotels or locations every few days, you have a taste of what your child is experiencing. Instead of simply being on a vacation or business trip, your child's experience of "home" is disrupted. For children on a visitation schedule, there is more than one home. Just about the time they are growing settled in one place, they move again. As a parent, you need to recognize how unsettled your child may feel. It is a good idea as part of this recognition to acknowledge to your child and yourself that your child has more than one home.

Many parents going through a divorce hear about "parent alienation syndrome."[5] Sometimes, parents read about it on the internet and decide that this is what they are facing. Be careful. It's a lot like diagnosing yourself with a dreadful, rare disease after going through some checklist you found on an obscure website. Although parental alienation syndrome does occur, in our opinion, it is typically more often a legal ploy than a medical or psychological matter.

Sometimes, attorneys find that accusing the other party of parental alienation is a useful strategy to employ in a legal proceeding. Keep in mind, however, that in most divorces there is understandable tension around the issues of custody and visitation post-divorce. Most parents do not really want to prevent their ex from having a good relationship with the children. After all, any additional tension is usually harmful to the children. Also remember that kids may take sides on the divorce even without the encouragement of your ex. Children try to make sense out of what is happening and may end up blaming you for a variety of reasons. So our advice is to be slow to conclude that Mom is trying to keep you from being with the kids. A good mother will want you involved. Not only is it better for the children, it will be easier for her if she is not the only one doing the parenting.

"I put them up after the divorce so he knows his father is still part of his life."
[comment enlarged for clarity]

Q: What if I am convinced about "Parental Alienation Syndrome"?

A: In the relatively rare case that your ex really is trying to alienate you from the kids, a legal remedy is probably your best bet. Talk with your attorney about the best way to proceed and the likely outcomes if you pursue a legal response. Some states have actually prohibited the use of this type of claim in custody cases because it is so difficult to prove and so easy to allege.

Having cautioned you as strongly as we can, we include a list of the symptoms of parental alienation adopted from Darnall.[6] Note that the symptoms are based on your observations of your ex-spouse's behavior more than on your observations of your child's behavior. Be aware that the presence of some of these problems is unfortunately fairly common post divorce. However, if you feel that these problems predominate your situation after your divorce, you may wish to consult with your attorney as to legal remedies.

SYMPTOMS OF PARENTAL ALIENATION

❑ Allowing the child to decide about visitation (when the visits are court-ordered)

❑ Telling the child "everything" about the marriage as a way of damaging the other parent's relationship with the child.

❑ Refusing to allow the child to transport possessions from one home to the other.

❑ Keeping the other parent from having access to school or medical records or to schedules for extracurricular activities.

❑ Blaming the other parent for financial problems, breaking up the family, or having a new relationship.

❑ Being inflexible with the visitation schedule or scheduling the child's extracurricular activities as ways of limiting visitation.

❑ Accusing the other parent of being abusive of the child without justification.

❑ Encouraging the child to choose to change residences.

❑ Promoting the child's anger against the other parent.

❑ Suggesting name changes or adoption to the child.

❑ Using the child to spy or gather information on the other parent.

❑ Employing secret signals or communications with the child.

❑ Using special treats or outings as temptations for the child not to visit the other parent.

❑ Reacting with hurt or sadness if the child reports having a good time with the other parent.

❑ Asking the child about the other parent's personal life.

❑ "Rescuing" the child when there is no legitimate threat to the child's safety.

❑ Listening in on phone conversations with the other parent.

Q: What about allegations of sexual abuse?

A: One of the scariest accusations is that of sexual abuse. Unfortunately, it is very hard to defend yourself against this allegation once it is launched. The best thing to do is to plan defensively. All dads, especially those with an angry ex-spouse, should seek to protect themselves from accusations of sexual abuse.

We are not saying, "Never touch or hug your kid again." However, angry ex-spouses often accuse fathers of sexual misbehavior, sometimes with relatively little justification. When sexual abuse is alleged, judges tend to err in the direction of caution in order to protect the children. It is hard to argue with the idea of ensuring the safety of kids, but the judge's actions may result in restricted contact between children and their fathers. In the worst case scenarios fathers may be required to have only supervised visitation even when there is no clear evidence of sexual abuse. In our experience, most of these allegations could have been prevented had the father used some basic common sense.

❏ When the kids are with you, don't walk around in your underwear, or even worse, sally through the house naked. Maybe it was in bad taste to do this before, but now it is courting disaster. This may seem basic, but many men continue to act as they did before the divorce. Sometimes these men think they have a right to act in any way they want. This is a good way to wind up back in court.

❏ Keep the bathroom door shut and locked when you are in there. The last thing you need is for your ex-wife to hear from the kids how they saw you naked.

❏ When the kids are in their underwear or naked, steer clear of them. If the kids are too little and need help with their clothing or in the bathroom, make your actions as matter of fact as possible. Minimize the time that you have to deal with them in these compromising situations. .

❏ If the kids are with you, don't have overnight guests. This just invites your ex to make a complaint about what the kids are witnessing.

❏ Make sure the kids have their own beds. Although it may have been acceptable before, it is not a good idea to have the kids sleep in your bed.

❏ If you are roughhousing with the kids, recognize that they may talk to Mommy about how you touched or hit them. The context of the touch may not be communicated in the child's description. This is especially problematic when you have an ex who is looking for an excuse to attack you.

❏ If you like to look at pornography, make sure that the children have no access to it when they are with you.

Frederick insisted that as a father he still had the right to take care of his toddler daughter. She was, after all, his namesake, Frederica. Angrily, he argued that he was going to continue to bathe her as he did before he was divorced from her mother. The mother filed a complaint alleging that he was sexually abusing their daughter after the child came home with a "rash on her privates." The mother, suspicious of the father, inquired if Daddy had "touched" the child down there. The child, of course, reported that Daddy touched her all the time when he was in the bathroom with her. Ultimately, the court determined Frederick's visitations with his daughter needed to be supervised for a period of time. Frederick acknowledges that he was so focused on exercising his parental rights that he was careless about how an angry, vengeful ex-wife might react.

Q: Can I withhold child support if she makes it difficult for me to be with the kids?

A: If your ex-wife keeps you from seeing the kids or makes visitation difficult, you may be tempted to withhold child support. You may see this as a logical response to her lack of cooperation, or may believe it would help motivate her to cooperate; however, the judge will see this as a violation of the court order. You do not want to be in the position of having to explain to a judge why you failed to pay child support. Nor is it pleasant to have to answer your kids' questions about why you didn't pay child support. Your ex-wife is very likely to tell them "If Daddy really cared about you, he would have paid your child support." Your little ones may then confront you about it; or perhaps even more difficult, your adolescent may start ignoring you. Both are unpleasant. Legally, you cannot win by tying child support to child visitation; emotionally, you lose if you try to connect the two.

Q: When should I go back to court?

A: There are times when it is appropriate to go back to court. However, as you have probably already figured out, our bias is that going back to court should be your last resort.

❑ Going back to court is expensive. You can easily spend many thousands of dollars on the endeavor.

❏ The outcome is rarely satisfying. Often *both* parties feel that they lost.

❏ The kids are hurt by their parents' ongoing conflicts. They invariably become aware that their parents are still feuding.

If you've ever seen a sculpture of the goddess Justice, you will note that she is blindfolded. Justice is meant to be blind (i.e., objective). Do not expect that in going back to court matters will be resolved to your satisfaction.

And yet, sometimes it is appropriate to return to court. Good reasons to return to court include:

❏ Your ex is putting the children in danger. Make sure that your concern over "danger" is a valid one, and that you are not overreacting to the situation. We have seen couples go back to court over minor issues such as sending the child to school with a fever. We can guarantee the judge will not be happy in such a situation. One way to monitor if you are overreacting is to describe your ex's behavior to other parents and ask if they feel that it is a genuine danger to the children.

❏ You have repeatedly tried—unsuccessfully—to resolve disputes with your ex regarding the original divorce decree. These often have to do with fundamental matters such as when visitation begins and ends, who has the children during holidays, and the amount of child support that must be paid.

Q: What if nobody believes me in court?

A: Some guys figure that if they have to go to court they will never be believed. The notion here is that the courts are biased towards women and mothers, so a man/father doesn't stand a chance. We have not generally found this to be the case. For the most part, we find that judges and the courts honor the role of both fathers and mothers. You are not generally at a disadvantage in such situations.

Your credibility can be damaged easily, though, if you:

- ❏ Lie to the court.

- ❏ Fail to follow the judge's orders.

- ❏ Argue with the judge.

- ❏ Are arrested for unrelated matters (e.g., DUI).

- ❏ Don't pay child support.

- ❏ Make a mountain out of a molehill.

If you return to court, your case will be strengthened if you have physical evidence or witnesses to support your position. Of course, you will do less well if it is just your word against hers.

> *Bernard, the father of three young children, was awarded sole custody of the children because the ex-wife made repeated, unjustified accusations against the father. Apparently, the judge eventually grew weary of the unsubstantiated allegations and decided that the Bernard was the better parent under the circumstances. You can imagine how this might have come out if the father had been the one making repeated untrue claims about the mother.*

"Get mad, then get over it."

—Colin Powell

CHAPTER 6

"Fatherhood is pretending the present you love most is soap-on-a-rope."

—*Bill Cosby*

PARENTING AFTER DIVORCE

Ok, so now, like it or not, you are divorced. If you have kids, though, divorce is still somewhat of an illusion. For the rest of your lives, you and your spouse will probably continue to interact around the children. You'll be dropping off the kids, she'll be calling you to switch weekends, you'll have to tell her where you are taking the kids for spring break, she'll be asking you if your parents are going to be at the *bat mitzvah*, you and your second wife will be sitting across the aisle from her at your son's wedding. Of course, you can avoid the hassle by backing away from your relationship with the kids, but we certainly aren't recommending that! Or maybe your ex will end her connection with the children if she remarries, but wouldn't that be terrible for the kids!

Q: What are my rights as a parent after divorce?

A: In general, as a parent you have certain rights regardless of whether or not the child is in your care. The court can choose to abridge or amend these rights as part of a legal proceeding. Every state has somewhat different standards in this regard, but the following list of parental rights, taken from the Texas Family Code, is fairly typical of most states.[7] Usually, both parents have the right to:

- ❏ Receive information from the other parent about the child's health, education, and welfare.

- ❏ Have access to the child's medical, dental, psychological, educational, governmental, and law enforcement records.

- ❏ Consult with a physician, dentist, or psychotherapist of the child.

- ❏ Communicate with the school regarding the child's educational status and welfare.

- ❏ Attend the child's extracurricular activities.

- ❏ Be designated as an emergency contact for the child.

- ❏ Consent to medical, dental, and surgical treatment or mental health evaluation of the child in an emergency.

In addition, if the child is in your care (e.g., the child is in your "possession" for the weekend), you have additional rights and duties:

- ❏ You are responsible for the care, control, protection, and reasonable discipline of the child.

- ❏ You can consent for the child to have medical or dental care, even in non-emergency situations.

- ❏ You may direct the moral and religious training of the child (e.g., You could take the child to church.)

- ❏ You must provide the child with clothing, food, shelter, and necessary medical care.

- ❏ You must inform the other parent in a timely manner of significant information about the health, education, and welfare of the child.

Keep in mind that the specific rules vary from state to state. In addition, the court may limit these rights or expand upon them.

There are also additional responsibilities and duties that the parents typically have which may be either shared by the parents or given to one parent. These typically include such things as the rights to:

- ❑ Designate the primary residence of the child.

- ❑ Make decisions regarding the education of the child.

- ❑ Consent for psychiatric care or psychological treatment.

- ❑ Represent the child in legal proceedings.

- ❑ Consent to the marriage of the child.

- ❑ Consent to the child's enlistment in the armed forces.

- ❑ Manage the child's financial resources.

There are many more details that could be discussed and may need to be decided between you and your ex-spouse regarding the children. The Collaborative Law Institute (2006)[1] has produced an excellent guide that addresses a wide array of such issues. Among the issues that you may need to resolve are:

- ❑ Telephone Access. *How will you handle phone calls from the other parent?*

- ❑ Transport. *Who will transport the child to be with the other parent?*

- ❑ Air Travel. *Can the child travel unaccompanied?*

- ❑ Summer Camp. *Who can make the decision regarding the child's summer activities?*

- ❑ Schedule Changes. *How much notice must be given when a change to the schedule must be made?*

❏ Discipline. *Will you attempt to implement similar discipline methods in both homes?*

Q: How can I effectively parent (or co-parent) after divorce? Is it really possible?

A: Post-divorce, parents should endeavor to work cooperatively, supporting the ex-spouse in the role as parent. Frequent contact focusing on the children (e.g., progress in school, medical condition, behavioral problems, and upcoming events) is necessary for optimal coordination between the parents. The single biggest predictor of the child's post-divorce adjustment is the level of cooperation between the parents. Of course, if you and your spouse cooperated well, you might not have gotten a divorce in the first place. While cooperating with your ex-spouse is an ideal, it is difficult to bring off in reality.

It is probably self-evident, but we will remind you that frequent visitation and contact with your children is essential to maintain your bond with them. Children who have regular contact with both parents are much less likely to develop emotional or behavioral problems after a divorce.

Constance Ahrons (1994) in her classic *The Good Divorce* describes four styles of parenting relationships post-divorce:[2]

❏ *Perfect Pals.* These couples remain friends and continue to respect each other. Their separation was usually a mutual decision. They plan celebrations and events together, discuss problems, and rely on each other for support in parenting. This is an ideal situation, but it is not possible for many couples.

❏ *Cooperative Colleagues.* These couples put their differences aside in order to work on behalf of the children. Their commitment to the kids outweighs their negative feelings. They share in decision-making and divide parenting responsibilities. If you cannot be "pals," then you want to aim for at least being colleagues.

❏ *Angry Associates.* These couples have not been able
to forgive each other. They continue to feel anger and
resentment towards each other. They only grudgingly
accept the other's parental rights. As a result, the
children are often caught in the middle of their
parents' struggles post-divorce. Things often blow up,
and the children suffer. Clearly, this is not the situation
that you want.

❏ *Fiery Foes.* These parents view their former partner as
an evil enemy that must be defeated. They frequently
return to court in an effort to win custody or just
to limit the privileges of the other parent. Often,
other family members and friends are drawn into
these conflicts. The children are invariably put in the
position of choosing sides, and they may lose a parent
in the process. This is the worst possible outcome for
all parties.

Q: How should I handle my time with the kids?

A: It is somewhat of a shame, but we men often become better
fathers *after* a divorce. Prior to divorce, fathers often leave much of
the parenting duties to their wives. Even in the 21st century, in most
marriages, the wife performs more parenting duties than does the
husband.[3] It is usually the wife who takes the kids to their doctor's
appointments, who fills out the permission slips from school, and who
escorts the children on field trips. After a divorce, however, the father
is usually put in the role of having sole possession of the child during
more extended periods of time. For example, the father may have the
child for an entire weekend, three times a month. This means that Dad
is now the one fixing meals, transporting the child, and overseeing their
homework when the child is in his "possession." Quite often, this is a
big change for both the child and the father.

We would encourage you to take a "hands on" approach to
parenting wherever possible. Don't rely on others (neighbors, friends,
babysitters) to do the parenting. Especially don't rely on your ex-wife
to help you out with parenting. Fathering can require big sacrifices and

schedule changes for dads, but the resulting relationship with your child will be worth the costs. Dads who throw themselves into these new roles usually do them quite well.

One common problem area centers on extended visitation periods. For example, your children may be with you during six weeks of the summer or for extended holiday visits. Some dads respond to this by simply hiring more help or farming the kids out to relatives. Quite often, fathers put their kids into daycare or summer camp for the duration of their "visit." Not surprisingly, most kids dislike this. They usually would prefer spending more time with you! Dads in this situation are well advised to take vacation time so they can be with the children. It may be inconvenient, but the results are worth it. Every child wants to feel loved by their dad, as well as by their mom. Spending time with your children is the best way to communicate that you love them. Don't make the mistake of thinking that "quality time" somehow makes up for a "lack of time."

Q: But what do I do if the kids are interfering with my work?

A: You could probably be a better worker if you abandoned the kids, but then you wouldn't be a better man. Being a parent always means juggling multiple responsibilities. To be a good dad, you have to spend time with the children. Yes, that will probably interfere with your work at times. Remember your relationship with your father. Did you get as much time with him as you wanted, or needed? If he was a good dad, he made time for you. In principle, we may know that our fathers loved us, but we need more than that to feel loved.

At times, work will have to take precedence over family time, but be careful about your prioritization. Humans are masters at self-deception. We have met many men who essentially believe that their particular job (e.g., physician, CEO, lawyer, plumber, whatever) is simply so important that they can't spend as much time as they would like with the children. Don't fool yourself. Parenting is the most indispensable job. Be there for your kids. The consequences of being too busy to be with the kids can be devastating to your children's future. It puts them at greater risk for dropping out of school, teenage pregnancy, substance abuse, depression, and criminal behavior. Furthermore, the quality of your relationship with your children can be permanently damaged. To paraphrase a common aphorism: no parent of grown children complains about spending too much time with their kids when they were growing up.

> Rebecca told us about how her four-year old reacted to her father. "Who is that nice man?" the child asked after her father left for yet another business trip. And this was in a family where the parents were still married. Don't be "that nice man." Be Dad for your children by being there for them.

Q: How do I handle it if my kids don't want to spend time with me?

A: It is very painful when you are looking forward to spending time with your kids, and they seem disinterested. Often fathers in this situation blame the problem on mothers' influence. It is common, though, for kids themselves to object to visitation. You won't hear such vocal complaints from younger children; they may be unaware of the whole process, simply going where they are taken. Toddlers and elementary age children usually look forward to their visits with the noncustodial parent. However, as kids get older and busier, going to see the other parent is less of a treat and more of a chore, and an "interruption" to the life they've developed. This does not mean that the kids don't care about you. It does mean that they are becoming more interested in being with their friends than in being with you. This development often hits noncustodial fathers especially hard. They may feel that they have already missed many opportunities to be with their children, and now it seems that the children don't want to see them at all.

You should also realize that the whole process of going back and forth between households can be a real pain for kids. In some ways, it is a reminder over and over again of the divorce. Just like it may be hard on you to drop the kids off at their mother's house, it is hard on the kids to switch back and forth between homes. They often wish they could just stay at one place. Try not to take these kinds of feelings too personally. Often, their unhappiness is about the situation and not about the parents.

Sometimes, dads in this situation take their ex-wives back to court in an effort to force visitation. In general, though, this is not a satisfactory solution to the problem, particularly because in many cases the child's motivation is more the issue than their mother's influence. Such legal actions cause further animosity, making your ex-wife even less cooperative. The children invariably become aware of the court action, and they often then blame you for hurting Mom or for interrupting their activities. Needless to say, this does not make them more eager to see you.

If your kids are resistant to seeing you, forcing them to visit does not necessarily make things better. You might get them there, but they can make things unpleasant as a way of expressing their anger. In some situations the child may tantrum or actively resist going with you.

> Carol Anne's parents had a very contentious divorce. As a result, it was written in the divorce decree that rather than the father picking her up at the mother's home, the child would be exchanged by the parents at a neutral site such as a fast food restaurant. Carol Anne, though, resisted visiting her father. When they arrived at the restaurant, she refused to get out of the car. The father could have physically forced her to come with him but that would have both alienated the child further and perhaps also have given the mother another cause of action against the father. With coaching and continuous support from his men's therapy group, Tom committed himself to the long, tortuous and seemingly unrewarding task of regularly inviting Carol Anne. Twelve years later she asked her parents if she could live with her father and his new wife for the last two years of high school. You can't really force someone, even your child, to want to be with you.

The best way to handle this situation is to talk directly with the children about your concerns. Let them know that you want to continue being a part of their lives although you realize that they are busy and have other things to do. You may be able to work things out with them by:

❑ Allowing your child to bring friends for overnight visitation.

❑ Making sure that you do things that are in line with your children's interests.

❑ Being the one to take your child to his/her various events/activities (e.g. games, concerts, movies).

❑ Rearranging the visitation schedule to accommodate your child's special events.

Q: I don't think the visitation schedule is fair. What can I do?

A: It is common after divorce for *both* parties to feel the visitation schedule is inherently unfair. You may note, for example, that she gets to put the kids to bed at night more than you, while she may feel that you get the kids on weekends when there is less schoolwork to be done. Probably, both of you have lost out on some of the things you enjoyed doing with them. Sadly, this is one of the costs associated with divorce. You simply miss out on some of the positives (as well as some of the negatives) of raising children. The best you can do is to make the most out of the time you have with your children. While you could go back to court to try to get more three-day weekends or the like, the financial and emotional cost of the legal process is usually greater than the potential rewards if you win your case.

Q: What do I say if the kids blame me for the divorce?

A: Sometimes kids will blame one of the parents for the divorce. It can be the result of the other parent's influence, but often it is just a conclusion from the child's own evaluation of the situation. For example, if you had an affair, your child is more likely to feel that you betrayed the family. Extenuating circumstances such as the fact that you and your ex-wife have not had sexual relations in years will not be understood by the child.

Children cannot be expected to be objective about such matters. They have limited understanding, experience, and judgment. For them, things are more black and white with little shades of gray. Their TV programs reflect this, always showing "good guys" and "bad guys" with no mistaking which is which. Children seek to explain the upheaval that divorce has caused in their world, and they may conclude that you are the culprit for reasons that might make little sense to you. They may blame you for the divorce because:

- ❏ Mom is usually the one who takes care of them.

- ❏ You are the one who moved out.

- ❏ You traveled more than Mom.

- ❏ Mom is a girl, and girls are nice.

- ❏ You don't see the children as much as before.

With young children it is best not to argue the point about who was at fault in the divorce. Simply reassure them that you love them and you know how hard the divorce has been on them. Over time, they will judge you based on how you treat them, not on the fact of the divorce.

With older children it is more tempting to explain "your side of the story," especially if you believe they are being fed misinformation about what led to the divorce. Usually, though, this is not helpful, and it risks putting the child in the middle of the conflict between the parents. Here again, we would recommend that you simply acknowledge to the children that you understand their disappointment about the divorce, but that you want to remain a steadfast fixture in their lives. There may be a day when you will have the opportunity to explain your perceptions about the divorce, but this will probably come much later, usually after the children are well-grown. In the meantime, what counts more is to demonstrate your abiding love for them through your actions. Make the focus of your emotions your love for the kids and not on your anger at your ex-wife.

Q: How can I avoid problems with my ex-wife about the kids?

A: At the very least, you should not speak ill of your ex to the children. This particular point is always stressed by family attorneys in talking with their clients and in the various programs offered to divorcing parents through the courts or through other organizations. Most men seem to grasp the literal meaning of this (i.e., "I can't call my ex a b----"). However, many parents say things that, although they are less explicitly negative, are still understood by the children as criticism. Subtle character assassination is still inappropriate and harmful for the children. Your kids are smart. They can figure out what you really mean. They are also very sensitive to such remarks, almost—but not quite—as sensitive as your ex-wife. Imagine how your ex will react when your kid comes back to her reporting, "Daddy said you were the one who wanted the divorce. Why, Mommy?"

Another common problem occurs when the kids overhear something you say to someone else about your ex-wife. We have often seen men who made derogatory remarks about their ex-wives to their friends or family, sometimes on the phone, sometimes in person, which their children overheard. Then all hell broke loose, especially when the kids reported the remarks to their mother. Don't take a chance by talking about your ex when your kids are with you. Better yet, don't *ever* talk ill about her. It doesn't make you look good. Remember, you once loved her. She is the mother of your children. What do you have to gain by talking badly about her? If the two of you divorced, it is already evident that the marriage wasn't going swimmingly. You don't need to detail her shortcomings as a spouse, sexual partner, or parent to others. They won't be more impressed with you as a result.

If your kids live predominantly with your ex-wife (i.e., you have "visitation rights"), it is exceedingly important for you to be consistent in keeping those visitation obligations. This means, for example, that if you are supposed to have the kids for a particular weekend you keep that commitment. It also means that you are punctual both in picking up the kids and in returning them. Ex-wives are often very reactive to dads who fail to follow the visitation rules stipulated in the divorce decree. In addition, these are very black and white stipulations, simple to document. It is easy to attack you for failing to follow the court's mandates when you are lackadaisical in these regards. You open yourself up to assault. Probably more importantly, you convey to the children that you are less than enthusiastic about seeing them. Above all, don't get in a power struggle with your ex around visitation times and schedules. Otherwise, you may get to visit with your family attorney again when your ex takes you back to court.

Q: How should I handle phone calls to the kids?

A: One of the ways to stay in contact with the children when they are not living with you is through phone calls. However, phone calls can also be the source of a lot of hard feelings.

Some fathers want to talk with their children by phone each night before bedtime. While this is an endearing idea, practically speaking, it is problematic. As you know, bedtime is one of the most important and difficult times when parenting young children. A phone call coming every night as your ex-wife is attempting to get the child in bed often becomes an event dreaded by both the mother and the child. Instead, plan with your child and your ex-wife when are good times to call. Respect limits that they request regarding your phone calls rather than taking them as an affront.

Remember, too, that older children are usually not very interested in conversing on the phone with a parent. Try not to take their diffident attitude personally. Recognize that they will probably treat their mother similarly when she calls. If your child is old enough, you might consider purchasing him or her a cell phone. A cell phone ensures that your child can call you if the child desires, and it gives you a private method of communicating with your child.

When you are talking with your child on the phone:

❏ Avoid the guilt trip. *("Why haven't you called?")*

❏ Don't become overly emotional *("I miss you so terribly much!")*

❏ Avoid broad, general questions. *("How was your day today?")*

❏ Remember what they told you so that you can refer back to it next time *("You said that Coach Smith quit. Has he been replaced yet?")*

Q: To tell you the truth, I don't like being with the kids. Will it hurt to skip seeing them sometimes?

A: Some dads, although they may not admit it, really don't like being with the kids. Kids are noisy, smelly, and constantly into mischief. They drive us crazy! Maybe the kids remind you of your ex-wife or of the marriage that ended. Perhaps you would prefer to focus on your future, on the single life, on dating again. The obvious point is that you are still responsible for these children that you helped bring into the world. They are certainly not responsible for your predicament. Girlfriends (and sometimes even wives) come and go, but our children are a permanent legacy.

Everyone gets tired of their children at times. Look for ways to make your parenting experience less unpleasant:

- ❏ Become involved in your child's special interests (e.g., music, baseball).

- ❏ Team up with other parents to engage in fun activities, impossible to do on your own.

- ❏ Read a book or take a class to become more knowledgeable about child development.

- ❏ Make time for yourself (e.g. to exercise, read) during times of visitation so that you won't "burn out".

- ❏ Consult with experienced parents about how they deal with typical parenting challenges.

- ❏ Forgive yourself if you sometimes get frustrated with the kids.

Q: Why do my kids always need something that is at their mother's house?

A: We have seen many formerly married parents get into big hassles—even protracted legal battles—over a science book left at Mom's house or the school uniform that was forgotten at Dad's house after a weekend with him. This is silly. If you start running into these kinds of headaches, we recommend that you simply buy additional items so that you don't have to transport them back and forth. Kids (as well as adults) commonly lose or forget things. It's too expensive to do this you say? Believe us. It will be cheaper to do this than to have one phone call to your attorney about the matter. When couples keep struggling over such matters of possessions, it frequently results in the involvement of lawyers. So unless you enjoy an ongoing argument with the ex and possible legal fees, just buy items to reduce this problem

Q: Every time the kids are with me they seem to need something that their mother is supposed to be buying. I already pay child support! How much more do I have to do?

A: Maybe it seems unfair to you that the kids seem to always want or need something when they are with you. In this case, we are talking about things that kids actually need (e.g., clothing, shoes, athletic equipment) rather than toys or luxuries. "Mom is supposed to buy you your shoes," as one parent told his son. Unfortunately, your children are not likely to buy this argument. To them, you will probably just seem like a skinflint who doesn't want to spend money on them. You may be technically right, but you will probably create hard feelings with your child. Of course, it is perfectly legitimate to tell the child that you cannot afford an item, but don't blame their mother or put it off on her (i.e. "If your mother hadn't taken all my money..." or "Tell your mother to buy it"). Instead, talk about what you *can* do:

❏ Buy it for them next time.

❏ Buy a cheaper version.

❏ Save up so that you can afford it.

❏ Find an alternative way of getting it for them (a used item, asking another relative to help, etc.)

Q: I feel taken advantage of by my kids. How do I stop being just a banker or an entertainment center?

A: Many dads feel that they simply dispense "goodies" to the children. They lament that their children seem unappreciative of them while at the same time expecting fathers to "cough up the dough." In these situations it may feel as if your child has little emotional connection to you. You may feel like the banker or a giant entertainment system for them.

There are several factors that can contribute to creating and maintaining this problem. In our materialistic society, children (as well as adults) are encouraged to always want "more." Often, parents get into the mode of meeting all of their children's wants. This is typically more of a problem in affluent families because they have the additional resources for non-necessities and luxuries. Unfortunately, dads often are responsible for this "gimme" attitude by providing too much to the child (the new game system, a TV in their bedroom, expensive clothes). Sometimes, fathers are overly generous as a substitute for the emotional presence that the child really needs. Dads who suffer from guilt because of their travel schedule or workaholism are particularly prone to providing too much in the way of material possessions as a substitute for their involvement with the kids. If this was the pattern in your marriage, the children quite naturally expect it to continue.

Emotional factors also can promote this pattern. The children may feel depressed as a result of the divorce, and parents sometimes try to cheer them by buying them expensive things or taking them to new and exotic places (e.g., Europe, Disneyworld). Alternatively, the children may be angry at you for the divorce, and you may therefore be tempted to try to win their favor by buying them things. Some parents even try to entice the children to live with them by pointing out the material advantages (e.g., "I have a pool"; "You'll have your own bedroom"; "I'll buy you a car").

Our advice: Don't get into the mode of trying to buy your children's affection. Don't let guilt about the divorce or your work habits lead you to buying the kids things. Don't purchase the expensive toys or take them on the elaborate trips in order to please them. In the short run, it may make them happy with you, but it will make you both unhappy in the long run. It will only spoil the children. They will constantly want and expect more, and you will probably become resentful. The emotional connection that you actually want and that they need will still be missing. If this has been your pattern in the past, resolve to change it now that you are divorced. Instead, plan to spend more time with the children post-divorce. Time is the only irreplaceable commodity. Invest it in your children.

Q: Child support: I hate it! Can I skip a few payments?

A: If you are a non-custodial parent, you will probably be paying child support. The exact formula for determining the amount to be paid varies from state to state.

Many men object to paying child support. You may have found yourself saying one of the following:

- ❏ "The amount is too high."

- ❏ "My ex-wife does not use it on the kids."

- ❏ "I would rather have direct control on how the money is spent."

- ❏ "My ex-wife has sufficient income of her own and does not need the money."

- ❏ "My ex-wife has remarried, and her new husband makes a lot of money."

- ❏ "She doesn't care about the kids anyway."

- ❏ "The courts are biased against men."

- ❏ "She doesn't cooperate with me about visitation, so why should I have to pay child support?"

- ❏ "My income is too unstable to consistently pay the amount ordered by the court."

Whatever your feelings are, you are required to pay what the court has ordered for child support. Even if you don't agree with a speed limit, you still get fined if you violate it. Remember that if you had not divorced you would be providing monies for your children's needs. The situation has not really changed in this regard.

Q: What about alimony?

A: In many states, alimony or spousal support is paid in addition to child support. If you have trouble with paying child support, you'll probably take even more issue with helping out your ex financially. There is some reason for it, though.

If you have been the breadwinner for the family, while your wife has been at home, she may have been out of the job market for quite awhile. Her job skills may have eroded, or she may never have acquired the education and proficiencies necessary to make an adequate living. Like it or not, you and your wife had a tacit, if not explicit, agreement that she would not have to work to support herself. Now the situation has changed. She may have to work, and the courts typically recognize that she will need time to transition to this new status. As a result, the court may grant her financial support (paid by you) during this period. Of course, this support may be reduced or waived if she is already adequately employed or has the prerequisite abilities to become adequately compensated. Most courts, for example, are not going to require you to provide financial support for a woman who is a practicing physician, teacher, or attorney. If you have been in a marriage where she has been supporting you, the judge might even order her to provide financial support to you as you transition back to work.

Q: There's a new man in her life, and he's around my kids! What can I do?

A: Lots of guys feel renewed angst when they realize there is another man in their kids' lives. You probably knew it was going to happen, but that doesn't mean it's not painful, especially if he gets to be with the kids more than you do! Rather than hating the fellow, try to see him as a potential ally in the joint endeavor of raising the kids. We all have had coaches, uncles, teachers, and youth directors who helped us along the way. This new man can perhaps be a positive influence on your ex-wife and your children. You *want* him to be a good guy. You *want* him to be successful with the children. You are not in competition with him. If you are a good dad, you will not be replaced. Ideally, your kids will see him as another good man, a person who genuinely cares about them.

Some dads even form a level of friendship with the "new man." After all, you share the responsibility of parenting the children. Often, he can be more objective and understanding of your position than is your ex-wife. That doesn't mean he will become your best buddy, but at least work to not make him your mortal enemy.

A few years ago one of us attended the 50th birthday party of a man who had been the step-father to several children. Gordon's step-children, now all grown, attended the party. At one point in the festivities each attendee was asked to tell a story about the honoree. One of the step-kids who had initially disliked his step-father, used the opportunity to thank the man for being such a role model for him. Although this young adult had maintained a close relationship with his biological father, he came to also appreciate the step-father's discipline, guidance, and concern. Later, he elected to pursue his step-father's career field. Although the biological father and the step-father never became friends, they both served vital roles in raising this boy to be a man.

Q: What if one of the parents moves?

A: If either you or your ex moves, it obviously puts a much greater strain on the ability of the non-custodial parent to have meaningful involvement with the child. Frequently, one or both parents will want to move in order to escape reminders of the past, to be closer to family, or just to improve their job prospects. Sometimes, a former spouse wants to move to avoid what they feel is excessive control by their ex.

You may feel threatened by the prospect of the other parent moving. Sometimes, former partners attempt to block such moves through provisions in the divorce decree or subsequent legal action. These actions may include prohibiting the custodial parent from moving more than a certain number of miles away, limiting the geographical region or area where the custodial parent may live, or requiring a reopening of the custody issue if the custodial parent moves. Sometimes, these requirements have time limits or age limits (e.g., within two years of the divorce or until the child is at least 14 years of age).

We have mixed feelings about such sanctions. On the one hand, we agree that the children benefit from having easy access to both parents. On the other hand, things happen, and life goes on. If you or your ex gets the opportunity for a big promotion, shouldn't you or she be able to consider taking it? And what if you (or your ex) remarry and desire to live in another area of the country (or world)? Furthermore, these kinds of provisions are difficult to enforce. Once the other partner has moved, particularly if it is across state lines, it usually requires a court action to bring about a reversal. It may be hard to get the authorities in another state to be particularly concerned about what a family court said in your state. Frequently, it is simply not worth it financially nor psychologically to bring your ex to court over this. Even if you win, it may be a pyrrhic victory because she will probably then make visitation more difficult for you.

Jonathan attempted to prevent his ex-wife from moving out-of-state with their child when the couple divorced. His attorney accurately told him that such prohibitions could be included in the divorce decree. However, the attorney did not point out the potential psychological risks in this legal maneuver. The mother, a professional in a very specialized field, needed to be able to relocate in order to advance in her field. His repeated trips to court to enforce the residential restrictions created enormous animosity on her part toward him.

Eventually, Jonathan relented and agreed that she could move out of state, but the damage was already done. Rather than supporting him in his role as a father, she resisted doing anything to facilitate visitation. She did little to promote contact or to accommodate his schedule because she was resentful of how he had tried to restrict her. Ironically, he, too, eventually decided to move out-of-state to pursue another job opportunity making the whole matter moot.

Before attempting to restrict your ex in some way, consider the impact of this action on your ability to collaborate with her in other areas in the future.

The best approach is probably to talk with your ex-spouse if either of you are considering moving. Your divorce decree will have built-in provisions about how to handle visitation if the two of you move further apart. Typically, these include such things as extended visitations during the summer and less frequent but longer weekends with your child. In any case, if you and your ex live far apart, provisions should be made to allow for more meaningful contact between the children and the non-custodial parent.

IDEAS TO PROMOTE CONTACT WHEN THE KIDS LIVE FAR AWAY

❑ E-mail

❑ Internet cameras

❑ Toll-free telephone numbers

❑ Cell phone paid by the non-custodial parent

❑ Frequent "snail-mail" with little gifts (e.g. stickers)

❑ Videophones

❑ Financial support from the ex for air fare

Q: The big switcheroo—what if my kids want to live with the other parent?

A: As the child matures, he or she may need or want more contact with the non-custodial parent. During adolescence, kids often decide they want to try living with the other parent. This may be related to curiosity about the other parent, a desire to connect more with the non-custodial parent, and/or to an effort to explore him or herself more fully by increased contact with the less known parent. At other times, the child simply hopes to "cut a better deal." The "bargain hunter" child may feel that the custodial parent is too strict, or the child may simply believe that the noncustodial parent will be more lenient or fair. In some states, the child may articulate a desire to live with a particular parent, and the court will often honor this when the child has reached a certain age (which varies according to state law and practice).

If you were the non-custodial parent, you may have hoped that your child would eventually come to live with you. For you, this may feel like a dream come true. However, the adjustment of the child to living primarily with you is often difficult. The child may react differently with you now that you are the one more responsible for such things as discipline, homework, and medical appointments. The adjustment can be complicated by numerous differences between the two parents' homes:

- ❑ Lifestyles of the two parents (e.g., one of you is vegetarian).

- ❑ Methods of discipline (e.g., one of you is lenient, the other strict).

- ❑ Socioeconomic status (e.g., one of you is wealthy).

- ❑ One of you is married, the other is not.

- ❑ Your child doesn't like your new partner.

- ❑ One of you lives in the country while the other lives in the city.

❑ One of you lives in a place considered "cool," the other does not.

❑ Your child has friends in one place and not in the other.

❑ The schools are better in one area than the other.

❑ Your child is engaged in elite athletics or music programs not available in the other area.

If, on the other hand, your child has been primarily living with you, the prospect of him or her choosing now to live with Mom can be very threatening. You may dread the possibility of them asking to live with her. You may even feel that it would be unwise for your children to live with their mother because of her personal habits (e.g., irresponsible behavior, anger). Nonetheless, it is best not to try to dissuade your child from this option. If they really want to live with their mother, you probably cannot persuade them out of it through logic. The issues are likely to be more emotional than rational. Nor should you attempt to prevent their moving by promising your child special treats or privileges or by talking negatively about their mother. Remember that, in any case, your children will eventually leave you anyway (or at least you hope they will!). It is normal for them to want to spend time with the other parent, but that doesn't mean they are no longer interested in you.

Obviously, this sort of change is a big deal, not to be taken lightly. On the other hand, it is a normative event. Don't look at it as a disaster, but as a test. It is rather like the challenge facing you when your child is of age and would be moving out to go to college or to start work. We tend to think of kids doing this at around age 18, but for various reasons many kids move out much earlier. If your child moves to the other home, it will not be the end of your relationship, but it will require adjustments. On the other hand, if the child is coming to live with you, it may be a joyous reunion, but it will also mean new issues as well.

CHAPTER 7

"The worst loneliness is not to be comfortable with yourself."
—*Mark Twain*

LIVING ALONE

One of the common fears that men have about divorce is adjusting to living alone. The longer you have been married, the more daunting this may sound. This chapter is intended to help you think through the challenges of flying solo again.

Q: How can there be anything good about living alone? It sounds awful!

A: Many men dread the idea of living alone. Often, divorced men have not lived by themselves in a very long time. Sometimes they have never lived on their own. Robin Green (2005) points out that divorce may mark the first time in your life that you identify yourself without reference to a family.[1] Perhaps you have been married for years and are now returning to the single life. Some men have lived in dorms or with buddies in an apartment before marriage, but they have never really lived alone.

Strangely enough, unless you are comfortable being alone, you probably are not ready for a new relationship. If you like yourself, you are more able to have a good relationship with someone else. We believe that the best relationships grow out of a desire to be with a particular person, not from the fear of being alone. Think about it from the perspective of sexuality. Is it more of a turn-on to be wanted by someone (i.e., because they desire you) or would you prefer being needed (i.e., as a way of relieving their sexual urges)?

To be comfortable with yourself means you:

❏ Don't feel depressed when you don't have someone with you.

❏ Can take care of your own basic needs.

❏ Don't need someone else to entertain you.

❏ Can deal with not having a regular sexual partner.

If you are not comfortable with yourself, you tend to become too needy, settling for a relationship to make you feel less lonely. Yet later on you may wish you were alone and not with her! There's a line in a country song by Bobby Bare (1980) that expresses that idea in a more earthy way: "I never went to bed with an ugly woman, but I've woke up with a few."[2]

Q: I'm not ready for dating, but I'm lonely. What should I do?

A: Ah, now we're getting somewhere. Let's hold on to the dating idea and deal with loneliness a bit. *[We'll talk about dating in Section III].* Are you "lonely" or are you "alone"? That may seem like the same thing, but they are different.

Aloneness is a number. You look around the room, count the number of people in it, and end with "one." There's no feeling about it. Some people, however, have not learned that there can be good feelings attached to being alone. They feel lacking and rush to join others, whether it be dating or other activities. No wonder some people don't enjoy dating. They don't enjoy the aloneness, but they don't really enjoy the togetherness either because they are too concerned about being alone again. They are constantly seeking something else.

In contrast, "loneliness" is a feeling state. It is the sense of missing or lacking, most often seen in states of bereavement. Scientists have noted that even animals are capable of grieving. Waterfowl such as geese and swans will go through a prolonged period of bereavement when they lose a mate, and they may not seek another.

Loneliness has nothing to do with the number of people in the room. We may complain about loneliness when we are alone; however, some of the saddest cases of loneliness involve a person who is lonely in the midst of a crowd. So, analyze your state. Are you alone or lonely— or both? Understanding the distinction can help put you in the right direction for dating.

"There's something you need to know about me, Donna.
I don't like people knowing things about me."

Q: So, I guess you're talking about just being with people for now?

A: Yes, if that's what you desire. If you don't want to be with people, then get some alone-time, which ironically prepares you to fully enjoy being with a group of people.

The only important time to pursue being with people is if you are still depressed. Most depressions are self-limiting. In six to nine months, most persons get out of them. During that time, there is a tendency to isolate, to get by oneself and "lick your wounds." The isolation found in depression is a way of protecting oneself from further harm, and can be a valuable tool for introspection. However, isolation can be problematic because it also tends to protect you from good things in life.

Clinical therapists who specialize in the treatment of persons with depression often use the Cognitive/Behavioral model, addressing "cognitive errors" depressed persons make when they talk to themselves.

When someone says, "I'll do it when I feel better" yet that "feeling better" time doesn't come for six months, they are operating from a depressive framework. Consequently we recommend re-wording motivational tactics. Rather than promising, "I'll do it when I feel better" we recommend acknowledging, "I'll do it regardless of how I feel now, knowing that afterwards—by doing it—I will feel better."

Now, just "being" with others can be hard for some people, particularly for men. As men, we have been trained to "do" things with others, not just chat. "Doing something" is the main way in which guys spend time together. If there's free time during the week, guys might get together with buddies and develop a poker night. They may eventually chat as much as women do, but it's organized around an activity. Other men go bowling, often through a league. Or, if there's a little bit of time, two guys may go out to the driving range and knock out a bucket of balls before having a sandwich. In a sense, these activities make it easier for men to get involved with each other because the activity is taking precedence. This is characteristic of men regardless of their age. When men, as teenage boys, begin interacting with women, the formalized date starts with an event, an activity. So we recommend that you find activities that you would enjoy doing with others as a way of building more connections.

COGNITIVE ERRORS ASSOCIATED WITH DEPRESSION[3]

❑ Self-Downing: global rating of self based upon arbitrarily picked traits, performances, or abilities: "Because I can't date easily, what good am I?"

❑ Shoulds, oughts, musts, have to, need to: unrealistic, absolutistic self- and other-expectations and demands. "I shouldn't be so weak and dependent."

❑ Negative forecasting: "The future is bleak and there is nothing I can do about it."

❑ Joyless outlook: "There's no joy or purpose to my life....What's the point of going on?"

❑ Negative filtering: all positive aspects are filtered out. "I can't do anything right anymore."

❑ Catastrophic thinking: gross exaggeration of discomfort, pain, or inconvenience ("awfulizing"). "The food here is just awful!"

❑ Low frustration/discomfort tolerance: "I can't stand being here."

Q: So I should just start "doing stuff" again?

A: Glad you are with us, although you may have skipped one element—time. Often, men respond with, "I'm too busy" or, "I couldn't do it on that night" when they should be taking advantage of personal time to "do stuff" with others. True, your time is frequently spoken for, especially if you have children. Often those periods of time are dictated by your divorce decree. Thus, the time allotted for being with the children may have more rigid boundaries than the time to be alone or with others.

We all have the same 24 hours in a day—no more, no less. Time is our most valuable commodity. While it is difficult for men to balance the time requirements for work, children, social life, and being alone post-divorce, achieving that balance is perhaps the most essential task for good mental health and recovery.

Q: Connecting with men is difficult because I get too competitive. How can I change that?

A: In our culture, we are educated—from our earliest years—to view situations as competitive. This is especially true for men. Many men participate in team sports where winning is the major emphasis. Competition is just as great in the so-called individual sports. Schools even hold competitions in the arts for bands, cheerleaders, and theatre productions. Our academic institutions are a great competitive arena, not only in sports, but also in scholastics. Awards are given for eminence, and college-bound students look to their class ranking, as do the colleges to which they are applying. Because of this intense competition grades have been inflated and teachers prodded to give glowing recommendations, so that students can get into the "better" or the "best" colleges. University professors respond to the same pressures, and grades in colleges have been inflated, too. One Ivy League school has cut down on the number of Summa, Magna, and Cum Laude graduates because too many students were achieving the grade points needed. And, professors have taken defensive steps against being sued by students who only got a "moderately glowing" recommendation. Our culture, then, is reminiscent of Garrison Keillor's hometown where "everyone is above average."[4]

Other cultures do not push competition so highly, although as this was being written, the Winter Olympics were on TV, and we were bombarded by beautiful yet immensely competitive people from all over the globe who are healthy and strong, and embody the Olympic Motto: *Citius, Altius, Fortius* ("Swifter, Higher, Stronger")

One of us (GS) was fortunate enough to be among a group of mental health professionals touring (Communist) China just after Richard Nixon opened travel to Americans. We saw schools and colleges recently opened after years of inactivity due to the Gang of Four political oppression. We skipped visiting the tractor factory and instead visited a mental health sanitorium, learning that China uses the same mental health criteria we do for serious psychiatric illnesses such as psychosis and schizophrenia. However ,their treatment plan for neuroses such as anxieties and depressions is different than ours. Anxieties and depressions need political re-education.—no psychotherapy. So, neurotics get "talked to" from their group, and if that fails, then a member of a larger group talks to them, then a larger group and so on.

We also found that the meaning of competition was different in China. Their education about competition, as in the United States, begins early. During our visit to a Chinese kindergarten, we saw children at recess playing tug-of-war. Now, maybe this was the same kindergarten pictured in a film made by actress Shirley MacLaine. (The Other Half of the Sky: A China Memoir, 1975).

Ms. MacLaine had visited with a group of women leaders just a bit earlier than we did, looking at the condition of women in China. Her group included women of different age groupings, races, backgrounds, and political leanings. The children, like the ones that we saw, were also playing tug of war. The thick rope used for the game had a red flag as the indicator of the center point, and when it crossed one of two lines drawn on the concrete, then that would indicate the game was over. Win or lose, thought the women from our culture. One woman got so upset when the team nearest her was about to lose, and the flag was about at the mark, she jumped in to help pull the flag back to the center. Just then, the Chinese teacher blew a whistle, stopped the action, and took the woman aside. The teacher explained to the woman that they would not have really let the team lose, but, rather, would have blown the whistle just before that happened. The message that each team was getting, and the lesson to be learned, was that it was important to "pull for the team." There was no emphasis on "winning or losing." So, Vince Lombardi of the Green Bay Packers wouldn't fly in China with his advice that "winning isn't everything; it's the only thing.".

Our society, though, still tends to reward—with money, fame, and popularity—highly competitive recreational activities ranging from high school, college, and professional sports to game shows to hot dog eating to "reality television." Even board games like *Risk* and electronic games like *Warcraft* are intensely competitive.

In many, if not most, of our recreational pastimes the goal is to win, to excel over all other players. However, this model does not work so well when it comes to forming new relationships. See if you can tone down your competitive urges and emphasize cooperation as a way of becoming closer to others.

Q: Should I develop a new pastime? Are you telling me hobbies will help me through the divorce?

A: Yep. In order to connect more with others look for situations in which you can be yourself. Have fun, learn something, and in the process, make contacts. Developing pastimes can make a big difference in the length of your life, as well as in the quality of your life. Many of the people we see in nursing homes have retired after many years of work, yet they now feel lost. They have not developed hobbies or pastimes to carry them through the later years.[5] In fact, it has been noted that those without hobbies will often die roughly eighteen months after retirement. They have nothing to look forward to, nothing to keep them going. So develop good habits now by finding meaningful activities outside of your work.

In considering a new pastime you should look at the requirements of the activity. Consider, for example, what's involved if you're interested in picking up scuba diving:

❏ *You first need prerequisite skills.* If you are not a swimmer, then you probably need to hold off on becoming a scuba diver until you've developed enough skills in the water. You don't have to be a swim-the-English-Channel swimmer, just a good swimmer who can handle himself in the water.

❑ *Prepare yourself for what the activity requires.* Get prepared physically for scuba diving by weekly, even daily, exercising. Your local "Y" has programs in swimming, and encourages swimmers to meet goals by offering yearly prizes to those who swim 100 miles or more per year.

❑ *Find groups/classes/clubs that are in your area of interest.* Once you feel comfortable in the water, check out scuba programs. Most programs today are not like the "Marine type" programs that used to exist, where beginners were treated like grunts and few passed to become excellent divers (the rest being scraped off the bottom of the pool). Courses by the accrediting agencies such as PADI (Professional Association of Dive Instructors), NAUI (National Association of Underwater Instructors), or SSI (Scuba Schools International) are based upon psychological learning principles and the material is delivered in small increments.

❑ *Consider taking additional classes to improve your skills.* Each scuba diver learns the essentials in beginner classes and then re-learns material with more detail in advanced classes. Later, students are able to branch out into various categories such as deep diving, night diving, underwater photography, etc. For those who desire cave diving, special preparation is required. New technology makes even computer nerds feel happy underwater as they can log each dive and study minutia from their dive computers.

One hobby can play into another hobby. Maybe you like swimming, then learn scuba diving, but also like photography and thus want to learn about underwater photography. Finally, you may desire to travel to exotic destinations to photograph underwater sea life. Following this process, you've managed to combine at least three or four hobbies, and at the same time, you have gotten to meet interesting people from different parts of the world. By participating in an organized group such as a dive club, you can increase the number of people you know in your home area. Furthermore, clubs can organize activities (e.g. dive trips to foreign destinations) that are less expensive and tailored to your needs and interests.

> *George had learned to skydive while in his 40s, which was no small thrill. He discovered that it was fun to combine his new hobby with his life-long passion: photography. Now in his late 50s, he takes pictures of beginning skydivers making their first jump! What a terrific present (or purchase)! Every new jumper can appreciate (or laugh at, depending upon his facial expression) a picture of his or her first jump. George is frequently invited to photography clubs to present on his unique passion.*
>
> *In pursuing his interest, George first had to hunt for the right camera, learn how to mount it on his helmet so his head wouldn't be encumbered by the extra weight, and rig a triggering apparatus from the camera to his hand. He learned to do all those things and then combined it with his interest in public speaking and the pleasure he got from getting the chance to show off his gear. To boot, he meets a lot of interesting people.*

Q: How do I locate hobby clubs?

A: Often, word of mouth is good. You may already know somebody who is engaged in a hobby you have thought about, but never engaged in because of innumerable reasons: time, money, or other obligations. "I'll do it when I'm retired," you may even say. Now—as you have returned to a single life—is a good point in time to develop these new interests.

> *One of the happiest men that I (Glenn Sternes) knew was the Best Man at my wedding. He was older than I and already retired (I married late). He had had a responsible, upper-management position in a large firm and had always been busy, but in retirement, was even more so. His schedule included many daily hours of caring for his wife, who was a semi-invalid. He helped widows and other retirees who didn't know anything about computers to do their investments and completed their tax returns, and he would do handyman work for others. He researched articles for the local and*

national Masonic journals, and engaged in photography, having built a backyard darkroom where neighbors had their garages. He did not complain about his week's schedule. He said that in retirement, he was busier than ever, but would never trade it in to return to his work, because he was happy with what he was doing. The joy from his pastime radiated from his face, so much so that people he had never met spontaneously commented on it.

Some of you may enter hobby group meetings looking to learn something new, and may even consider them a waste of time if you don't. "I already know it." Remember that there is a dual purpose, to enjoy the hobby and to meet people. Additionally, we often need to hear things a number of times before they "stick." Meetings offer that opportunity.

My Best Man also taught me something about the learning process. He and I attended a lecture on a subject well known to both of us. While I was somewhat disappointed by all of the "chaff" (stuff I already knew) in the lecture, he was happy to have found a kernel of "wheat" from the same talk. He noted that if he learned one or two new things, then the session was worth it.

Other ways to learn about hobby and interest groups include:

❏ *Your local library.* Most libraries in greater metropolitan areas have a listing of such groups.

❏ *Local magazines.* Articles and ads about club meetings are a mainstay of local magazines.

❏ *Specialty stores.* Look for stores that specialize in selling items associated with the hobby (e.g., REI for outdoor activities; gourmet food stores for cooking). Some stores have their own clubs, or allow clubs to use their space. They also frequently post information about club activities or club locations.

❏ *Conventions, meetings, and festivals.* Interest groups may have a booth and hand out information about their organizations and activities at local fairs or conventions.

❑ *The Internet.* Most interest groups have at least a small listing on the web, so that you can use one of the search engines to find them. If you don't know how to do this easily, ask your local librarian for help. A frequently untapped resource, librarians specialize in helping people locate available resources, and they are happy to search with you, or point you in the right direction.

Q: What about other ways of meeting people?

A: Men usually form relationships through participation in some kind of organization. You may already be acquainted with business or quasi-business groups that meet before work hours for breakfast or have luncheon meetings. Often, these groups have a business agenda such as promoting, networking, or marketing one's self. Other organizational groups are associated with a particular trade or profession. Groups may also be formed around a particular cause such as eliminating blindness, helping the mentally retarded, or neighborhood beautification. Civic groups like the Lions' Clubs, Kiwanis, and Rotary can also be good ways to meet others while serving the community. Alumni or fraternity associations provide yet other ways to connect with people who have similar interests. Public speaking groups such as the Toastmasters can help you overcome the butterflies you may have in relating to large groups of people. Even in large organizations with a formal meeting agenda you can find ways to relate to people more on a one-to-one basis, perhaps after the official meeting or in subcommittees.

Other groups like the Elks, the Moose, VFW, and American Legion may be more varied in their functions and activities. These groups may have entry requirements such as having been in the service. Keep in mind, though, that clubs with multiple chapters can have an entirely different purpose and feel from location to location.

Political organizations always need help at the local level, and if you are interested, volunteering can be a way of meeting other individuals who have similar ideas. Religious groups and charitable groups also need help, and your local newspaper may have a weekly column devoted to volunteers, noting times and places and the qualifications needed.

You might wish to volunteer for a group that meets needs of yours that are not fulfilled at your regular job. If you do "paper shuffling" or make executive decisions all week, you might balance this out with a few hours of hammering and sawing as part of a "Habitat for Humanity" volunteer position. It's amazing how physical work can activate and enliven you.

Q: But I'm not ready to do this kind of thing yet. Can't I wait until I feel better?

A: Depressed persons tend to over-mentalize, telling themselves things like "I'll do it when I feel better." Recently divorced men are particularly susceptible to such depressive cognitions. Action is one of the best ways to rid oneself of the blues! Doing things gives you a spurt of extra energy, and is the best medicine for men in the early stages of divorce.

Remember that depressions are usually self-limiting. While most depressions lift after about six months—who wants to wait six months? Get going—get involved!

Q: How do I know if I am depressed?

A: Nowadays, it may seem that everyone suffers from depression. Some have called today's society "the Prozac Generation." We are not suggesting that every person needs an anti-depressant. Nor are we saying that if you are divorced, you must be depressed. However, it has become increasingly clear that the depressive symptoms of men are different from those exhibited by depressed women.

Women are far more likely than men to experience symptoms of depression such as weight loss, crying, feeling sad or blue for extended periods, moping around, loss of interest in sex, indecision, and preoccupation with death. Researchers like Terrence Real (1997, 2006) have stated that men experience more "covert depression," evident in such symptoms as workaholism, difficulty with intimacy, and rage.[6] Many typically "male problems" reflect efforts to cope with depression. The radio talk show host Dr. Laura Schlessinger echoes similar sentiments, "Women cry and talk; men don't ruminate on feelings, they try to do something about the situation."[7]

Psychologists John Lynch and Christopher Kilmartin (1999) point out that men and women are socialized to handle their feelings quite differently,[8] so it should not be surprising that they experience depression in different fashions as well. When something goes wrong in women's lives they have learned to look internally at their own failings, to focus on relationship problems, and to express their feelings openly. Socialization of women promotes introspection, encourages them to be emotionally expressive yet relatively noncompetitive, and promotes women to be focused on helping others. Men, however, are raised to be more self-focused, competitive, task-oriented, active, and independent. Rather than *expressing* our emotions, we men are likely to *control* them. We want to handle things ourselves. A man's depression is often characterized by a lack of awareness of his own feelings or emotions.

Furthermore, his depression may be expressed in behaviors that are destructive to himself or to his relationships. So, for example, a depressed man is more likely to take unnecessary health risks, to have difficulty forming close relationships, or to be overly angry.

Most of us guys would have a hard time recognizing depression in ourselves, much less in reporting it to a doctor or psychotherapist. It's somehow unmanly to think of yourself as depressed. If you continue to struggle with problems after your divorce, whether the problems are constant sadness or a desire to work 80 hours a week, you may wish to consult with a mental health professional who understands the issues of men. Maybe you need medication, or maybe you need a kick in the pants. In any case, consult with someone who knows about depression in men.

Chapter 8

"*Talk to a man about himself and he will listen for hours.*"
—*Benjamin Disraeli*

Groups for Men

In the last few chapters, we talked about what to do in the first phase after the divorce, and how to get yourself straightened out. We talked about the value of being with people without the immediate stresses of the dating situation. Getting one's priorities sometimes means being alone, while at other times, being with people is what is called for. Being with others can satisfy a number of social needs, while sharpening skills that may be a bit rusty. Being with others builds contacts. Being with others energizes. Sometimes this can best come from a group of men.

Q: I've heard something about "Men's Groups." What are they?

A: Joining a specialized group for men is a way of meeting many of your needs, especially in this early pre-dating phase after divorce.

Of course, not all men's groups are alike. Some groups are part of a larger men's association (e.g., New Warriors, Waking the Passion, or the Million Man Movement). Others are essentially services provided by a bigger organization such as a church (e.g., men's fellowships and support groups for single adult men). Men's groups may also be established and led by psychologists, psychotherapists, or counselors.

Some men's groups work within a mental health framework and are led by a professional. In these groups the leader tries to help the members overcome their mental/emotional problems. In the case of divorce, the group might focus on the emotional issues such as depression and anger that commonly are associated with divorce.

Other groups are more educational than therapeutic in nature. Although a person with a mental health background may lead such groups, the members are not seen as undergoing an emotional crisis. Rather, the members learn certain coping skills. The leader utilizes coaching tactics and teaching tips to help the participants.

Still other groups are more supportive than therapeutic or educational. In these groups, the leaders, if any, are members themselves, going through similar experiences. Divorce recovery support groups utilizing this model are fairly common in large churches. Often these groups follow a self-help model rather than employing a professional leader. If there is a leader, he is likely to be a lay-person who is experiencing a similar situation himself.

These three types of groups may have varying levels of structure. Groups with greater structure have more protocol about such things as the subjects that can be addressed or the amount of feedback members provide. Groups with less structure generally have fewer rules, although all groups have some rules (e.g., about confidentiality). Rules help the group remain organized and on-task. In some groups the leader will present the rules as givens. In other groups the leader may ask that the group consider and vote upon the rules to ensure group support for these binding actions.

Q: What can I expect to get out of a men's group?

A: Typical things that you might get out of a men's group include:

❑ *Learning that you are not alone in going through the divorce process.* Of course, in your head you know that you are not the only person to have gone through a divorce, but it is difficult to evaluate the divorce experience when you are by yourself. Unfortunately, we men typically do not talk a lot about our personal experiences, especially when those experiences are painful or embarrassing.

In a currently popular series of beer commercials, a group of men get together in a secret location to discuss the rules for manhood. Collectively, they refer to these rules as "man law." (For some reason, most of the laws have something to do with beer!) A real review of "man laws" would certainly include the rule about keeping stuff to ourselves, dealing with our problems without outside help. Regrettably, this latter rule creates additional problems, especially when you are going through something as emotionally difficult as a divorce. You may be surprised to learn that in a group setting men typically share more about their experiences than they do in an individual situation. The rules and atmosphere of the group promote candor, and as others talk about their lives, you become more able to talk about your own. Thus, you get a better understanding of how others have "weathered the storm".

❑ *Avoiding common errors in going through a divorce and recovering from it.* There are typical missteps—ways that men frequently get fouled up— when going through a divorce. However, you may wonder how you can learn anything from a bunch of other men who have the same problems as you.

In the first place, just because a person has the same problem as you (in this case divorce), does not mean that he has nothing to offer on the "solution." Indeed, he probably understands your problem in a more personal way than others would. Secondly, a great thing about group is that you get both positive and negative examples. You hear from men who have dealt with their divorce in a constructive way. You will make mental notes about some of the good things that they did to make the process less toxic and more positive. On the other hand, you will also hear about ways to make life even more miserable while going through divorce—mistakes that you will want to avoid. Hearing from real people about their experiences usually creates greater impact and learning than merely reading from a book. (The present volume, of course, is clearly an exception!)

❑ *Getting feedback about how you are doing in dealing with the divorce.* Another valuable function that groups can provide is to give you feedback about how you are doing. Let's say that you have been making some errors in dealing with your divorce; the group will probably confront you about this behavior. Perhaps, for example, you described to the group how you have been asking your wife to reconcile. The group, though, might give you feedback that your "asking" sounds more like "begging," an approach that is usually counterproductive. The guys may also suggest better ways for you to deal with the concern underlying your actions.

❑ *Holding you accountable for your actions.* The group also helps by encouraging accountability. As you begin to be known in group, the members will be interested in how you are progressing in dealing with your problems. They will want to know if you have been more successful or if you have persisted in a failed strategy. Many guys find this sort of accountability very helpful in maintaining their resolution to change their actions. In addition, as you make positive changes, the group will encourage you to keep going in the right directions.

Q: I don't like to talk about myself in public, especially with other men. How could I even fit in a group?

A: Virtually all men tell us that they don't think they would enjoy being in group. Usually, they will echo what you said, "I wouldn't feel comfortable" or "I'm too private." These are nearly universal feelings among the men we see. Yet, almost all of these men, if they try being in a group for a while, really like the experience. We think what happens is that after guys get over their initial reluctance, they find that the other fellows are pretty much like themselves; bright, interesting, wanting to make things better in their lives. Men often compare the experience of being in a men's group to being part of a sports team or a military unit. The spirit in these groups is usually "One for all; All for One." There is a camaraderie in these groups that most men don't have in their lives. So don't be surprised if you join one of these groups, that you actually come to like it.

Q: I've heard of men's groups in which they do drumming? What is that?

A: The idea about men drumming in groups became popular some years ago after the publishing of Robert Bly's (2004) book, *Iron John*. Bly, a poet, talked about the need for men to reconnect with their more primitive, inner selves. The idea was not to unleash a "wild man," but to experience masculinity in a more positive form.[1]

Bly and others argued that masculinity has gotten a bad reputation. It has sometimes been seen as synonymous with aggression, anger, and dominance. These writers noted that the positive aspects of masculinity include such qualities as self-sacrifice, hard work, wisdom, restraint, and helping the disadvantaged. Whether it is protecting the home and hearth or working long hours to provide for the family, we men do a lot of good things. If there is a noise in the middle of the night, we don't rouse our wives from their sleep to "check it out." We pick up the baseball bat hidden under the bed for just such an occasion and sally forth to encounter a possible burglar.

Many writers on men's issues note that masculinity seems less valued in modern societies than it has been in native cultures.[2] In indigenous societies, there are usually elaborate rituals when a boy makes the transition to manhood. By contrast, our urban societies provide little guidance or even give notice to men coming of age. In addition, tribal communities commonly have an association of the men (e.g., village elders) where problems are discussed and solutions formulated. These societies recognize the collective wisdom of men. There are few comparable associations of men in our complex urban world. The Jaycees, the Rotary Club, and the like are pale reflections of these earlier traditions.

Drumming and similar such rituals are seen as ways of emulating aspects of native cultures where manhood is revered. The overall goal of these rituals is to help men reconnect with positive views of masculinity. Drumming can provide cohesiveness and *esprit de corps* in a new endeavor. When done with others, drumming can give a feeling of oneness or cohesion (and a sense of power). This can help a man in a difficult situation like divorce when he feels pretty powerless and alone.

Certain rituals are part of any society, but if there are persons who make it, and are *in*, then that means that others haven't made it, and are *out*. And, there are usually feelings about being "*out*." You may feel like a member of the "*out*" group now that you are divorced. Groups can help you feel better about your situation and can help you feel that you are still "*in*." Group rituals like drumming create feelings of belonging.

Q: Aren't those group rituals kid stuff?

A: Many of us can relate to things we've missed in our childhood. This is not to become maudlin, and we're certainly not saying you have to go back and do a Freudian-type analysis of your childhood. Even if your mother dressed you funny, you can still have a good life; however, we may feel a sense of loss from our childhood that affects how we feel about our adult lives. Specific events, holidays, rituals, and ceremonies may remind us of important moments or feelings from our childhood.

As with most graduate students, my (Glenn Sternes) graduate-school years were characterized by putting off present pleasures in pursuit of a distant future goal (graduating). Most men have engaged in goal-directed behaviors, but for would-be psychologists that period of denial is pretty long, at least eight years, including internships and residencies. After four serious years, I decided to start throwing parties as a way of bringing fun into my life between the times of intense study. In my child psychology class, I discovered that other students had spent much more time than I had as a child doing finger-painting. So, I decided to make up for lost time. I hosted a finger painting party, complete with huge sheets of paper on the dining room table and plenty of paints. I quite enjoyed reconnecting with the lost pleasures—indeed moments of pure delight—I had had in first grade doing finger painting. To my surprise, other graduate students had much the same experience, reconnecting with important memories.

Rituals like drumming may bring back memories of Scouting days—good or bad—or things you missed or enjoyed. Don't dismiss it out of hand—try it if it's offered in a particular group.

Is it silly? We can't answer that, but if that's your response, maybe you can look at your life and see if there's a place for "silly" in it. Did you know that the person who can look at himself and laugh—loudly—has a much lower chance of developing a stomach ulcer than the serious, uptight fellow?

Martin never had a Monopoly set as a child. He had always played Monopoly at other kids' houses. So one day, as an adult, he bought his own Monopoly set, brought it home in the original cellophane, and ripped it open. Tears came to his eyes as he handled the race car, the top hat, and the other tokens. Now, Monopoly has taken its proper place in his life: mostly collecting dust on the shelf, but every so often pulled out for an evening of fun complete with that old killer instinct he had honed as a child. Nothing connects him quicker to that 10-year-old-Martin inside of him than the grandeur of being a Park Place tycoon. Quite by accident, he discovered his two children also enjoy an evening of Monopoly.

Q: What kinds of men would I meet in a group?

A: The kind of men that you meet in group depends, of course, upon what type of group you join. Members may vary across several dimensions: age, length of marriage, length of time they are separated or divorced, occupational level, and interests. The best answer, though, is that you will meet men like you. Leaders try to organize their groups so that the men have things in common. You will probably meet at least a few men that have similar backgrounds or experiences. In addition, you will have shared important milestones common to men: growing up as a boy, playing sports, going to school, marrying a woman, becoming a father, starting a career, dealing with parents as they age. When men get together and share their "stories," they usually find they have more similarities than they expected. In any case, we recommend that initially you focus more on those commonalities than on the differences among you.

As you grow to know the members of the group more, the differences among the members are an added bonus. After all, you can learn more from someone who is different from you than from someone who is just like you. Some of the best learning in group happens when you encounter someone who has faced challenges unlike your own. One of the common reactions for group members is to become more appreciative of their own dilemmas. Hearing the problems of others helps you put your own in perspective. Most people find that they would rather keep their own problems rather than exchange them for those of others.

Q: What's the difference between individual and group therapy?

A: Some people fear that joining a group is an indication that one must be *really* "sick." Unfortunately the media's popular representations of group therapy reinforce this stereotype. Probably the most well-known television representation of group was the old Bob Newhart Show.[3] On the show, Newhart portrayed a clinical psychologist who used group therapy in his practice. The group was composed of very neurotic people who were all outlandish caricatures of human problems. It was a very funny show, but not a good representation of what group is like. The people you meet in a group will seem pretty normal; they will be like you.

Being a group member is generally more demanding than going to individual counseling or psychotherapy. You must share the time with others rather than having a counselor's undivided attention. You also have to develop good listening skills as you hear the stories of others. Group members have to practice empathy, too. Understanding how others feel is a basic interpersonal skill, but one many men have skipped over. You learn to "walk a mile in another person's shoes." In other words, group is a laboratory for practicing relationship skills. Group enables you to hone your abilities for a future relationship. If you are still hoping for reconciliation, it is a wonderful place to get feedback from others on how you might best be able to accomplish that goal. Joining a group is also a very strong statement to your wife (or your ex) that you are willing to do whatever it takes to make the relationship better.

We believe that most men can greatly profit from discussing the process of divorce with other men. However, not everybody is ready for group. If you are too emotionally distressed, you may have difficulty waiting your turn or yielding the floor to others. Often new clients tell us that they don't think they would like being in a group. These men confide in us that they don't think they are the "kind of persons" who would talk in a group setting. However, once those same men try out the group experience, they usually like it. When a group is functioning well, the experience is somewhat like being on an athletic team or in a military unit where there is a common goal that you are working hard to achieve. *The common goal in group counseling is to learn about yourself in order to successfully cope with divorce.* The best groups feature both emotional support and challenge. Most men don't want or need a pat on the head nor a "pity party." They need practical tips on how to improve their situation. Sometimes that means challenging old beliefs and learning new tools for success.

> *The men in our groups get a lot of camaraderie from their participation. Much of that feeling is manifested in humor about the experience. In one particularly intense group meeting we discussed the various ways that men expressed anger. Each man took a turn talking about how his anger had been a problem for him. We asked the men to liken their anger to an object in the natural environment. One man stated that his anger was cutting like the edge of a sharp stone, while another man talked about how the person who had most hurt him was now dead. As each man finished his description, the group created a chant which the members then repeated out loud. The goal of the chant was to help the men ritually let go of these old angry expressions. As a result the group began to chant such things as "No more cutting!" and "He's dead now!" Others, in nearby offices wondered what the heck was going on in that group room! Afterwards, the group*

members suggested that the group should have tee-shirts made up declaring themselves "Free from Anger."

Q: Aren't men's groups just another "gripe session"?

A: This is one of the possible dangers to look out for in considering joining a group. Particularly in groups where there is no clinically-trained leader, matters may deteriorate to griping about the bad points of the spouse or ex-spouse. A leader is usually trained to recognize when ventilation of anger toward the spouse is helpful, or when it just seems to be repetitive and "stuck."

Women sometimes fear that a men's group will consist of "woman bashing." (Of course, men often fear that their wives do man-bashing as well.) If a lot of "bashing" is going on, you are in the wrong group. A well-functioning group focuses on the *self*, not on "what is wrong with her." If the session starts to devolve into criticism of ex-partners, usually the members themselves will correct the problem. Often a more experienced member will remind the others that you can only change yourself and that criticism of an ex-wife is not part of the group's process or goal. For the most part, men seem to appreciate these conventions. They ultimately see the logic in the position that you have to work on changing yourself, not your ex-wife.

Often, when one member articulates his anger about his wife or life, it brings up similar, unpleasant memories for other members as well. These memories can be handled in a constructive way, or they can begin a destructive spiral, focusing more and more on the negatives. Should you find that your own anger keeps coming out in such a spiral, get "unstuck" by looking for help from an anger management specialist. A referral from your physician or mental health professional can get things back on the right track. It is not helpful to be part of a group that gets stuck on detailing the inadequacies of women or the inevitable injustices of the legal system.

Q: What would I have to contribute to a men's group?

A: This is a common question from someone who has not yet participated in a group. When we were children, adults would sometimes ask us an unexpected question and the spotlight of unwanted attention would suddenly focus on us. You may wonder if you will experience a similar kind of awkwardness in group. What if someone asks me an "off the wall" question, or a question I'm not prepared to answer? Fortunately, most groups allow for easy entry of a new member.

When you begin a group, the first and natural response is to listen to the others talk for a while, getting a feeling for the subject of that session, and then introducing yourself and mentioning a few sentences about why you are there. If there is a leader of the group, then he may take over this introduction process, offering a ritual or process for integrating new members into the group. Also, the "old" members will probably be supportive, remembering their own first sessions. Sometimes new members opt to remain silent for a number of sessions before participating more freely. Gradually, the move from "new" to "old" member occurs.

Don't underestimate what you have to offer to others. Just because you are going through a divorce does not mean that you don't have a lot of insight about marriage, parenting, grief, and recovery. All of us have a piece of wisdom to share. In group counseling, we put those pieces together. Your piece of wisdom may be just the ticket for someone else in the group. Likewise, you may greatly benefit from his wisdom as well. It's a great feeling to help someone else who is going through a difficult time. As you help others, you help yourself.

Q: How do I know what to talk about in group?

Every group has its own way of deciding what to discuss. For example, in some groups, at the beginning of each session the members are asked to give a couple of sentences (or one minute) about what is currently going on in their lives. Groups may then take a vote about a topic they'd like to discuss. In other groups, the interaction is more "free form" with members simply bringing up an issue that they want to explore. Often, these issues reflect events that recently happened in the member's life (e.g., being served with divorce papers). The group then "kicks around" the theme with direction and oversight from the leader. At other times the members continue a theme that had been discussed in a previous session (e.g., "So what happened when you went to mediation?").

Still, in other situations, the group leader may bring up a theme for discussion. In our groups, for example, as leaders we often introduce themes around holiday times such as Father's Day or Thanksgiving. At other times, we bring up themes that the group has been seemingly avoiding (e.g., loss of contact with the children) or themes that might be relevant to a number of group members (e.g., anger management) and require further exploration.

Q: How long do groups meet?

A: Group sessions may meet for one or two hours per session. Some have a coffee hour after the session or go out for a bite to eat. When the group session is at least 1½ hours in length it allows the group to get into a topic in depth rather than just skimming the surface. Shorter-length sessions require those who talk to get right to the heart of the matter. Some members are more forthright in expressing their opinions. Other members may be slower to participate, or they may tend to remain superficial or diverge from the topic at hand. If you are in a group, and someone tells you that you are not staying on the topic, or being superficial, listen to him. This criticism may seem harsh or even cruel, but it is important for the group to make the most of its time. You can always ask if other members agree with this feedback. If they do, then take it to heart.

Q: What if I don't like what the other group members are saying to me?

A: From the very start most groups encourage members to give feedback to the speaker about what he has said. This feedback can be very helpful to you in understanding how your thoughts, words, and actions are affecting others, especially as you interact with women. This may particularly critical when considering interactions with your ex-spouse, or even your new dating relationship. Sometimes, you will receive positive feedback in the group, encouraging you in the paths that you are taking. At other times, the feedback may not be so positive. While it may be difficult at times to hear negative feedback from group members, it may be easier to hear it from them than from a woman. Usually others, especially women, are less willing to give you such important feedback so directly. Friends and family tend to be too biased to be objective in giving you feedback. In group, though, you are more likely to get the unvarnished truth about how you are being perceived. You don't have to agree with all of the feedback you get, but give special consideration to feedback if you:

- ❏ hear the same messages consistently

- ❏ hear similar messages from multiple people

- ❏ hear messages from people whom you especially respect

Take the feedback that makes sense to you and put it to use. The feedback that is less helpful from group (or from therapy in general) feel free to dismiss. Remember, though, that we humans are masters of self-deception. Try not to fool yourself. Instead, practice listening.

Q: When am I finished in group?

A: You may also want to know how long you should attend a group. There are two general models of groups: "closed-ended" and "open-ended" groups.

In closed-ended groups there are a finite number of sessions. Everyone stops after the number of sessions agreed to in the beginning. Usually, in closed-ended groups, the members start and finish together.

In open-ended groups the length of your participation is more of an individual matter, or a decision made between you and the therapist-leader. In some groups, members and the leader or members and the entire group jointly decide if a member is ready to leave. In any case, the last couple of sessions that you attend group are often the most important.

Usually, you are required to give notice before leaving the group. This is to prevent members from just disappearing into the night, never to be heard from again. Leaving in this way is very disruptive (and rude) to the other group members. When this happens, the group usually becomes preoccupied with why the member left in this way. "Why did ol' Joe decide to leave? Was it something I said?" rather than on their own issues. In addition the other group members may be disappointed that they can no longer get feedback from the now-absent member. The experience is a little like having a friend suddenly die.

To prevent these feelings, group members are exhorted to discuss their plans to leave the group during a group meeting. (In our groups we require a two-week notice before leaving.) While an individual may consider himself ready to leave, a look at how the others perceive the ending is in order. If there is a fee involved to be in group, there will obviously be legitimate concerns about pocketbook issues, but it is our experience that financial concerns mask deeper issues.

Sometimes a group member leaves after being called out or criticized, and leaves out of anger to punish the group or to protect himself from further criticism. When a member leaves precipitously without discussing the matter, the members generally cannot learn anything about the effects of their behavior on the departing member. More importantly, a member who leaves when angry may have missed learning something himself—something that will inevitably emerge in his interactions with ex-partner and/or children.

A group member may feel ready to leave, but the group can point out further things to accomplish that the group member had not considered. If he attends a final session, he may still consider it time to leave, but he will usually carry important feedback with him that he can either work on by himself, or return to that group (or another group) and continue when the time (and money) are better. Sometimes, men need time to digest new developments, particularly when they are in ourselves.

Saying "good-bye" is a normal part of every relationship, yet many times we leave relationships with regrets. For that reason group leaders often stress the significance of leaving group. Leaders encourage members to use leaving the group as a rehearsal for how to leave a relationship in the best, most healthy way. Members who are leaving usually get a lot of feedback from the entire group about their progress and continuing needs. Most often, warm feelings are exchanged, particularly from those members who have been in the group from the departing member's first sessions and have a good perspective of his progress. A sense of completion comes out of this, both for the individual leaving the group, and from the group seeing him leave. This can increase optimism, or at least maintain realism, for those members of the group who are in the earlier or middle stages of therapy. Members may tell themselves, "He can do it; therefore, so can I!"

A PRIMER ON MEN'S GROUPS

❑ Length: Groups may meet for a predetermined number of sessions with all members starting and ending together (closed-ended) OR for an indefinite number of sessions with members coming and going (open-ended).

❑ Session Times: Groups may meet for 1 to 2 hours per week, or they meet on a less frequent basis (e.g., monthly or even annually). Sometimes there are "after meeting" or informal gatherings at restaurants or coffee shops.

❑ Leadership: Groups may include a professional leader (e.g., a psychotherapist) or be peer led (e.g., support groups).

❑ Structure: Some groups specify the topics that will be discussed while others utilize more "free form" discussions with the topics offered by the members. Some groups limit the giving and receiving of feedback (opinions) of others, while some groups encourage such feedback.

THE SECOND PHASE AFTER DIVORCE—DATING (AGAIN)

CHAPTER 9

"You can make more friends in two months by becoming interested in other people than you can in two years by trying to get other people interested in you."

—*Dale Carnegie*

THINKING ABOUT DATING

Okay, now that you've gotten preliminary divorce issues out of the way, you're going to look forward ... to what? Dating? Other relationships? Let's touch base and see how many of the following items you can comfortably endorse:

❑ You can now consider the possibility of going out with a woman without masses of anger welling up in you.

❑ You have reconnected with people, especially with other men, in some concrete ways.

❑ You are not consistently preoccupied with thoughts of your previous marriage or the divorce.

❑ You can tolerate living on your own and being by yourself.

If you have done well in addressing the above items, you may be ready to look forward to dating. Of course, you may decide that you are still going to fly solo. That's OK, but most of us begin wanting to have a connection with another woman sooner or later. We'd like you to do some thinking about dating before actually plunging into it. Let's start with answers to some basic questions.

Q: Can I realistically look forward to a new relationship?

Many men start lining up prospective dates and bed partners even before the divorce is final. Indeed, as soon as friends see you as "single," they may be offering to "fix you up" with their co-worker or their cousin who is also just divorced. It can be flattering, and it can be exciting, but it is probably also confusing. You may not have dated in years, and many people find the whole process more anxiety provoking than fun. What happens if you meet someone nice? Can you handle it? Most people will say that they don't want to get into a new relationship until they are ready for it.

Q: How will I know when I'm ready to date?

A: Our general advice is to go slow. "G...O ... S...L...O...W." As we noted in Chapter 7, you first should be comfortable being by yourself. In Chapter 15, we will talk more about becoming serious again. For now, let's just say that you will probably want to be ready to date before you actually are ready.

Q: What if I get nervous around people, especially women?

A: In dating women, to be at your best, you need to be yourself. That is, you need to act like the person you really are, not someone you think she wants you to be. You are no longer a teenager, and you don't need to engage in the juvenile games that adults often play in dating and love. Trying to "look cool," "be hip," "act as if you don't care," "play jealous" to see if the other notices—are all typical adolescent games. We're not saying that you should wear your feelings on your cuff; too much transparency will scare anybody away.

Being yourself means taking a little bit of time to get to know yourself. In part, it involves knowing the activities in which you want to engage. Suddenly wanting to be a "big-game hunter" is probably not going to reflect who you are if you've never fired a rifle before. Maybe you want an activity that involves some physical stamina, but not too much. Do you want to do these activities in your home area, or to travel? If the latter, recognize that traveling cuts down on the number of people you meet, and the likelihood of keeping such friends is small.

Look at things from the opposite perspective. If you are not acting yourself, and you find a "special someone," she will like you for this "Not-You" façade. Later, when you inevitably begin to act like yourself again, she may not like you as you really are. Enough said!

> *Bob and Sue were going through a lot of marital problems, and decided to seek consultation. Bob began the session explaining that he and his wife used to play a lot of golf together. He had imagined that they would buy a house on a golf course, play nine holes together after work, and generally enjoy a country club sort of life. He was disappointed when his wife didn't want to purchase what he considered his dream home on the 17th green of a golf course. He couldn't understand why she never joined him on the links and objected to his playing a round with his buddies on the weekends. Then, when it came her turn to speak, Sue admitted that she had never played golf before meeting him. In fact, she took golf lessons so that she could spend time with him, knowing it was his passion. Now that they were married, though, she never got out her clubs. She exasperatingly explained, "I hate that game! I just pretended to like golf so I could get Bob."*

Q: So it's back to dating?

A: Dating is actually a relatively "recent invention," accompanying other inventions of the 20th century. For example, the automobile contributed to dating because it allowed for some bit of independence. Large cities created anonymity, making dating a way of getting to know people of the opposite sex and appropriate age. People in small towns, who knew everybody else, went to school together, and had daily contact with them, did not have this problem, but dating did provide a way to get away from the eyes of Mom and Dad. In addition, as people began to have money for discretionary spending, a fellow could treat his date to a movie or a burger. During the years of the

Great Depression, there generally was no extra money, but groups of young people still gathered together and engaged in pastimes, enjoying the group activity without excessive cost.

The current dating trend originated in the 1950's by the Baby Boomers and by the "unnamed generation" just before them. This was about the time that the "big movies" came out. Taking a girl downtown to see one of those Cinerama or wide screen "biggies" involved some money and arrangements either with a car or public transportation. If a guy did not drive or still had monetary problems, he might get another couple to go along, and maybe that guy drove—*voila*: the double date!

In those years, emphasis was upon giving the date a good time, and later possibly getting some action. Movies were a good first date because you could focus on activities other than yourselves and then have at least one commonality to talk about afterwards when at the malt shop, coffee shop, or at dinner.

Such a date required advance notice, and the learning of telephone etiquette came here. Don't call the girl too soon, or too late, and don't ask what she's doing on that night, but just go out on the limb, ask her out, hand her the saw, and see if she cuts you down by refusing, in which case you skulk away feeling lower than slime mold, or if she accepts the date, you feel like the man of the mountain.

Dress for this first date was often upscale, and behavior was likewise. Both of these have sometimes been termed "bow-tie" behavior. Imagine the guy just outside the girl's door, ready to ring the bell, and straightening out his bow-tie while practicing his best smile. Inside, the girl was at the door, or close, but not too close, so as to not appear too eager, and straightening her dress and hair, while practicing her smile—okay, you get it.

Later generations, some sooner than later, eased up on this formal style of dating, because of the strains put upon the dating couples. Sometimes it continued longer because of outside pressure from school and other organizations, due to commitments such as finding a date for the Junior-Senior prom.

More recently then, "regular" dating returned almost to the "Depression-style dating" with dates that are more casual and with more spontaneity, leaving the "big events" for more formalized dating. Such spontaneous dating includes going to a dance or having a get-together after a football game or such. Sometimes, it just means gathering or hanging together as a group, either with the same-sex or both sexes present. Dress is more casual, often what the person happens to be wearing at the time. This has many of the advantages of the "Depression-style" dating, allowing you to get to know a whole bunch of people without any commitments. Of course, they get to know you, too. Thus, when single-dating occurs during later adolescence, there are not as many of the awkward first-date scenarios mentioned above.

College often re-shuffles this, as a person is placed in a new situation in another part of the country (unless he or she goes to junior college and lives at home), and single couples dating may be the style. However, separation of the sexes became less common over the years, and the *in loco parentis* attitudes of colleges disappeared. In their place come co-ed dorms, allowing for various other educational, sleeping, and bathroom arrangements not foreseen by former generations. Not that this was always desirable. Probably, many potential dates were scratched off the list because they were seen without their hair combed, make-up on, or shaved.

One undergraduate philosophy professor said that college was the only place where the "guilty go free while the innocent were locked up." He was referring, of course, to the *in loco parentis* days where college girls were not chaperoned, but had "hours" and they got "late minutes" if they came back from a date later than the designated time.

Q: Why do we have to go through this dating stuff, anyway?

A: Every society wants its people to get paired off and eventually reproducing. This is fundamental to that society continuing into future generations. Just as the politician's first duty after getting elected is to get ready to be re-elected, a society is interested in continuation of itself. These rules have nothing to do with how you feel and the aches in your loins, or sometimes, the butterflies in your stomach.

One of the best societal codifications is found in the Bible. Many of the Biblical rules, prescriptions and proscriptions, are to make sure that the tribes of Israel stayed strong. Rules about how often to have sex, depending upon one's vocation, are there to help both men and women stay happy and thus producing. And rules against homosexuality (at least male) are because such seed that is spilled is lost because it cannot be deposited in a female and thus increase the strength of one's tribe.

In other cultures, we see that they have solved the "problem" of meeting others in quite different ways. Maybe you have heard of the arranged marriages in Far Eastern (Oriental) cultures, where the bride and groom have never met prior to the wedding day. Wonder what stresses they had to put up with in learning to accept almost a total stranger? Maybe their lower divorce rates are because they are not allowed to divorce, and one partner just caves into the other, giving him (yes, often the guy) his way.

Or maybe you remember the arrangement in the Bible where Jacob had to labor for seven years to win his love, Rachel, and then her father changed his mind and had him marry the older daughter, Leah, first. Jacob then had to work seven more years to marry his chosen one. Different times and different cultures.

European cultures did allow dating, but always with a chaperone, either a pesky younger brother or an old maid aunt, or assorted cousins. That put the damper on adolescent passion!

All of these elements of dating are changing, and we cannot always see the changes because we are so immersed in our own culture. Not as often do we have large dance halls or theaters today; they evolved into movie theaters as places to meet someone; churches have shown a renaissance as a place to meet someone, but couples are often meeting in coffee shops, at schools and colleges, and in the workplace. Methods of meeting someone today also have gone to the use of the dating service, computer dating, and internet communication.

Q: Is dating the same as when I was a teenager?

A: No, because over the years, you have changed (and matured) in your personality, and most likely you will not have to date vast numbers of persons to form your selections as you did when in your teens. You don't have to re-invent the wheel. You know things now that will help short-cut this process of getting the one that you want.

Q: So, what do I know about dating?

A: You already know that dating is a way to meet people—people that you like and people who like you—people you want to spend time with and share interests, activities, talk, and....maybe love. You know quicker how to eliminate the other categories: People you don't like and who don't like you (that's the easiest!), people who like you but you don't like (this often involves diplomacy, or at least assertiveness), and people you like but who don't like you (this is often the hardest).

Q: What if I want to be more spontaneous in dating?

A: Remember when you were dating as a teen? If you waited to call a girl until the last moment, so you could be spontaneous and do what you felt like doing, you ran the risk of her being booked up, either with another date or with another activity, family obligation, etc. If, on the other hand, you called much sooner, she may have accepted, but then you didn't always feel like doing the thing you agreed to in making the date in the first place. Only in later dating, when you are past the "bow tie" stage can you call a little later and have a spontaneous-type date because you both know that you will not be dating others.

Q: I remember being very kind to my ex when we were dating, but what if I don't want to do that now in my dating?

A: Are you still angry over (perceived) slights from your ex-? Have you really given up on her, or could you possibly be trying to "get even" with the next female for what your ex did to you.

A quick way to get out of this is to see that both of you are in a new and strange situation together, and need information about each other to solve some problems. No magic signposts are there to tell you how to do this, but if you can remain yourself during this process, then she can figure out whether she likes you, and if you do the same, seeing her presenting herself as she really is, then the beginnings of a relationship may be there.

Q: Do men and women relate differently as they get older?

A: Yes. Remembering back when you were in your early 20s, what was the importance of physical sex to you back then? Depending upon when you had your first sexual encounter, you may have been focusing upon this event to the exclusion of others. Men's sexuality peaks in their late teens and early 20s. Sadly, this means that our peak years are in the rear-view mirror of the lifetime drive. Women's peak years are in their mid- to late- 30s. Now, maybe this means that God has a sense of humor, maybe even ironic, because even if you meet someone now who is perfect for you sexually, your graphs will not stay at the same point five or ten years from now.

In counseling couples, we often liken the relationship to building a fire. At first, things in a relationship cannot be hot and heavy; there has to be a phase of finding similarities, of liking—what has been earlier termed as the "bow tie" phase with lots of smiling and pleasant chatter or small-talk. This is analogous to starting a fire with newspapers and small kindling. Anything too heavy or too big in the early stages of a relationship puts out the "fire", just as too much wind or suddenly dropping a big log on a new sputtering campfire puts it out.

Next, the relationship settles in to a more comfortable stage, where there is a chance for a real "sparking". The kindling now comes in terms of bigger sticks, which can emit lots of fire and crackling noises, and the relationship is in the "being in love" or infatuation phase.

After this, the big logs may be put on the fire. Now the fire settles down, and there may not be the popping and crackling, but the relationship, like the fire, is capable of real heat. In terms of the marriage, there may not be all the hourly or daily indications of affection, but each partner knows that the other is true, and the love can endure hardships, just as the fire made with big logs can last the entire night without replenishing the logs.

Some persons do not understand these changes over time, and seem stuck at the earlier levels. They want the pops and crackles and excitement, and may even become upset if their partner does not give them the adulation they want. They may even trade their partner in (via divorce) to find another partner and stay at this "being in love" or infatuation stage, thus short-changing themselves in the long run from experiencing the "big log" stage.

Q: Who is in control of sex in dating?

A: This is an important question as you reenter the dating scene. It involves an essential part of Western life and values, particularly with regard to religion and how we men comport ourselves.

Control of dating, control of sexuality. Women have had more of the latter, although since the days of the Pill, women have had more freedom, but still have the responsibility of the pill for contraception. This may be a sore point with them, and many women ask, "Why don't they develop a contraceptive pill for men?" The problem is analogous to the question "Which is easier—guarding a castle against one attacker, or guarding a castle against one thousand attackers?" Actually, the example should be enlarged upon because the average ejaculate contains thousands, maybe millions of sperm, and the male is capable of more than one ejaculation per month, while there's only one egg per month.

Western theology emphasizes control of our emotions and our sexuality. Going to church means limiting our sexual urges (at least temporarily), and some churches limit this by dress codes. Psychologists know that dressing up makes us feel better and act better; just ask school teachers whose schools have dress codes. Other churches, synagogues and mosques segregate the sexes, putting men and women in separate portions, or typically, with the women behind, or behind and above, the men. (We know who is more likely to have sexual thoughts during the services). You may be interested to note that Eastern theology does not always share our same cultural findings about sexuality.

> *One of us had the privilege of traveling to Khajuraho in India. This city is notable for its erotic temples. Carvings of humans engaged in copulation in various and sundry positions make for interesting slide presentations (and you thought that family pictures were always boring) and tall tales. Why would such carvings be placed on a religions' place of worship? Apparently, the people of those times knew our weaknesses better than we do. The reason they created this sculptural pornography was that they thought that by presenting such images, the attendees' thoughts and longings would be worn out and they then could concentrate on religion. What a revelation! Perhaps such an idea might help priests, who for centuries have struggled with their basic lustful urges while attempting to remain celibate, often feeling guilty when they fail to do so.*

Total control, then, of sexual urges does not work with humans. In men, dreams may lead to nocturnal emission, involuntary seminal ejaculations (i.e. "wet dreams"). Some men have learned to feel guilt about this, but this, too, can be unlearned.

Now don't go to the other extreme and think that we are endorsing a total lack of control either. We are not suggesting that people should be lying around, humping furiously on the carpet and floors, without much regard to who is engaged or what is taking place. Our cultures, and other cultures, have prescribed what is considered appropriate. It's just that our culture says that the genders can interact with each other in non-sexual ways without a concern of whether there is always the goal of sex when two people meet. Prominent citizens get headlines and are censured when they say differently. Take, for example, a judge who declared that "the woman was asking for it by the way she dressed" and therefore dismissed the charges of rape against a man. Needless to say the judge got in trouble over that ruling. Another example was a politician who glibly declared "If a woman is going to be raped, she might as well lie down and enjoy it." He then got "raped" at the next election. These kind of comments sound like things fraternity brothers say.

In our culture, we do not go to the extremes of segregating women from men once the girls reach puberty. We do not dress them in shapeless bags and hide their faces. However, we may go to the other extreme, in part, leading to a "look but don't touch" mentality. And some few persons in our society do not have the cognitive controls to follow this.

Our Houston scuba group gave a whole sex education to a bunch of Jordanian boys. We were the first American group to dive in Jordanian waters. The beaches there were beautiful and only three miles across were the equally fine beaches of Israel, which we visited the next year. The young boys quickly gathered to watch divers returning from the cold waters of the Red Sea and doffing their full wet suits before they got too cold, and then could warm up in the 90+ degree weather. The women were, of course, wearing bikinis, or at least, two-piece suits. The boys had never seen grown females wearing anything except the chalabas, full-length clothing that included a head cover.

Going into town was also a sex education. A woman friend and I had gone into town in Jordan, and she had disregarded my suggestion that she not wear a sleeveless top, but dress more conservatively. She was striving for independence on this trip, so disregarded my advice. Buying some trinkets, we met a man who had doubled for Omar Shariff in some of the Arabic movies. This good-looking man ran a souvenir shop and helped her look at an Eastern costume. While she was trying the costume on, the man came to me and asked if she were my wife. When I said no (she was not under my protection), I knew what was to come next. She came bursting out of the dressing room, indignant that he had groped her. Of course, he was operating according to their culture, and according to them, she was "obviously" one of "them" (i.e., a wanton woman) since she was not my wife and was wearing no long-sleeved clothing. That being so, she was fair game for being groped, with hopes of more.

While we're talking about culture, control and sex, think about what the dating situation means to you. Some men use dating as a way of deceiving women. Anything (trickery, lies, etc.) is fair game, as long as you can get into their pants. If this describes you, then maybe you are viewing life as a competition, with women as trophies to be won by the man with the most prowess or the best pick-up line. If so, you are probably headed towards a second bad relationship.

Q: How do I tell people (especially women) that I am divorced?

A: First of all, we remind you that your divorce should not be a source of shame for you. After all, about half of all marriages end in divorce. You are not wearing a "scarlet D" on your forehead. On the other hand, you need not advertise it as if it is the essential definition of your life. "Hello, I'm Sam, and I'm divorced." As you begin to date and meet new people, moments will occur when it will be natural to describe your status. When those moments occur, don't go into long-winded explanations or time frames. Just state plainly that you are divorced. Later on, when and if it is relevant, you can explain what happened. Most importantly, don't use this as an opportunity to tell others how badly your ex-wife treated you. A new acquaintance will probably sense this as overly defensive on your part, and perhaps even conclude that you are being either naïve or untruthful.

Q: What are some warning signs to look out for when dating?

A: Many men tell us that during dating either a) they didn't see any warning signs about the woman or b) ignored the warning signs they saw. Our feeling is that usually indications about potential problems in the relationship are manifested during the dating process. Of course, you are much more likely to recognize these warning signs if you date for a longer period of time. Our second piece of advice is: "Don't dismiss your concerns." Don't tell yourself that her annoying habits (e.g., always being late) won't really bother you later in the relationship. If anything, they will probably bother you more. That is not to say that you must find a faultless creature (not much risk of that!). Rather, you must accept her for whom she is, not for whom you *wish* she were. Of course, the same thing goes for her. She is better off accepting you with all your warts, rather than planning to shave them off later. Have you heard the old joke about marrying the perfect person and then trying to change them?

Yet, there are some warning signs you should consider. What may be a warning sign for you, though, would not necessarily have the same ominous meaning for someone else. If, for example, you pick up on the idea that your new love is, shall we say, a tad too materialistic, that could be a big issue or a relatively small one depending on your attitude about such matters. If you are very cautious about money, accounting for every expenditure to the penny, her cavalier attitude about money would eventually drive you crazy. If, on the other hand, money is no great object to you (i.e., you have plenty of it and like to show that off), you might actually like having someone who can appreciate the finer things of life. In short, it depends. So, you must first know your own self in order to give proper credence to the hints you glean about her. With these caveats, though, here are some of our thoughts about "warning signs":

❑ How does she handle money? Will her money habits make you crazy?

❏ Does she like sex well enough to suit you? If the answer during dating is "no," it will probably be no during marriage, too.

❏ Do her personal habits (e.g. smoking, health, weight, exercise) concern you?

❏ Is she a heavy drinker? Does she abuse alcohol or other drugs? The "party girl" doesn't necessarily make a good lifetime partner.

❏ Does she have a history of being unfaithful to previous men? If so, she is more likely to eventually be unfaithful to you.

❏ What is her involvement with her family? If she calls her mother twice a day, she will probably continue to do so even after you become a couple.

❏ How honest is she? Does she tell the "little white lies". Does she shade the truth or hold things back? If she lies about little things now, she cannot be expected to be truthful about big ones later.

❏ How does she manage her anger? Does she have a fiery temper? Does she make cutting remarks? How did her last relationship end? Even though her anger may not be directed at you now, you can expect that her anger will be similar in style when she is upset with you.

❏ What is her emotional stability? Is she highly moody? Does she have a history of being abused? What kind of mental health treatment has she received? Has she ever been suicidal? Today, it is not uncommon for people to take antidepressants or see a counselor, but if her problems have been severe in the past, she is likely to have periods of severe problems in the future as well.

❏ How does she balance parenting with being in a relationship? Can you be a priority for her?

❏ (If you have or want children) Can you picture her mothering your child? Does she seem to object to your kids? Does she share your desire for children? Or, conversely, will she be content with not having children?

❏ Is she invested in a career? If she is career-oriented, is that acceptable to you? If she is not, will that be a problem?

Q: What do I have to look forward to in life?

A: This chapter does not end with us crying in our beer, bemoaning our lost youth. Just as we are no longer able to run the 100-meter dash at the same pace we did in our teens and early 20s, we no longer retain the same interest in this ability. We move on to other things. It is that flexibility, of moving and changing with our changing abilities, that marks good mental health. However, if we rigidly stay with things despite changes in our environment and ourselves, then we show the hallmarks of mental problems. We can set ourselves up for depression, anxiety, or other mental health issues.

Men have often told us that as the push for physical intercourse lessened over the years, they discovered the wonders of touch, of giving and receiving caresses. The changes in the sensitivity of their nervous system which led to a decrease in speed of physical climax now allowed them to take the time (if they allowed it to happen) to learn to give and receive love, thus opening up a wonderful new world to them.

It is easy to see the second half of life as a time in which all of the abilities and talents you have learned in the first half are slowly going away. However, at the same time new talents and abilities can now appear that have been hidden by these earlier ones. Your previous experiences of dating, usually characterized with much anxiety and self-conscious learning, can be improved upon. While we still describe the process with the same word "dating", thankfully, it need not be a repetition of that prior difficult time.

CHAPTER 10

"Women are like cars: we all want a Ferrari, sometimes want a pickup truck, and end up with a station wagon."
—Tim Allen

PRIORITIZING AND DATING ISSUES

Before taking the plunge back into dating, we encourage you to give some serious thought to your priorities about relationships, about women, and about yourself.

Q: What priorities should I be setting in dating?

A: Younger people who start dating look for commonalities: similar music, similar likes among movie stars, similar classes in high school and college, and possibly, similar occupational training. While these may be important at that age, should it take prime focus at your age? You may be looking for these commonalities already in people you meet. At all ages, the concept of *similarity* is one of the major ways in which we select a person we like, and therefore, eventually, a partner.

The Greeks had this idea that we are all born as twins, but we become separated from one another before birth, and we then go through life searching for the other, a "soul mate" if you will. As adults we often seek persons who are like us.

For example, many of us begin relationships around music. Music, being very connected to emotion, is one strong way in which we share who we are. If a new friend has similar musical tastes, you may quickly begin to feel connected. If on the other hand, she has very different musical interests, then you have to be more broad-minded. You might alternate listening to her music with her listening to yours.

Similarity in other areas (e.g., religion) may also be important. Some people who grow up exposed to only one religion react very strongly and negatively if asked to consider another's religion, particularly if it is quite different. Religious groups themselves have educated their parishioners about this. They often put impediments in the way of marrying outside the group, either by preventing the marriage in the church, synagogue or holy place, or by excommunicating or otherwise sanctioning the member. Often, persons who are single or single again, play the "marriage roulette" game, denying that religion (or some other belief) may be important. They may feel that choosing only from among people of similar beliefs denies them a chance at a full selection of potential mates. Later, when they see whose "number" comes up, they will deal with the issue of religion. If religion is very important to you, you may want to save yourself and the other some hurt. Decide before the emotions get too strong that this is not your cup of tea and select instead only from persons within your religion. Likewise, you have to look at your similarity to the woman on other variables, behaviors, or qualities.

Let's take the example of smoking. If you are a smoker, should you only select from women who are also smokers, and if a non-smoker, what about dating a woman who smokes? You may again do a denial trip, and say you want to keep the lines open as much as possible, but the issue of smoking or not smoking says a lot about that person. For example, smoking may indicate how anxious this person tends to be, and how she handles anxiety. Smoking may also reflect her feelings about maintaining her health and how she views her body. Thus, her psychological sophistication, body image, and health attitudes may be signaled by her smoking behavior. Don't interpret this to mean we are snobs, for all of us know some very sophisticated persons who are smokers. However, the general trend in our society is to be much less interested in smoking with each passing year. In the United States less than 25% of the population now smokes. Furthermore, nonsmokers are less likely now to passively tolerate a smoker as they realize that passive or secondary smoke can harm non-smokers.

> *As a comparison you might consider how schools have dealt with smoking. Schools went from prohibiting smoking for students (and tolerating smoking among teachers, but in a special location) to "allowing" and "understanding" smokers' needs and providing a special location for both teachers and students to smoke, to a return to the first position. In high school, we used to joke with one teacher who smelled like a chimney and often was late to class, asking him if he'd changed to cigars. But there was still the negative reaction to being near him and smelling the strong smoke odor, although he was one of the better high school teachers.*

Thus, in prioritizing, you may initially think that dating a smoker is okay, and even like initial kisses, but later on you may start thinking that she will smell this way all of the time and not just at "sexy" times. You may wonder what it will be like in other health modalities. For example, if she smokes, is she less likely to take up the healthy hobby I like, and so I'll miss out on my mountain climbing or scuba diving, or have to do them on my own?

You may have other priorities such as racial and ethnic backgrounds for finding your "soul mate." Some of these personal attributes may overlap with your religious preferences, and it may be important for you to consider these as well. Can we suggest what is right for you? By no means. But, a little bit of reflection now can save you some time, money, and trouble later.

Sometimes, we try to fool ourselves into thinking that we have an unlimited amount of time, and thus we can just wander from one pleasant woman to another. But just like in the business world, the man with the plan will be ahead of the one who meanders from place to place. A few persons will end up in satisfactory relationships without a plan, but you increase your odds with preparation.

We recommend that you consider the twenty areas listed below (in no particular order) in forming your priorities. Not all of them will be important to you, but you should pay attention to the ones that are.

You may, of course, have some other priorities not listed, but we have found this to be a good starting place:

- ❏ Age

- ❏ Race

- ❏ Religion

- ❏ Ethnic group

- ❏ Cultural background (e.g., raised in the city, or adopted the traditions of the old country)

- ❏ Occupational status

- ❏ Health

- ❏ Desire for family and children

- ❏ Importance of hobbies

- ❏ Intellectual interests

- ❏ Interest in travel

- ❏ Pet ownership

- ❏ Language

- ❏ Verbal communication style and skills

- ❏ Cultural beliefs

- ❏ Comfort with physical touch (e.g., holding hands, cuddling)

- ❏ Need for sex

- ❏ Social habits (e.g., smoking, alcohol, and drug use)

- ❏ Connections to parents and other relatives

- ❏ Need for money/economic status

Q: Why should I care about such trivial matters as her occupational status?

A: Many of the priorities we suggested for you to consider are associated with personality traits, values, and attitudes about the world. Her occupational status suggests many of her qualities such as the values she has placed upon higher education and her willingness to delay gratification to obtain such education. By considering occupational status you also learn something about her abilities and her cognitive or attention skills. On the other hand, her having a high occupational status *per se* is not a guarantee that she will make a good future mate. It's much like the old movies who showed us that rich people had just as many foibles as the rest of us. Often, we seek partners whom we feel are similar to us in their educational or occupational status. Don't fall into the trap of thinking, though, that more money or more education means a better person. Often, luck or chance is operative in terms of occupational or monetary status; and some people directly choose against monetary gain for the added prestige of a profession that meets another, stronger need. For example, those in the teaching and helping professions may choose them for the rewards of seeing others better themselves rather than for the salary they earn.

Similarly, other priorities we have recommended for you to consider will suggest qualities about your potential partner. Her interest in travel, her health habits, her ethnicity all will tell you important things about her. Some will be more vital to you than others. Just don't dismiss them out of hand thinking that "Love conquers all." It may start out that way, but the love is unlikely to be sustained unless you are compatible in vital areas. Remember, though, that compatibility does not mean equality. She can (and will be) different from you, but you need to be comfortable with who she is, not who you wish that she were, who you thought she was, or who you hope she will become. Keep in mind, too, that your own occupational status will suggest aspects of yourself and your values to her.

Q: Does this mean I should seek a woman who has no needs?

A: Good news! There are no such women (or men). All of us have needs, but the precise needs we are seeking to fill vary from person to person.

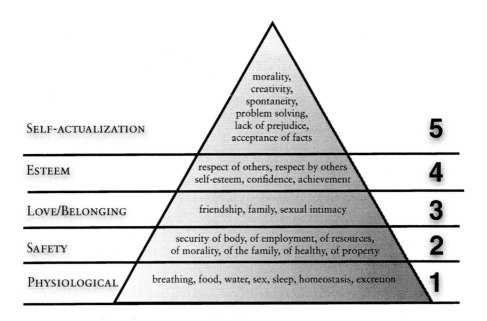

MASLOW'S HIERARCHY OF NEEDS

Think of a triangle with horizontal segments, labeled from the bottom, as: physiological needs, safety and security needs, love and belongingness needs, status needs, and self-actualization. Most people in the world are at the bottom-most level spending the majority of their time worrying about eating and drinking. These physiological requirements are our most basic needs. As Maslow so convincingly pointed out more than half a century ago,[1] until these needs are met, nothing else seems important. If we are able to meet those physiological needs, then we focus on the next level of needs: safety and security. Safety and security needs include housing as well as other things we need to feel safe. Nowadays, locks and keys, fences and gates, security cameras, guards, etc. may be part of our needs for security. When you move to a new place, you typically become quite aware of those security needs. Indeed, real estate advertisements often describe the security features of the apartment or neighborhood. If we meet our safety and security needs we come to the next level in Maslow's hierarchy: love and belongingness. Feeling loved and a sense of belonging only become important to us when we can meet our physiological needs, and we feel a sense of safety and security in our world. Many people are involved in clubs and groups as part of fulfilling a need to belong. If we meet our physiological, safety, and love needs, we are apt to focus on status desires. We don't want just any old auto, but it has to be the best Cadillac, Lincoln or Mercedes we can get. Of course, people find status in different ways. Maybe you drive a clunker, but you achieve status through other purchases or through accomplishments. Lastly, at the summit of Maslow's hierarchy, we have a few persons who having met all of the lower level needs, are then free to devote themselves to their own desires regardless of what others think, regardless of the status, etc. These people are described as self-actualizing. They use their own creativity and intelligence to the best of their abilities because their lower level needs have been met.

Perhaps, you may have the financial wherewithal to support someone at her self-actualization level. Your partner then can be free to do whatever she chooses because the money coming in from you allows her to concentrate on creativity and experiencing the world. If, however, a war or natural disaster such as a Hurricane Katrina came to the neighborhood, she would most likely have to (at least temporarily) stop being at the self-actualizing level, and come down, possibly even to the physiological level. The people in New Orleans who lost their jobs, their homes, and all their belongings, had to start over and were reduced to meeting their most basic needs of food, housing, and security.

Now, don't think that only rich people are the ones who can self-actualize. Maslow himself described a woman who did not have an extraordinary income, yet was able, with extremely limited means, to decorate her home creatively and set an attractive table for her guests. She kept her other needs humble, so that she could remain at the actualized level.

What we are saying is that you might consider Maslow's hierarchy of needs when sizing up a potential partner. Let's say that prior to meeting you she has existed at the physiological level for the most part. You might think, then, that it would be easy to please her. Not only will you feed her, you'll give her a house, and even sign her up for gym class! She'll love you forever, right? No, because as we meet lower level needs, we become more focused on the next higher unmet needs. So before long, she may be complaining about the unmet needs that she had not even considered before.

In short, humans tend to focus on what is missing from their lives more than on what is present. Once one level of needs is met, we begin to focus on the next level that is as yet unmet.

One situation where we have seen this issue of changing needs become important has been with men who marry women from third world countries. These men are often attracted to these women, in part, because they seem to have simple needs. These women may come from places where their needs have been at the most basic levels of Maslow's hierarchy. Perhaps they felt fortunate if they had food enough to eat or a roof over their heads. Their American husbands expected that their brides would be thrilled and grateful to their benefactors for providing them so much. Initially, it is usually that way. The wives from these impoverished backgrounds are very happy to leave their previous circumstances, and they show this appreciation to their new husbands in abundance. Later, though, these same women often grow dissatisfied because their other needs are not yet met. In particular, we have noticed that they often become much more concerned about needs for status. Perhaps they had low status in their home country, but there was no way to change that status. In the U.S., though, physiological and security needs are pretty much a given. As it becomes clear that they no longer need worry much about those basic needs, they may then turn to focusing on their status. Their husbands are often dismayed by this change in focus, naively expecting that their wives would always remain humbled by what their benefactors had provided for them. Now, though, these women may expect their husbands to also provide their wives with the symbols of status such as expensive homes and jewelry. These husbands may resent these new expectations or feel that their wives only care about them because they are "rich Americans." This change in need focus is often the root of significant conflicts for these couples, not infrequently ending in divorce.

> *Fridel, a concentration-camp survivor, came in for psychotherapy to help as she considered a new marriage. She had been "rescued" by an American soldier at the end of World War II, and she was forever grateful for his having saved her. They enjoyed married life for over three decades before his untimely death. However, she still struggled with self-doubts. The damage to her self-esteem from her imprisonment and treatment by the Nazis was immeasurable, and she could not fathom how her late husband could have ever wanted to have her as his wife. She never was able to feel herself an equal in the marriage, even after thirty years of "freedom" in the U.S. She feared the same unshakable self-doubts if she married again, but courageously wanted to try.*

Q: Should I try to find virgins to date?

A: For many men, the woman's need for sex is a priority in considering potential partners. Some, even after being married before, desire to find a virgin (i.e., a person who has not experienced the sexual relationship, coitus). These men assume that a virgin would bring minimal baggage from previous sexual relationships. While nowadays this may limit you to dating very young women, there are some not-so-young virgins as well. Finding a virgin has increased importance in certain religions, and maybe it is your own religious beliefs that are coming forth if you are seeking one. In our practice, we occasionally meet people (men and women) who describe themselves as "born again virgins." These people mean that although they have been sexual in the past, they have made a decision not to engage in sexuality again until after marriage.

On the other hand, you may have some concerns about not wanting to be with an "experienced" woman who could compare you with other men with whom she has slept. Some guys particularly like being the more experienced person in the sexual relationship as they feel it gives them an element of control. If you have such feelings and are not in your twenties, examine whether this is an "old feeling" that was laid down in your teens. Sometimes, it's just a lot better to have someone at your same level of experience.

Just because a person is not very sexually experienced does not mean she is free of significant issues around sexuality. Indeed, she may have avoided sexuality because of those issues. Don't make the assumption that just because she is virginal (or a "born again virgin") that she is ready to be taught the "ways of love" by you.

Q: I definitely do not want to be with a virgin. Is that a problem?

A: Your statement may indicate a more realistic approach in view of these sexual times; however, it may also express hope of having sex with a woman who is more experienced, a woman who will "be more sexually uninhibited." It suggests a focus on the sexual aspect of the relationship, rather than on the whole-person concept. We recommend that you look at the person and laugh a bit, learn a smidgen. Get to know her, and let the sexual stuff develop. Then find out what sexual "baggage" she is carrying around. Find out how many times she's been married, and how long she has dated. This may be important not only for the sexual information, but also for what problems led to the dissolution of her relationships and/or marriages.

Some men say they don't mind when they know that a woman has been with several previous men, when in actuality, her previous sexual experiences make them anxious. They may rationalize that if she has been married, she was bound to have had sex before! These guys can allow that she might have slept with one man or two, but they may have an upper limit in their mind as to the number of partners she has experienced. Or they may be concerned that she has been with bigger, younger, stronger (or fill in the blank here with your own favorite anxiety) men. If you are like this, the issue that you are ultimately facing is whether or not you will measure up to what she may have previously experienced. Rather than fearing that you might fail in this comparison, try to relax and enjoy her company, both sexually and in general.

Other men sensibly realize that in these days of sexual contraception and equality of sexes the women they are dating may have had as many or more sexual partners than the men themselves. Women can and often do like sex as much as men. Some guys really prefer this kind of woman, the lusty girl who is comfortable expressing her sexuality and is ready to experiment with new sexual ideas. Other men would find this intimidating or a turn-off. The important thing is to get to know yourself, and where you stand on this issue of her sexual experience. If you are anxious about it, one way or another, try to address your own feelings rather than wanting her to somehow be different so you won't be troubled by your feelings. At the same time, don't dismiss your feelings about her level of sexual experience as unimportant because they will likely come back later at an inopportune moment.

How do you address these feelings? You could go to a counselor to discuss them, but you can also talk them over with trusted male friends. How have they handled such feelings? You can also read books on male sexuality by well regarded authors such as Dumas, Saul, or Zilbergeld for ideas on how you might consider these issues in your life.[2] The key point is that if they are *your* feelings, *you're* the one that has to fix them, not her.

Q: I can't stop comparing women I might date to my ex-wife. Why do I keep doing this?

A: To make sense out of dating you must be able to spend time with a woman without comparing her incessantly with your ex-wife, seeing the similarities or looking for exact opposites. To help you understand how this works, let's consider a bit of basic psychology. Often the first way a person achieves independence from a situation is by being negativistic, going against something. Negativism means "no-saying."

Developmentally, the first time that a person achieves some independence is in the second year of life. The infant, who has no language, begins to use "telegraphese," a shorthand way of communicating. With just one or two words marked by intonation, an entire communication can be sent to mother or father. Often, it is "no" or even "NO!" This negativism ensures that the child no longer has to placidly accept whatever the parent offers, even if it is something he wants, and mother and father now have to accept the fact that he is an individual. Parents often believe that their child, whom they believe to be special, will certainly not behave in this manner. It is a rude awakening to find that a quiet and accommodating child, who formerly could be taken anywhere in public, has developed his own independent voice, and practices it at seemingly awkward moments.

The second period of negativism leading to independence occurs during adolescence. The teen may no longer happily go along with his parents, instead spending time with his peer-group. Teens loudly protest attempts to get them to do things simply because it is the parents who are doing them. The "no" gives them independence. They may not know what they want to become, but they profess loudly to know what they do *not* want to be.

> My first merit badge in the Boy Scouts was the Cooking Badge. To earn it, I had to prepare a meal independently of others. My parents suggested that I bring photos of this preparation and meal to the merit badge counselor for evidence of passing this step. I loudly protested, one of the first times I ever did so that strongly. On reflection, I don't know why I was so adamant. There must have been something about photos not being the way the other guys had passed their tests, but the truth probably is that my parents were asking, or telling me to do this which I disliked. Grudgingly, I took the photos, and sheepishly I had to report back that the counselor really liked them and had praised me for this aspect of my accomplishment.

In adulthood, we have periods of negativism, too, although they are not so culturally universal. For instance, people in the workplace often become entrenched in their positions and do not want to change, saying "no" to new ideas. The "no" is an assertion of independence. As the saying in business goes, "Many people can say 'no' to a project, but only a few have the guts to say 'yes.'"

In dating, this process of independence-through-negativism can operate around your divorce and your ex-wife. You may seek to create independence from your previous marriage by comparing potential dates to what your ex was like. If you cannot look at a woman without making sure she is the opposite of your ex, maybe you need to spend a little more time freeing yourself of your old feelings. If you note that the women you find "attractive" are all blondes and your wife was a brunette; or tall women are what sets your heart to beating, whereas your ex was average or shorter-than-average; or small-breasted women, like your ex-spouse, make you dream of big-busted women, then maybe you are not yet free. You are not considering the women you are going to date as individuals, but whether or not they belong to the category: *not* my wife!

Q: I'm finding myself attracted to women who resemble my wife. What does that mean?

A: After divorce, some guys seem inevitably to be drawn to women that are remarkably similar to their ex-wives. The similarities may be physical in nature or may reflect psychological, emotional, cultural or background characteristics. If you find yourself dating women who remind you of your wife, it could mean that you have not yet separated from your ex. You are trying to re-invent her. This is a warning sign, suggesting you have not adequately dealt with your feelings about your ex. Unfortunately, we are often blind to this process. We may literally be unaware of the similarities, although those around us may be whispering behind our backs, "Can you believe how much his new date is like his ex-wife?"

We recommend that you consult with your "buds" about this matter. Just ask them if your new girlfriend seems similar to your ex-wife. By the way, female friends (non-girlfriends) are often even more able to perceive such similarities.

Of course, we are not saying that you should find women that are either the opposite of your ex-wife or a clone of her. What we are saying is that your perceptions of those similarities and differences may be unconsciously affecting your choices of whom to date. You want to be choosing dates (and potential mates) based upon who they are and not upon comparisons to your ex. So check out your choices and perceptions of women with others whose judgment you trust so as to get a "second" opinion.

Q: Ok, you've mentioned several things to watch out for in choosing a woman. Are there other things I should watch for as well?

Our reasons for being attracted to a particular woman can be healthy, neurotic, or problematic. Let's go over a few of the other common reasons men find a specific woman enticing, and then let's look at the risks related to each choice.

MORE GOOD WAYS TO CHOOSE A BAD WOMAN

❑ Comparison Shopping. This, in itself, is not a bad idea. It makes sense to compare your experiences with different women that you date. The problem is that guys, especially after divorce, tend not to shop long enough. Make sure you have squeezed all the melons before you put one in your shopping cart.

❑ She's Pregnant. Perhaps, you thought this only happens to teenagers. Well, you are old enough to know better, but it can still happen to you. You certainly know how to prevent pregnancy, but if it should happen to you, don't rush to the altar. Take some time to consider how the marriage will work out in the long run. Better yet, make sure that this is not an issue you have to consider.

❑ The Old Habit. Usually, what happens here is that you date someone for a very long time, and she insists that you marry. At some level, it feels like an ultimatum, either marry me or the relationship will end. We see a lot of guys who wind up marrying as a result of this kind of pressure. At the time of the marriage they seem OK with the decision. Later, though, they often regret it. Then, typically, they blame her for pressuring them and decide they never loved her anyway. Divorce usually follows. If you have been dating someone for a long time, but you are not sure you want to marry her, you need to figure out why that is. Maybe, you just don't want to be married. Maybe, you know at some level that the marriage to her won't work. Maybe you would like to marry her, but you are still too anxious. Answer the questions about your reluctance and then resolve the relationship one way or another. At the very least, tell her if you are not going to marry her, even if that ultimately costs you the relationship. To not tell her is simply unfair if she is still hoping for a lifetime union, especially if she wants to have children by you.

❑ Just Like Dear Old Mom. Some guys decide that what they need is a woman just like the one Dad found: Mom! Of course, most of us would be appalled to sleep with our mothers, and this may be how you feel, too, after a time. It's a better idea to look for women who possess some of Mom's better qualities, rather than to find one who could take her place. Otherwise, pretty soon you'll be feeling like a rebellious adolescent.

❑ Groucho Marx Syndrome. You may remember the old Groucho Marx line that "I wouldn't join a club that would have someone like me as a member." Some men have such low self-esteem that they jump at the chance to marry any woman who would have them. After awhile, though, they come to realize that no one else can improve their self-esteem. They resent the woman for not making them feel good. Divorce may follow. If you have poor self-esteem, your first task is to learn how to feel better about yourself. This must be accomplished before you can make ANY relationship work well.

❑ Damsel in Distress. In this approach the guy seems to seek women who need "help." The more that she is in need of rescue, the stronger is his attraction. Frequently, at some level, the guy expects Ms. Damsel to be eternally grateful for rescuing her from that dragon, the mortgage payment, or her wicked step-parents. Unfortunately, there is not usually a "They lived happily ever after" ending to this story. After awhile, the guy (Prince Valiant) begins to see that she had some role to play in her own distress. Indeed, she usually demonstrates some of these problems in her new marriage to the Prince. For her part, she may begin to resent him, especially if he reminds her of how he saved her. Conflict may be bitter leading to break-up. Be careful about damsels. They might need frequent rescuing, and you may get tired of that action. Better to find a self-made duchess.

Q: Why is focusing on health important in dating?

A: You are now in the process of sorting out and prioritizing those elements that you value in a relationship. Valuing good health in another can be an important aspect of valuing yourself. You probably would not place yourself in a dangerous situation unless you believed you could emerge from it safely. Even in the so-called "extreme sports" that many people now seek, participants use safety devices. The pros always use such safety mechanisms. Every circus performer who is shot out of a cannon, walks the high-wire, or enters the cage of wild lions and tigers knows the amount of preparation needed, and maintains continual vigilance. One slip up or absent-minded moment and, "sorry about that, Roy!" Similarly, paying attention to health—both hers and yours—during dating serves to protect you.

In the olden days of the American frontier, men had the longer lifespan than women. Women often died in childbirth, and men frequently had to find another mate to help rear the children. Today, though, women live longer than men—on average about 7-8 years longer. These differences tend to be partly genetic, partly lifestyle.

Scientists know that 150 boys are created for every 100 girls, but due to "mistakes" leading to spontaneous abortions, only 105 boys are born for every 100 girls. Males are more prone to genetic problems, mainly because there is less genetic information carried on the little Y-chromosome, the one that makes us male, than on the bigger

X-chromosome. Remember that women have two X-chromosomes. Thus, a recessive trait causing some disease or condition is more likely in males than in females. For example, color-blindness occurs in 5% of men but only in 0.5% of women. This is because women have a second chromosome to help out if one is defective, whereas men have only one X-chromosome. If that chromosome is defective for color vision, for instance, the corresponding spot on their Y-chromosome offers no protection, because it is does not have space—it is too little—to carry all of the genetic information as the X-chromosome. So, women must have two defective X-chromosomes in order to be colorblind, whereas men only need one.

Lifestyle has a larger effect on lifespan once the early years are survived. By the 20th century, many of the perinatal maternal deaths were prevented (due to good sterilization of hands by the doctor or midwife), and men died earlier than women because of lifestyle choices. Occupational hazards in male-dominated jobs have always caused many deaths, and this remains true today. Mining catastrophes, machinery mishaps, shipping calamities, and farm accidents are all large causes of loss of life. But, men are also more likely than women to make other risky choices during their lives: smoking, drinking (in excess), eating (in excess), and engaging in dangerous pastimes (skydiving, parasailing, mountain climbing). Furthermore, we men are much less likely than women to get regular medical check-ups or to go to the doctor when we experience symptoms. As a result of these lifestyle choices men, on average, die sooner than do women.

You generally do not have choices about your genetic makeup, although you may be able to find out about it so as to make adaptations in advance. For example, if there is a family history of diabetes, you should be careful to have your doctor monitor your blood sugar levels. However, in some extreme cases, this kind of advance knowledge makes for difficult options. Parents-to-be now sometimes must choose between abortion-versus-birth during a pregnancy because they acquire knowledge that the fetus is defective in some way—maybe the resulting child would be mentally retarded due to a trisomy (extra chromosome) on chromosome 21. Before the advent of such prenatal tests as amniocentesis, parents were not presented with such dilemmas. These genetic issues sometimes do not manifest at birth or in childhood, but may develop later in life, shortening or impairing a person's life. Huntington's chorea, a neurological disorder that leads to death, is an example of such a condition. We now know that Huntington's is transmitted according to genetic rules, and if a parent has it, there is a high probability that his or her progeny will later develop it, typically in mid-life. The musician Arlo Guthrie has had to face this risk since his famous father, Woody Guthrie, died of Huntington's disease.

On the other hand, you (and she) do have choices about lifestyle events. You can limit your exposure to the sun's rays, drink only a moderate amount of alcohol, and cease your tobacco use (and for some of you, this includes chewing and dipping). You can also go to the doctor from time to time. Popular self-deceptive statements we've heard from guys for engaging in self-destructive behaviors or for putting off medical check-ups include:

"I'm going through a stressful time."

"I'm going to cut down soon."

"It's not much."

"It's only temporary."

"I'm too busy."

"I have to have at least one vice."

Q: So, you're saying that I should be selective in dating?

A: Yes, you certainly should be selective as you reenter the dating world. As we said before, you now have knowledge that you didn't have before when you first dated as an adolescent or young adult. With age and maturity, you know that you don't have the limitless time-horizon you thought you had as a teen. You also should be more aware of who you are as an adult, whereas when you were younger you were not yet "finished." This again underscores the importance of being genuine or true to yourself as you begin dating again, something that was much harder to do when you were younger. You don't need to date everyone you meet, willy-nilly. Instead, select dating partners from those you meet based on the priorities that are important to you.

Q: How can I get more contact with eligible women?

A: Things are likely better than you think. Hopefully, you have spent time getting ready to date by practicing "negative feeling removal." Ideally, you have also broadened your circle of friends (of both genders) to increase your chances of meeting someone either directly, or indirectly, in the clubs, sports, and hobby-groups you've joined.

It is true that when you were college age, the campus was an excellent place to meet motivated, upwardly mobile young people. If you attended college, you probably met many interesting, eye-catching women. If you did not attend college, you still probably hung out in places that attracted single, young women. One thing you might consider is going back to college to take some more courses to further your educational or occupational aims. Broaden your educational experience. Who knows, you might meet someone in the process. If you've not obtained a degree, then get an Associate's or Bachelor's degree. If you have a Bachelor's, then consider graduate work.

If college or university options are not appealing, consider taking some continuing education or Leisure Learning™ type courses (e.g., cooking or kayaking). Nowadays, divorced and single adult men and women commonly take formal and informal classes, sometimes finding more than just a degree plan. You could be eliminating a good chance of meeting someone if you discount this possibility.

If you are interested in achieving some formal credentials, many universities have programs that tailor-make your educational experience, and they may even give you credit for the "real-world" experiences you've obtained on the job.

George came to see us for our expertise in dealing with a "mid-life crisis."

He was in his middle years, and was working in the oil brokering business, making good money. Unfortunately, however, his career had also earned him a stomach ulcer. He knew that the industry was entering a turn-down phase, and his ulcer would likely last longer than the income. He now had the resources to do what he really wanted to do.

He first completed vocational testing, assessing his interests, aptitudes, personality, and motivation. The findings suggested that he either return to school to get a Master's degree in a related field so that he did not have to do the actual brokering, or work in the Federal Government where he had good contacts. The testing also identified some personal "hot button" issues that merited consultation.

George used his time wisely while attending counseling sessions by inquiring about a Master's programs at a nearby university. He found that they would tailor-make a course of study leading to a Master's Degree in his very field of interest. Wonderful! Should all of our choices involve a win-win situation like his did.

Q: I was shy before my marriage—I feel even more so now. How can I change?

A: Most of us know little about the psychological concept of shyness, except we know that for years people may have been referring to us as "shy." After a while, we believe it about ourselves.

Psychologists have found that although there is a strong genetic contribution to shyness, most shyness is a learned condition that may begin in early childhood, about the second year of life. When children are confronted with a new situation, most show some hesitation, checking things out before engaging in much interaction. Early in life, this hesitation has adaptive qualities, ensuring survival in those beginning years. There is adaptive value in holding back and looking to parents or others to see if it is okay. Frequently the young child will shuttle back and forth between something new, like a desired toy, and the caregiver, usually the mother. The child can get a chance to explore, yet also maintains contact with the mother, assuring safety. For instance, in her studies of young children, Mary Ainsworth (1978) found that when the caregiver was instructed to leave the room, the child shows increased anxiety, begins to act lost, and no longer wants to play, waiting for the security figure to return.[3] Even if another adult attempts to be reassuring, the child remains anxious until the mother returns.

A secure basis with a constant caregiver lowers anxiety in the child, making tough situations tolerable.

The salutary effect of consistent caregivers was well demonstrated during the London blitz of World War II. Because of the nightly bombing by the Nazis, children were evacuated from London and moved away from their parents; however, these kids did okay away from Mom and Dad if they had others who were like Mom and Dad in their consistency and dependability, not just the "camp counselor for the day."

Children who do not receive as much of this kind of adult reassurance during early childhood are more apt to be shy as adults, having not as successfully overcome those early fears about safety in a new situation.

Another time when anxiety may manifest itself is in later childhood when you are faced with an unpleasant situation, withdraw from it, and someone (like a parent or other adult) labels it, thus: "Gee, you sure are shy!" Or, maybe you overhear one adult saying to another about you: "He sure is shy!" As a child, you are still learning about aspects of your identity, and since adults are seemingly "experts" about all things, if they say you are shy, then you must be shy. It's like a kid who overhears someone saying that "you are crabby just like your Grandpa Frank", and so, by golly, it becomes a self-fulfilling prophecy.

So, they try to become the best crabby person just like Grandpa Frank is. If adults during your childhood described you as shy, then, by all means, you probably worked at that shyness. The strange thing is that you are probably not even aware of all the ways you have adapted to become this way.

Now, it may sound strange for a grown man to be shy, but shyness is usually found only in certain situations. When teaching Assertiveness Training, which helps deal with shyness, we have found that some persons are shy in business (and only certain types of business areas) while being assertive in their social lives. Other persons are shy in their personal lives while being assertive in their business lives. Only a very few persons are shy in both their business and personal lives. This latter group can benefit from specialized assertiveness training on an individual (one-to-one) therapy basis, while the rest of us can draw upon our strong area to help with our shy area, after a few group sessions in assertiveness.

Actually, we prefer to talk about people not being shy, but having learned shyness. While this may sound like we are splitting hairs, our language often betrays our choices and our viewpoints, our power or lack thereof. Thus, if you think "I AM shy", then underneath it all you also may be thinking, "this is the way I am, and I cannot change." However, if you say "I have LEARNED to be shy" then the implication is that, since you learned shyness, you can UNLEARN it." Much more optimistic.

Look at what you tell yourself. Any time you say "I am _____," this implies you were this way yesterday, are that way today, and will be that way tomorrow or the next week, too. For example, think of having learned shyness rather than of being shy.

So, if you feel that you are—or have learned to be—shy, there are specific things for you to unlearn, mainly centering about the thoughts that control (or limit) your behavior. If you label yourself "shy," then when you get mad enough about it, (and lonely enough) you may say, "I'll just go out to a party and meet a whole bunch of people. This will be so much better than being miserable home alone." So, going out to a large party, you force yourself to meet a whole bunch of people, search around the room, exchange names (which you forget within a minute or two), find yourself around the food dishes or liquor, smoke cigarettes (if so inclined), and come away from the party with another unpleasant incident which only proves to you that you really are shy since you didn't have a good time.

Well, what did you expect? Did you really expect to be at ease around large numbers of people that you don't know and with whom you have little in common? Somehow, we forget this obvious fallacy and think that "others" do it (i.e. are comfortable in this kind of social situation), so the fault must lie within us. As a result, our (natural) tendency toward retreat is now labeled as "shy" and so we again punish ourselves with "see, you just can't make it around people." This makes it even harder the next time to venture forth meeting new people.

Why punish yourself? This only reinforces the concept of "shyness" and makes it all the harder to unlearn! Let's instead examine some of the other elements of this common social scenario.

It is NOT comfortable to be around large groups of people you don't know. That is true for virtually everyone. Don't forget that. In such a situation, you may plan to reduce your anxiety by seeking the nearest exit. Another possibility, though, is to try to find someone with whom you can share, someone safe, so as to reduce your anxiety. Often, we do this by finding the one person in the room whom we already know. Of course, if you choose this route, you won't meet anyone new!

If you hope to meet people as a way of potentially developing a new relationship, a better alternative is to try to find an unfamiliar person who appears interesting and looks "less fearsome". Get to know this ONE person. Spend some time talking with her, rather than lamenting that you are shy.

Q: How will I get to know multiple people if I'm just going to meet one?

A: We met one man at a party who was nice to get to know, but after 5 minutes, he excused himself and was seen "getting to know" others, again for 5 minutes. He got to meet a whole bunch of people that evening, but on a very superficial level. He probably had the same end feeling we have had, when we have done this. Not good at all! Again, look at the long run—if you meet one person well at a party that would be 12 people in a year if you attended one party per month. Most of us do not have 12 really good (intimate) friends—maybe only 1-3. And we don't mean intimate as in "sexual".

Q: I think I'm ready for dating—how do I know?

A: Guys who are not yet ready for dating will be looking for a woman based on their resentments, fears, or penile erections.

It takes time to get ready for dating after divorce. Marriage counselors sometimes talk about the first year after a divorce being a time of "craziness" and of "getting things out of your system." To some extent they may be referring to sexual behaviors, but that doesn't mean we want to engage in bad decision-making. We especially caution you not to focus too much of your dating plans below the belt.

Sex researchers have made an interesting observation. Statues of Adam and Eve, populating almost every art museum in the country, have traditionally displayed fig leaves covering the genitals. However, they observe that today's generation might well create statues with fig leaves covering their eyes, not their genitals—people blindly copulating, but not knowing each other. You can do better than that!

Q: What about dating the woman who is still married?

A: You must like to live dangerously. Some find a special thrill in dating the married woman; others believe they have found "true love" —a love that transcends any formal or legal arrangements. Whatever you may think about your relationship with her, technically it is an affair. The research findings are clear.[4] Only about one of ten relationships beginning as an affair ever leads to marriage, and, of those that do, only about one tenth of those are long lasting. Whenever we point this out to guys who began their relationship in this way, they are quick to point out how the particulars of their situation make it an exception to the rule. They say things like, "She actually hasn't loved him in five years, so it's like they were already divorced." In our business, we call this a rationalization. Our best advice for you is to wait until she is truly available. If the relationship indeed is so promising, it can be resumed when the matters become less complicated.

CHAPTER 11

"Instead of getting married again, I'm going to find a woman I don't like and just give her a house."
—*Lewis Grizzard*

BEGINNING TO DATE

Okay, your head is clean. You're not selecting women because they do or don't look like your ex. You don't have your ex partner's voice echoing in your head all the time, and you haven't even mentioned her name this entire week. In this chapter we go beyond *thinking about dating* to *"doing it"*—dating that is. We now assume you've considered what you want from dating and you have thought about how you will handle sexuality while dating.

Q: What do I talk about on a date?

A: Beginning chatter on a date comes under the heading of "small talk." Before you dismiss this notion by saying that small talk is worthless, remember that the purpose of small talk is to preface the "big talk" later. Just as most books have a preface, telling you what you will be reading about prior to the main chapters, small talk serves the same function in our spoken communication.

Q: Don't others resent or look down at someone doing "small talk" with them?

A: Maybe they do, but you will be looking for the ones who don't. As with all communication, there are a number of "levels" involved. The "surface level" of communication involves the words that we are saying, while the "subsurface level" of communication involves our feelings and emotions. Imagine yourself at a party and you see this attractive woman whom you approach. You might start, for example, by doing small talk, talking on the surface level about the weather: "Gee, wasn't it hot today! Seems like we're having a very mild winter." At the sub-surface level, though, you may be indicating that you are somewhat uncomfortable but would like to talk to her and "start something."

If she is receptive, she may then continue with the conversation, saying something at the subsurface level like "I'm a bit uncomfortable, too, at this large party, but thank you for noticing me, and I'd like to continue this conversation in order to get to know you a little better." But of course, this is not what she says. She will talk to you at the surface level and so she may say something like "Yes, we've had quite a mild winter, and all of my azaleas are blooming early this year." Now, although this is at the surface level, you have had a message of agreement to continue talking, which has now become a dialog, but also you have an added piece of information. She has let slip (maybe not so innocently) some information about flowers. Maybe she is a gardener. Maybe you are too, or maybe not. Even if you are not a gardener, though, you still might like to focus on this subject in order to continue the talk and possibly build a friendship (or relationship). If so, then continue, with other thoughts on the subject of gardening.

On the other hand, maybe her response turns you off. If so, you can either drop the subject, or if you still value the possibility of a friendship, you might switch this subject to see if the two of you can find another topic on which you can agree to talk. Or, maybe she is the one who nixes the furtherance of this relationship. If she responds to your comment about the mild winter with a comment like: "No, it hasn't been mild at all", you might start thinking of moving on at the party and trying to begin another conversation with others.

We often wonder how we "hit it off" with someone, male or female. Look at your friends of both genders. During the getting-to-know one another stage, there was probably a beginning that was almost magical, in which layers of information were processed, starting with small talk. Some theorists have likened this to the peeling of the layers of an onion. Imagine that you (as well as she) have an onion in your hands, and as you tell something about yourself, you peel another layer off. It is the willingness of the other person to accept you, and give you another bit of information about himself/herself (peel their own onion) that continues the process. If you or the other stops this process, then the peeling, and the relationship, also stops.

The search for commonalities through small talk is often why, at parties, men congregate in one room, while women meet in another. Women may be talking "kitchen" (e.g., "I have this neat new blender") while men are in the living room talking "auto repair" (e.g., "My Chevy has been trouble free for 102,000 miles. How's your Dodge doing?"). We are often unaware of how our culture has trained us in the use of small-talk, but see how the comfort level changes when a woman starts talking with the men about Dodges or Chevys, or if a man starts comparing Warings with Osterizers with the women in the kitchen.

Q: I don't have trouble with small talk, but after I reveal myself, the relationship stops! I get hurt and am puzzled. What am I to do?

A: Maybe the problem is that your relationship has not been an equal one. An unequal relationship feels uncomfortable; therefore one or both parties push away.

Imagine what happens in a relationship when one of the two of you peels your onion much faster than does the other, so that one of you is way into the "soft, tender insides" of the onion while the other person is still at the papery outer layer of the onion.

In this situation perhaps the other person has been reluctant to do much "peeling" (i.e., revealing of herself). However, often what has occurred is that you have spilled your guts too quickly and pushed beyond what is equal and comfortable. Both parties are then left feeling hurt because not enough of the relationship was developed to deal with the sudden increase of feelings put on the table.

> *A year after his divorce, José had finally begun to venture out again beyond parties and group activities to dating. He was particularly attracted to Serena—until she started talking. She began to blurt out her life history on the first date, and in effect, wanted him to learn all about the members of her (rather large) family. He told us: "That was just too early in the relationship for me. I had hardly met her!" He was unprepared at that early juncture to become so involved with Serena's family history, much less think about meeting them. As a result, José was not interested in continuing the relationship, and certainly not interested in learning the names and birthdates of her brothers and sisters.*

If, on the other hand, you are more like the person who is slow to reveal himself, look at what this reluctance might mean. Maybe you feel that revealing yourself is like handing the other person a weapon to use against you. If this feels true to you, maybe you learned from earlier years that self-disclosure leads to being hurt, criticized, or made fun of. You have learned something important for your protection, but you may be over-generalizing this lesson.

We have often found that people who describe themselves as sensitive, easily hurt, or shy, are fast-learners. They are smart—it doesn't take long, usually only one experience—before they learn the connection between two things. The problem, though, is that they also tend to over-generalize. After initially being "burned," they may retreat from any situation that has the slightest similarity to the original one. Thus, they *retreat* or *withdraw* from any situation that might pose an analogous risk.

The problem with this strategy is that those who withdraw over and over again don't learn anything about the conditions that differentiate situations. They don't learn when it's good to withdraw and when it's worth hanging in there—they simply withdraw at the first sign of threat.

Back in our graduate school days, we learned that some personality theorists described three types of people based on their reactions to stressful situations.[1] For instance, consider your reaction to someone throwing a punch your way. One way to respond is to immediately punch back; a second response would be to dodge the punch; and a third response might simply be to take the punch.

The first approach is that of a "fighter," and the second might be characterized as the "withdrawer." Strangely enough, the third approach has been termed the "lover, " perhaps because the person opts take the punch in order to maintain the relationship.

Most people prefer one of the three styles, expressing surprise or even shock, at the idea of adopting one of the other two positions in a stressful situation: "I couldn't do that!" It has been found that lovers and fighters are more similar to each other than they are to the withdrawers. How can that be!?!

Response to stress in both lovers and fighters, is followed by an interaction with the other, either by "moving toward" (lover) or by "moving against" (fighter). So, both lovers and fighters get to know, at least at some level, about the different types of people around them. But the only thing the withdrawer learns is to withdraw, which he does quickly, and so he never sticks around long enough to get to know the different types of people. As a result, withdrawers have a more elemental type of personality, less differentiated than either the lovers or the fighters. And they remain more isolated, less connected with others.

Q: Okay, I can get through and unlearn that withdrawing stuff, but what should I say when I meet someone?

A: Many guys withdraw in social situations at the first sign of threat. For instance, you may be self-conscious about your words around a woman whom you assume might criticize you, because you were so frequently criticized by the previous "her" in your life.

Those of you who went through unhappy stages leading to your divorce know that women who are angry often express it indirectly through being critical—of you, your clothing, your jobs, your ideas, and even your language. After a while you came to expect this criticism. Criticism is often a woman's way of dribbling out her anger, much like being constipated leads to having one's bowel movement come out in "little balls of s----." Women are more likely than men to express their anger in this way, while we men are more infamous for their tendency to express anger in physical ways. Now that you're out of that old marriage, don't adopt a similar pattern of expressing anger yourself! If you find that you are a critic, too, see a good anger management specialist.

Finding An Anger Management Specialist:

Anger management specialists work with individuals and couples to save angry relationships. This new specialty involves a program of training and voluntary certification. Such a program is not licensed by the various states, nor is it limited to a specific discipline in the health sciences. Psychologists, psychiatrists, and social workers have become specialists through completing training, attending programs or conferences or reading on the subject, although certification is often used by the court system when referring persons having problems with anger control. Therapy programs vary in their length, format (group or individual sessions), and their use of workbooks).

Most people start by looking through the Yellow Pages. Asking the professional whether they have expertise in anger management is probably the best way to selecting a therapist. Newton Hightower, Director of the Center for Anger Resolution, Inc., and author of "Anger Busting 101", also suggests that:

❑ You don't have to "believe" in therapy for you to get something out of the experience. The focus should be on results (i.e., what you learn).

❑ Even if you are court-mandated to go to anger management training, you can still get a lot out of it. Fear of consequences can be a great motivator for learning.

❑ Avoid therapists who are too eager to diagnose (and/ or prescribe meds), and too slow to give direction and feedback.

❑ Avoid therapists who assume that every man is dangerous or abusive.

The most important thing is that the therapist believes that his or her consultation with you can improve your ability to deal with your angry feelings.

By being smart and reacting quickly to your environment, you have finely tuned your system to respond immediately to any perceived anger or slight on the horizon, especially from women. But don't over-react. Not everyone has these same critical tendencies. There are plenty of people (men and women) that are not ready to jump on you for what you say or think. When you think about a wonderful relationship in your past, you will remember that things just seem to have "happened." Looking closer, when your words were simply accepted by the other person, ideas flowed freely. You weren't worried about whether you were speaking formally or informally, thinking about educational differences, etc. You just talked! And she listened!

Often this kind of easy flow of communication happens during good first dates. Sometimes, though, women mention later that they let the man run on and tell all about himself, but they really wished the conversation had been more balanced. Yes, women with this complaint need to take responsibility for their part in this interaction and speak up more to get their needs met. However, we men also need to take our share of responsibility for keeping this budding relationship balanced, and our onions peeled equally. So, watch out for running off at the mouth while she is silent. If you sense this is happening, put the brakes on telling her about your football exploits and ask something about her.

Of course, sometimes these roles are reversed. She is talking endlessly about herself, seemingly forgetting that you are present. It's like she is talking to a tape recorder or transcriber. She doesn't need you except as an audience. If this is your experience, don't suffer in silence.

Look for an opportune moment to interject with an aspect of your life that connects to something she has said.

It may be easier to practice this balancing act with other men at first. It doesn't have to be in a formalized group of men—just do it with men in an informal get-together. Remember, we need listeners as much as we need talkers.

> *I remember one Christmas celebration when I invited two guys who were the "life of the party". I just knew they would be even more stimulating together at the same function, you know, both playing off each other. But you know what happened? Instead of stimulating each other, they competed for attention! Each gathered his own group of listeners, and one went upstairs while the other held sway in the kitchen. So much for that brilliant idea. Both were good talkers, and they were excellent entertainers, but neither was much for listening.*

Q: My shyness is a little different—it's like dating is so important! How should I handle my anxiety about it?

A: Any time we make a big deal out of something, we place pressure upon ourselves. In business life, we're used to handling the stress. We can do well, because we've handled this before. But, in a new a social situation, if we focus too much attention on it, we only magnify the problems.

Did you ever do this as a kid? Hold your hands straight out in front of you—no big deal, right? Now, have someone examine them to see if you are shaking. As the other person looks at them, and as you look at them, the slightest tremor soon appears, and even if you are in good shape physically, it soon magnifies. This unconscious movement is similar to the unconscious movements noted in persons who are working with a Ouija board. They quickly learn to answer "yes" or "no" to the questions put to them, miraculously!

So, if you are paying extreme attention to the dating situation, relieve some of the pressure. Are you thinking ahead too much? Is this just a date, or are you already thinking of what this might mean in terms of a relationship? Sex? Marriage? Telling the relatives? Kids?

Ease up. Dating right now should be thought of as just that—a date—just a way of sharing some time with another. Of making a pleasurable lunch-dinner-evening-coffee with this person. Don't make it into a lifetime commitment—at least not yet.

Q: So how do I get started dating?

A: In the old days potential partners for dating would typically either be co-workers, fellow students, or members of social groups to which you both belonged. Of course, many possible partners are still met in these ways. However, there are some problems and limitations with these traditional pools of eligible candidates.

People are more reluctant today to date people from work. After all, it can be very awkward to break up with someone whom you have dated and then see her every morning at work. Some companies even try to forbid romantic relationships at work (perhaps unintentionally making them more attractive!). It's even more complicated when you are her superior or subordinate. If you contemplate dating a subordinate, keep in mind that after a break-up you could be vulnerable to an accusation of sexual harassment (i.e., coercing her to be in a relationship with you). Dating someone who is your superior could be safer for you but probably not for her. Even dating a peer can be problematic if someone else accuses you or her of having your decisions compromised by the relationship (i.e., a conflict of interest).

Despite these problems we are not saying that you should forget about dating someone from work. After all, work is traditionally one of the places where you are most likely to meet a potential marriage partner; however, you need to be aware of the potential complications.

Social groups remain a good place to meet potential partners. Here again, though, a future breakup may make continued membership awkward.

We have known men who gave up their cherished membership in clubs or organizations following the breakup of their relationship with someone they had met in that setting.

Meeting at church, at the synagogue, or through another religiously affiliated association is no sure bet either. After all, once you break up, you may feel strange about seeing her there again.

Probably, the best you can do in all of these situations is to discuss this issue with your new girlfriend early in the dating relationship. Of course, at that point the whole matter is theoretical. The relationship is new, breaking up is not in your mind, and you may underestimate the complications, but you are establishing the topic as an important one for discussion. As your relationship progresses, you will need to revisit the theme. It may sound crass, but you must think about your exit strategy at the beginning of any new relationship, whether the relationship is business-related or personal.

As with a job search, you should first begin to think about the resources already at your disposal. You may already know women in whom you might have an interest. She might have been waiting for you to become "available." Women always seem to know the "status" of a man. You have an advantage in that a single man (especially one as handsome and nice as you!) is a scarce commodity. This is true for men almost regardless of their age. When you are ready to date, there will be women interested in you. The bigger problem for most men is their tendency to become committed to a new relationship too quickly.

Q: Where are some good places to meet new women?

A: The idea of starting dating is quite daunting to many of us. When we are in school, we easily become acquainted with new and interesting people. As an adult, however (and especially as a post-divorce adult), we may feel there are few ways to meet someone.

Volunteerism offers one possibility for meeting "Ms. Wonderful." Not that you should volunteer to help the homeless for the sole purpose of meeting a potential mate, but, rather, think about your special interests and concerns and then donate more of your time and energy to that cause. You will meet new people, folks who have similar interests to you and who have the luxury to give some of themselves to others (a good sign!). People who are concerned about others are more likely to be interested in you, too. While participating in a political campaign or charitable cause, you get the added benefit of connecting with people who have comparable interests. Consider which kinds of volunteer activities would be most likely to bring you into contact with eligible people. For example, volunteering at the senior citizen's center, while noble, may be less helpful in meeting an eligible female than volunteering at a children's charity auction.

Similarly, you might consider participating in social groups that are organized around a common recreational interest (e.g., scuba diving, biking, or cars). If you join a group of people who like the same recreational things as you, chances are good that you will have other things in common as well. In addition, they have at least some free time available for building a possible relationship. If they didn't have such time, they wouldn't participate in these leisure activities.

Another good place to meet potential mates is within a professional association. If you are an accountant, for example, there is probably a local, as well as a state organization for accountants. The people who participate in those organizations will have significant things in common with you. Of course, many of them will already be "attached," but others will not be. Again, you shouldn't view these organizations as some kind of dating service, but they could provide you with introductions to people who have similar backgrounds and interests to you.

We are less optimistic about the utility of finding a good woman while cruising the bar scene. Finding a compatible person in a bar is more of a "crap shoot." You start with little information about her except that she goes to bars (at least occasionally). A friend who assures you that, "You'll like her. She goes to a lot of bars!" is probably not giving you the best recommendation for a potential partner.

Q: Should I consider a personal ad?

A: Personal ads have long been a method for people to seek potential mates. Today, we tend to think of them as attracting a rather seedy lot or perhaps just the very lonely. After all, many of the ads describe their authors in terms of their lusts or fetishes. Maybe they are a good way to meet a one-night stand, but probably it is not the right method to find a long-term partner. Of course, if you are just looking just for a one-night stand, we commend you to them, but be sure to bring your protection!! In a large city, there will be one or more such publications catering to personal ads. In addition, there are various electronic versions of these personal ads.

Q: What about dating services?

A: Dating services have become a very popular way for people to meet new potential partners. Some are purely "for-profit" clubs, while others are affiliated with religious institutions, social clubs, interest groups, or alumni from universities. Most of them utilize the internet to both assess the members and to provide communication among the members.

The "for-profit" groups are corporations whose primary product is to "sell" you on joining their club so that you have access to their list/pool of eligible people. These corporations typically have you complete various surveys and questionnaires intended to identify preferences and personality characteristics. In some cases, they attempt to match you with potential partners based on the results of these instruments. In other cases, you are given access to the results of the other members, and you make your own attempted matches. The specifics of the information that is shared among the participants varies from service to service. They usually give you options about what you wish to share and how actively you wish to be involved. For example, whether or not you will allow people interested in you to send you e-mail. These corporations often spend a lot of money on advertising their services, sometimes making bold promises. Some even have research psychologists on staff seeking to improve their assessment tools.

In our experience these commercial services emphasize the importance of finding a compatible partner, someone who either is a lot like you or fits with you like tongue in groove. In our opinion, though, this type of compatibility is less crucial in the long run. Early in a relationship, we are drawn into a closer bond because of these kinds of perceptions of compatibility, but standing the test of time may be more related to such factors as tolerance, patience, management of anger, conflict resolution, and the ability to make up after a fight. In the beginning, we tend to pay less attention to the negatives especially if we are in the heady rush of passionate attraction. The real test of a relationship comes when the "blush has gone off the rose," when the differences and incompatibilities become more apparent.

The noncommercial dating services are typically offered as an additional service or benefit for being affiliated with a larger group. One advantage of this type of dating service is that there is at least some beginning common interest for you and your new "date" (e.g. ,you are both alumni of Big State University, or you both hope to save the baby tree frog). Furthermore, they are usually much less expensive than the commercial services. However, they still are based on the notion that initial compatibility will ensure relationship success, and as you have seen, we question that premise.

Q: Do you have suggestions for those of us using dating services?

A: In some ways, dating services provide a real boon for those seeking a new relationship. They enable you to avoid some of the risks associated with dating people from work or from groups to which you belong. Perhaps more importantly, they enable you to make choices about relationships from a much wider field, from people that you would otherwise not know. Although our modern society makes it possible to come into contact with many more people or potential mates than in previous ages, simultaneously there are more restrictions and limits on the types of relationships we can develop. Dating services enable you to do the sort of initial screening for yourself that might have been done in earlier times by your parents or by a matchmaker.

It should come as no surprise that commercial services can be quite expensive. We recommend that you do some comparison-shopping before committing to a commercial service. In addition, listen to their claims with a healthy dose of skepticism just as you would any other advertisement. If you are unsure about the value offered by the service, you might look to find a free or low-cost dating service offered by groups or clubs. Some men use the cost of the dating service as a screening device. They reason that a woman who can also pay the high entry fee of dating service will be a better "catch."

A common complaint about dating services concerns "truth in advertising." People notoriously under or over report the truth on electronic dating services. Is she really 41? What does she mean when she says she is "fun loving"? There are probably no easy answers to these kinds of questions short of getting to know her in person. Of course, deception in dating is not limited to the internet either. When they begin relationships, many people "forget" to mention details such as the fact that they are not yet divorced or that they have an STD. They generally decide to tell a "little white lie" or leave out a detail because they fear that telling the truth will cause the budding relationship to stop dead in its tracks. Internet dating services may create even more dishonesty because the increased anonymity prompts people to be less forthright. Advertisers, regardless of what they are selling, generally point out the best points of their products, not their weaknesses in comparison to competitors. Similarly, when people begin dating or describe themselves on a dating service, they focus on their strengths and minimize their deficits. With regard to yourself, though, we recommend you maintain a greater level of honesty in describing yourself if you use a dating service. Better to be rejected in the beginning than later when you have become more attached.

A particular concern that often comes up with internet dating services is whether or not to post your picture. Members who are concerned about their appearance are more likely not to post their picture. Others may post pictures from an earlier era or pictures that convey a particular image that they wish to convey (e.g., crossing the finish line of the marathon). If you decide to post your picture, we would suggest that simple is best. Let your personality be conveyed by your words and actions, not by your photo. We also recommend that the picture be current, not aspirational or historical in character. Keep in mind that if you don't post your picture, others may interpret this as a negative sign about your appearance.

Q: Are personal internet websites a good idea?

A: Another common phenomenon of our internet age is the personal website. Here people, especially young singles, create a personal web space address with information about themselves. People may post their own writings, pictures of themselves, videos of their pastimes, and descriptions of their interests. They usually allow on-line visitors to post comments and reactions. Some people are using these as ways of beginning new relationships. They become sort of like private internet dating services. The person who creates the site may hope that you will contact them in an effort to get to know them better or to potentially hook up with them. This is a little like fishing. You never know what you will catch. It could be an old boot. It might be someone with a mental health problem, or it could be a diamond-in-the-rough).

Just 10 minutes into the evening, Betsy resolved to cancel her online dating membership.

The relative anonymity of the internet seems to encourage people to be more risqué and self-disclosing in their postings on these sites. This results in postings that are far less structured than the offerings of an electronic dating service. Therein lies both the promise and the risk of such sites. You get a more spontaneous view of the person who has created the website, but, on the other hand, you may not get a clue about issues that are of interest to you.

If you are going to create such a website for yourself, keep in mind that you probably have little or no control over who sees it. More than a few people have found themselves having to answer embarrassing questions to potential employers or lovers about what was found on their website. More and more people are doing internet searches about people before they begin either a business or personal relationship with them. So be sure that what you have posted on your website will not start things off badly.

Q: What about internet chatrooms?

A: Internet chatrooms are an even more anonymous way of meeting people on the internet. Initially they were a way to have virtual meetings of people with similar interests (e.g., ham radio operators), but they are now almost synonymous with cybersex encounters. On the bright side, you won't get an STD from internet chat, but on the down side, it is hard to find a potential mate, too.

We are encountering more and more couples who met in one way or another through the internet. Some met through electronic dating services, while others met in a chatroom of one form or another. We suspect, though, that few long-lasting relationships begin from chatrooms whose focus is on sexuality. In the long run, knowing about someone's sexual preferences, while useful, is not the key to marital bliss. If it were so, then prostitutes would make the best wives.

Q: Some guys now get "mail-order" or internet brides. What are the risks of getting a woman from overseas?

A: Some men figure that the problems that they have had with women stem from the fact that they are dealing with "American women." By this, they mean "uppity" women—women who are too feminist or independent. These guys long for the "good old days" when women were more subservient and obedient to men. Some seek a solution by "importing" a woman from a third-world country (e.g., the Philippines, Russia). Usually, these men believe that the relationship will be maintained by:

- ❏ Her gratitude to him for "rescuing her"

- ❏ A tradition of female subservience

- ❏ Her unfamiliarity with American ways

- ❏ Her economic dependence on him

- ❏ His superior position as an American citizen

A number of these men use a "mail-order" service of some sort in an effort to find a more "exotic" woman. Catalogues exist for such things, but this is more often done on the internet today. For example, maybe they were always attracted to Asian women so they find a service that puts them in contact with women from Thailand or Malaysia. A lot of these men have the notion that a woman from another culture will be less sexually inhibited. Although that's possible, there is certainly no guarantee that she will be a sex expert simply because she comes from another place.

Some of these mail-order relationships probably work out "just as advertised," but there are no sure bets. The woman's lack of familiarity with American culture often creates unrealistic expectations for her. She may come expecting "a land of milk and honey" with you as the provider. That may be all right in the beginning, but what about five years down the road? Or what happens if you have an economic downturn? She may become dissatisfied if you don't fulfill what she sees as your end of the bargain, and she may have a very naïve view of the economic realities which can lead to bitter disputes.

Nor should you underestimate the significant cultural and language barriers that the relationship will pose. The language of love is nigh universal, but so is the language of anger. Couples formed in this way have all the issues of other couples. They struggle around issues of money, children, sex, and in-laws, but their views on these subjects are formed in totally different environments, making understanding much more difficult, especially when language and communication differences complicate matters. You also should be aware that women in other cultures have their own ways of exercising power in relationships. These methods may be less direct than the more egalitarian style of American women, but this does not mean that women in other societies are powerless. They will naturally seek to exercise their influence and power in order to meet their needs in the relationship. The relationship will still have to be bilateral (meeting the needs of both people). If it does not, it will soon prove to be unhappy for both of you. She may then seek to change the marital arrangement that you sought in the first place as she becomes more aware of the greater direct influence exercised by American women.

Finally, we are biased in the belief that you are more likely to make a good relationship when you are very familiar with the personality of the other person. The nature of "mail-order" relationships makes it highly unlikely that you can know her well in the beginning. Even if you communicate extensively by internet, have an occasional visit, and learn to speak her language, you will still not know her well enough to judge how the relationship will go. It is more or less a roll of the dice.

Q: What about blind dates? I've had offers to be set up by friends, parents or relatives.

A: Maybe you are remembering times in your adolescent years when you had double dates and were "set up" by the other partner. Perhaps the person who arranged the date told you that your blind date had the dreaded "nice personality," while you were looking for a nice body.

Remember that going on a date is only a short-term "commitment." It need not involve a big amount of money or time, just a "get to know you" period of time. If the friend or relative who offers to set you up with a new girl has a terrible track record, then by all means, tell them you are not interested. Remember, though, that we are not talking about a commitment to marriage, and this other person might not be interested in you either! You may find that although you share interests with this new woman, there still may not be the chemistry necessary for a long-term relationship—which, of course, could happen in any new relationship.

We recommend that you think of this kind of date as a chance to practice new behaviors and a time to hone old skills of politeness, civility, friendliness, and finding out about another person. If she does not wind up to be "the one," she suggest you to somebody that is "the one" (or closer to it).

Q: I've heard something about "brief dating." How does it work?

A: A recent fad has been "brief dating." Essentially, a group of single women and men meet at a location such as a bar or restaurant, and then spend a brief amount of time (typically around 10 minutes) with each person of the opposite sex getting to know them. The idea is that if you find someone initially attractive or interesting, you get her phone number or e-mail and follow-up later. Certainly, you can quickly meet a number of people this way. It also has the advantage that you meet them in person rather than on-line, and this is probably a better way to test your initial attraction to them. It is also more spontaneous as opposed to the structure of an on-line screening system. However, most people find this face-to-face kind of meeting system anxiety provoking. If you suffer from social anxiety or you hate the thought of rejection, this kind of dating can be very stressful. No wonder that it is usually done at a place where they serve alcohol.

Q: Does it make a difference where you meet a woman for the first time?

A: As one of our mothers put it, you meet a different class of woman in church as opposed to a bar. Of course, many people begin a relationship with someone they met at a bar. Some even marry that person, but when you meet someone in a bar, you might want to look at her goals for being there. Maybe her goal was to get "picked up." Maybe her goal was to get drunk. Or maybe her goal was just to celebrate happy hour with her friends, or she was cheering for her college football team on TV. Each of these goals for being at a bar has different implications for a relationship that you might develop with her, and some of the implications should send off warning signals to you. In contrast, if you meet someone through work or through a mutual interest, you begin with some commonality (not just alcohol) that says something about your values. Finding someone who shares your values is one of the key ingredients to marital happiness.

Q: What about the first date?

A: Remember your "first date history"? If your experience was like that of most of us, it was not altogether pleasant. Maybe you'll break out in a cold sweat just thinking about it. What if she says "no" when I ask her out? What if she doesn't like the place I take her? What happens at the end of the night...a good night kiss or...? These kinds of memories might make you want to never start dating again.

Try not to make too big a production out of your first dates. Don't expect too much, and you are less apt to be disappointed. Sometimes, spending a lot of money on the date sets up a dangerous precedent. Do you spend less on her later? Have you set a "high bar" that you now must exceed? Have you given her the expectation that dating will always involve lots of spending? Are you attracting a person who is interested in you or in how much you will spend?

Keep in mind that women also struggle with first date issues. If the man spends a lot of money, does that mean she is "beholden" to him? Should she offer to pay for part or all of the expenses?

We would encourage you to use first dates as a time to begin getting to know each other. A meal together is better than a movie for this goal. (Of course, you could combine the two.) A shared experience is nice, but the opportunity to talk, interact, and ask questions is more important. On the other hand, sometimes you will learn a lot about a person from observing her in a situation. For example, if she is rude to the wait staff at the restaurant, you should figure that later she will be rude to you. Don't ignore the "data" you collect while dating. After all, she and you are on your best behavior while dating, especially in the beginning of a relationship. If you see issues or problems at the beginning, they will probably persist later in the relationship. That does not mean you should look only for "perfect matches," but you should remember *caveat emptor* (buyer beware).

Q: What if she asks me out?

A: Today's woman might decide to ask you out. That's certainly a sign that she's interested, but it doesn't change any of the fundamentals of dating. There will still be the anxieties about her reactions to you, still the questions about sexuality, and still the implications about the future inherent in your conversation. Keep in mind the fears of rejection that you probably experienced when you have asked women out for a date. That's probably what she will be feeling.

The "rules" about women asking men out are not well established. For example, if she asks you out for a date, who pays? Are there connotations about sexuality (i.e., is she more interested)? What if she makes more money than you, should she pay? Should you go "Dutch treat" (i.e., each person pays for their own meal)? It is best not to make assumptions about these matters. Rather, you will probably have to sort them out as they develop. Ask her what she would prefer to do. Establish a precedent that her opinion will count in the relationship. If she prefers a more traditional arrangement where the guy pays for everything, you will at least know how to handle matters, and it gives you some insight as to what she would expect in the future. On the other hand, if she insists that she pay her own way, you will know that maintaining her independence is very important to her. Either way, you learn about her. Then compare who she is to whom you are seeking.

Q: But what if she is beautiful?

A: We are so glad that you asked this question. We have seen many men in miserable marriages who, ironically, describe gorgeous wives. Listen up, Bub. She may look good on your arm, but you live with the personality. There needs to be some level of physical attraction between you, but if it is the sole area of compatibility, you will probably get to read this book again. It is OK to be interested in her initially because she is cute, pretty, or "hot," but being with someone for an extended relationship requires some other attributes. In the old Dudley Moore comedy, *"10"*, the main character becomes infatuated with a gorgeous woman (played by the then very beautiful Bo Derek). He becomes so entranced that he leaves his marriage, making a total fool of himself. In the end, when he finally has an opportunity to be with the woman of his dreams, he finds that she is a total "ditz" and beats a hasty retreat. This is not to recommend that you follow the advice of the Jamaican song by Jimmy Soul "If you wanna be happy the rest of your life, be sure that you marry an ugly wife."[2] Beautiful is fine, if she is beautiful in personality as well as in appearance.

Q: I'm not ready for sex. What do I say?

A: Some men decide that for moral, spiritual, or personal reasons they are not ready to engage in sex while dating. They may be fearful of contracting an STD, or they feel wary of the level of commitment implied by beginning a new sexual relationship. Some men believe that it would be wrong to engage in sex outside of marital vows. Whatever your reasons for this choice, we respect your decision. Yet, your trials have just begun. You may be sorely tempted to change your plan when she shows sexual interest in you. Furthermore, many women today expect you to express sexual interest early in the relationship. If you don't, she may conclude that you are not attracted to her or that there is a sexual issue on your part (e.g., is he gay?). We advise you to talk with her about your position on sexuality as soon as the sexual signals begin to appear. Most women will respect this choice, at least early in the relationship. After all, they usually have had a lot of experience in trying to rebuff unwelcome sexual advances.

Q: When should a dating relationship become sexual?

A: In today's world sexuality accompanies dating for most people. We have heard both men and women cite that one of the reasons they sought to become sexual early on in a dating relationship is to find out if they will be sexually compatible. People are much more concerned about this issue than they were in times past. Furthermore, a lack of sexual compatibility is often a reason for marital and relationship breakups. However, you should not be pressured into being sexual before you are ready to do so. Of course, the same applies for her. Don't pressure her into being sexual when she is not ready.

Some guys find that having been married before makes it easier to think through the sexuality issue, and makes it easier to be comfortable with their own choices. Others feel the opposite, believing they have been out of the "dating scene" so long that they don't know how to think about their own preferences for sexual involvement.

For many people, becoming sexual implies a level of commitment. A woman may feel that once you have been sexual as a couple she can expect some greater investment from you: "Aren't you spending the night?" "Why didn't you call me?" "When will I see you again?" The earlier that the relationship becomes sexual, the sooner she may hope for signs of commitment from you. Men, though, more often seek the freedom to leave the relationship without such lasting commitments, and we are typically slower to make these commitments anyway.

This common difference between women and men sets up the basis for many relationship quarrels. In his perceptive book, *The Moral Animal,* Robert Wright points out that men are biologically pre-programmed to seek sexual freedom so as to increase the opportunity of passing on their genetic lineage.[3] On the other hand, Wright noted that women are pre-programmed to seek commitment so as to increase the likelihood that their children would receive adequate provision. Of course, our behavior is affected by more than just genetic programming. Human behavior is also determined by psychological and moral constraints that are essentially the result of learning. We are not automatons controlled by the waxing of the moon or hormonal variations. Nonetheless, the genetic tendencies do exercise some effect on us.

Of course, we realize that the expectation of a connection between sexuality and commitment is not the sole province of women. We have known many men who felt the obligation to be committed to a woman once a sexual relationship was established. Some men even go so far as to feel that they must marry a woman if the relationship has become sexual. More common, though, is the belief that if the woman becomes pregnant, the man must marry the woman and shoulder the responsibilities of being the father of the child. Our point is that for many people, sexuality begets commitment. So when you become sexual, you will be more likely to experience pressure about commitment, from her, and perhaps from yourself.

Many religious groups recommend no sex outside of marriage. Some people simply disregard this prohibition. Others don't follow it but feel guilty consequently. Some do maintain celibacy unless they are married. Sometimes this can lead to real conflict for a dating couple. If the issue occurs in your dating relationship, ask to talk about it with your partner. Ask about her beliefs and explain your own. See if the two of you can agree on how you will handle this matter in a respectful and mutual fashion, rather than imposing one person's values on the other.

This also brings up the Clintonesque question, "When does sex begin?" Comedian Jerry Seinfeld answered this by saying, "When the nipple makes its first appearance." If intercourse is not acceptable to one of you, how do you and she feel about other forms of sexuality: oral sex, mutual masturbation, "petting", or even kissing? You are most likely to get into an embarrassing or frustrating situation when you and she have not talked openly about your feelings with regard to these issues.

Q: My ex (or the kids) seem to call whenever I am on a date. How do I handle that?

A: Just when you are having a good time, there goes that darn cell phone. Maybe it's her kids suddenly "needing" to talk to Mommy. Could be it's your kids. Or maybe your ex-wife knows just when to call to interrupt your evening. We recommend that you and your date develop a policy of how to handle such intrusions. This is not something you would realistically do with her on the first date, but if your dates develop into a relationship, it makes more and more sense. For example, you could elect to turn the phone off!! Remember the good old days when no one could reach you and the "emergency" had to wait until you got home? There is also that wonderful invention of "Caller ID." You could look at the number, see who is calling, and elect not to answer. But what if it is a "real emergency"?

First of all, if the call is about the children, either they are old enough to pretty much take care of themselves, or they should be left in the care of a responsible adult. If so, and there is a real emergency, 911 is the right call for them to make. You can be informed later. Instruct the kids or the caretaker that they are not to call except in the event of an emergency: "An emergency does not include a fight with your sister or that the fact that you cannot find your ball glove. An emergency is a situation where 911 (police, fire department, or an ambulance) must be dispatched because of a fire, break-in, arterial bleeding, choking, or poisoning." If the children continue to violate this policy, appropriate discipline should be administered when you (or your date) return home.

If the call is from your ex or her ex, simply ignore it. That is one of the nice things about having an ex.

Q: How do I break up with someone if I see she's "not the one"?

A: Many men struggle with the idea of breaking up. They don't want to hurt the woman's feelings, but they know inwardly that the relationship is not sufficient for them to be happy. Whether the issues for you are about her personality, about the sex, or about some other concern, it is essential for you to practice ending relationships that are not working so that you may find one that will. We are not recommending that you bail at the first sign of trouble, but we do think that if you decide that the relationship is not going to work for you, you should act promptly and decisively. Vague suggestions (e.g., "We need a break" or "It's more about me than you") do little to either explain your position or avoid confrontation. We recommend simplicity and directness.

Simplicity. Say simply that the relationship remains unsatisfactory for you, and you have concluded it is not likely to become substantially better. Don't fall into the "why" trap (i.e., "But why?"). No explanation will be sufficient to make her say, "OK, now I get it!" She will almost certainly feel disappointed and may perhaps become emotional. An emotional reaction by her should not change a rational decision by you. Stick by a simple message: "I have decided to end it."

Directness. Don't beat around the bush. If you are breaking up with her, be clear that this is what you have decided. Don't seek to defuse her reactions by being subtle or indirect. Avoid the use of terms or descriptions that imply there is still hope as a way of "letting her down easy." They just prolong the pain for both of you and amount to a mixed message at best.

SECTION IV

BECOMING SEXUAL (AGAIN)

CHAPTER 12

___

"Don't have sex, man. It leads to kissing and pretty soon you
have to start talking to them."

—Steve Martin

THINKING ABOUT SEX

In the last section, we discussed things to think about as you
begin dating again. Now let's take a look at some of the things you
should think about before becoming sexual again. Yes, we believe you
should think first.

Q: You talked about love; what about sex?

A: You should know that our culture, in the post-pill decades,
has put a priority on sex. If you have any doubts, just look at your
morning newspaper, or TV. The ads are full of sex—sex is used to sell all
kinds of commodities. The advertisers know that we will pay attention,
and hoping that by grabbing our attention, we will buy!

We understand your push for what you may have been missing,
perhaps for quite a while! You may be especially needy because—like
many guys—you may have used sex as a comfort, to help you feel
better when you have been feeling bad or down. And just at the time

when you are having one of the biggest downs of your life—the divorce process— the person to whom you would normally turn for comfort is not available.

Men who have been in a sexless marriage for a long time, are often surprised and shocked about sexuality when they begin dating again.

> *Smitty had been sexually dissatisfied in his marriage for years. Soon after becoming divorced, he began dating for the first time since his college days. He found that a lot had changed since college! He was stunned by the readiness of women to go to bed with him so soon after he first asked them out, sometimes on their first date. On one hand, he was pleased. No more sexual frustration! On the other hand, he didn't feel entirely comfortable with this rapid progression to the bedroom. He wanted a companion as much as a bed partner. He also found that after a woman was sexual with him, she typically expected him to be "exclusive" with her. As he noted, "She might be very nice, but if I decide so soon to see only her, maybe I will miss out on something even better around the corner."*

Sex without love is more easily found in our society today, but that does not mean that there are no costs.

Q: Costs? Are you talking about paid sex?

A: Not exactly, although many men do use the services of prostitutes and have "paid sex." The word "costs" also refers to non-monetary factors, such as by engaging in "risky sex." Risky sex increases the likelihood of getting hurt or killed.

If sex includes the possibility of losing something valuable, whether it is your health or a personal possession, it could be characterized as high risk. Some prostitutes have been known to leave during the "afterglow" with wallets and rings, credit cards, or keys. Sometimes they even take your clothes, so that public embarrassment is added to the situation. Even worse is the story of a famous duo that used to "patrol" the interstate freeways, dressed provocatively, and seeking to get a hitch. When the man saw what looked to be a vision "too good to be true"—willing women who were attractive and "ready"—it really was too good to be true. The women pulled their guns, and the police found the bodies of their victims later. So if you are about to protest that you are too big, or fast, or too smart to be caught up like that, just slow down a little. There's more.

"I want more than anonymous sex. I want anonymous intimacy."

One of the biggest costs that fall under the heading of risky sex is the possibility of contracting a venereal (love) disease. The term used today by most professionals for this category is STD—Sexually Transmitted Disease.

Maybe you had a college course in "Marriage and the Family" that included more than information about the economics of a household budget, or maybe you saw the high-school films about syphilis and gonorrhea, and think that these risks are down (or gone) because of medical advances. But, just like the flu, which changes its form annually, and becomes immune to drugs in order for it to survive, so, too, have the STDs changed. In addition, while medical researchers have accomplished a great deal with the two headline STDs (syphilis and gonorrhea), there are many other types of STDs which also pose major problems. Problems such as venereal warts, chlamydia, and herpes (among others) should be mentioned here. Some of these have no cure, and no symptoms of early infection.

Men are often especially curious about herpes, which has become the subject of many television advertisements. There are actually several different herpes viruses, four of which are sexually transmitted. However, we used to think of herpes as either —Type I "above the waist" or Type II "below the waist." Type I was the canker sore found on the mouth or lips, and was easily treated although it tended to reemerge from time to time. Type II was the herpes virus that was most often manifested in genital lesions. Now, due to varied sexual practices (e.g. oral/genital contact) both types can occur anywhere on the body. And with herpes, you cannot always tell when symptoms are dormant, so you cannot see it in your partner, but you are still vulnerable to "catching it." The medications prescribed by doctors, the ones advertised so heavily, only alleviate symptoms and make it less likely that the STD can be transmitted. They do not cure the condition. Once you have herpes, you will always have it.

It is not that the "bad girls and boys" have STDs and "good girls and boys" do not. So many adults have STDs that dating services catering to persons with these conditions have been developed. These enable couples to meet without the worry of having to tell their potential partners that they have an STD—the secret is out! We know of such services both for people diagnosed with herpes as well as for those who are AIDS positive.

We have saved the biggest risks for last: that of AIDS, or Acquired Immune Deficiency Syndrome and its precursor condition, HIV (Human Immunodeficiency Virus) infection. AIDS refers to a collection (syndrome) of symptoms and diseases that take opportunity due to lowered immunity of the body. AIDS is acquired through the transmission of the HIV virus through body fluids, including blood and semen. Remember that your body is warm and dark inside, a perfect place for diseases to proliferate, and they would do it all the time if it were not for your immune system. Our immune system protects us from these diseases, except when it doesn't work.

An amazing amount of detective work was done to find the "cause" of AIDS—quite quickly, too. The first cases reported primarily involved the transmission of the disease between homosexual males, and so AIDS was first talked about as being a "gay disease." Some went even further and attributed AIDS to being a punishment from God for homosexuality. But now that we know its causation and how it is transmitted, we recognize that it is simply another STD. Indeed, the statistics in Africa show AIDS to be primarily a disease of heterosexuals.

Having sex without love is more risky because protection against STDs and/or pregnancy is less often used. Maybe it's a lack of caring ("we'll never see each other again") or a lack of understanding about a need for protection ("do we still need it these days?"). Sometimes a condom tears or is not put on until later, or perhaps the use of a condom is guided by the belief that protection is for (anti-) procreation purposes and not for (anti-) disease purposes. Note that "the Pill" used by women does not protect against AIDS. Nor does the cervical cap. Only barrier methods (such as the condom or the diaphragm), which serve to isolate bodily fluids, should be used to protect against AIDS.

Q: You haven't scared me. What if I'm planning to only have oral sex?

A: Aah! You haven't been listening. Bodily fluids also include saliva, such that oral sex is also risky sex, as is anal sex. While saliva itself is not implicated, so kissing is not a problem for AIDS, oral sex with an infected person can lead to AIDS or other STDs.

Q: How do I ask my new woman about STDs? What do I need to know?

A: You should think of this long before you are on a couch or in a bed in a clinch with clothes half off. This isn't the time to discuss who has or doesn't have an STD.

Hopefully, your relationship will involve a mutual caring so that you can, at the appropriate time, indicate you desire for intimacy and your wish to clear the air by discussing some important matters. If this sounds planned, well it is! You are no longer a teenager in heat who gets into a problem situation over his head without thinking. You have to be in "adult mode."

It is true that some women may react with anger or even make accusations, but you need to explain that your statements and questions about STDs reflect your care and concern for her as well as yourself. If she remains upset about you bringing up the matter, she may be less mature and more worried about her own guilt feelings than you thought. If so, you perhaps should be looking elsewhere for a partner. Most mature women will appreciate openness, allowing them and you to make sexual choices, despite the subject matter being difficult. Even if there is a risk of losing this partner because of your sexual history—or hers, isn't it worth it now rather than later? Would you really like having her say, after sex, "Oh, by the way, I didn't tell you I have chlamydia (herpes, etc.), but it's not active now." By then, you've lost some decision-making power.

Q: What do I do if the woman I'm with mentions that she has an STD?

A: Thinking of this before the fact allows you to clarify your values. In early dating, if you learn she has an STD, you may not have yet "invested" much in the relationship. Consequently, it may be relatively easy to decide what you want to do based upon the hassle factor (i.e., how much trouble versus pleasure is involved). Learning later in the relationship about an STD means that you have stayed around because of other factors. In this situation you have more invested, so a decision may be more difficult to make. Important considerations include:

❑ Is there an active disease ongoing?

❑ If not, what problems remain after this disease leaves the active phase?

❑ Will the condition reoccur?

❑ What precautions and protections need to be taken to prevent transmission to me?

❑ How important is a sexual relationship to you (and to her) in the relationship?

❑ What possible modifications in the sexual relationship will be necessary and will they be satisfactory to us both?

Randolf came to see us soon after meeting a new woman. He was intrigued with her and thought she might be "the one." Never married, he had become doubtful that he would ever meet a woman that met his stringent criteria: good looking, smart, fun to be with, similar political beliefs, financially successful. Then he found her! She seemed perfect. Some weeks later, though, he came to his appointment looking troubled. Just when things seemed to be moving to the bedroom, she stopped the "freight train" and told him that she had an STD: herpes. She had had the condition for years with only occasional outbreaks. However, Randolf was exceedingly careful about his health, a vegetarian who exercised faithfully and was careful about anything that he put in his body. For him, her revelation proved to be a huge issue and dilemma. After much deliberation, and much more discussion with her, he elected to continue the relationship but to use precautions so as to limit the likelihood of contracting the ailment. It was a very difficult decision for him, and he would most certainly have not done it unless he really loved her. Think about how the relationship would have gone had she not told him until later.

Q: I have an STD. When should I tell my date?

A: It's not "when," as on a particular date, but "when" in terms of your relationship. If you are thinking "one-night stand," then by all means, that talk better be done on the first date. However, you may risk a lot of rejection from women.

If you have more than a few dates with a woman and you grow close emotionally so that you are thinking about those urges below your belt, and you are aware that the feelings are mutual, then that would be a good time to discuss some "important issues of caring." If you delay such a talk, however, for fear of rejection, then you are wasting both of your time. If one or both of you are uncertain after the talk about what you should do in your relationship because of a lack of information about the particular STD and precautions, then, by all means, schedule an appointment with a sex therapist, or in smaller cities, your medical doctor. Many younger physicians have had courses in human sexuality, disease and dysfunctions included in their medical school curriculum, although, in earlier years, there was resistance to this by their professors. "There isn't enough time to learn all of this—they have to learn their medicine first!" was a common statement at that time. But now physicians see the importance of knowing about such subjects.

We hope that this chapter will start you thinking and communicating with that significant other, or soon-to-be significant other. Some of you may have questions about STDs that we have not even come close to addressing. Remember, though, that there is no cookbook about these matters. We men, particularly with our mechanical bent, like the idea of a logical sequence which we can follow. From boyhood on, we want to know that if you push this button, touch this breast, and tickle this clitoris, then the woman you're with will "bang your brains out." However, women don't come with mechanical instructions, and you shouldn't expect that you will react the same way every time either. A mutual exploration of options on dealing with STDs is in order.

HOW TO SELECT A SEX THERAPIST

The factors involved in selecting a sex therapist are similar to those in selecting any other professional; however, some aspects of sex therapy make such selection a bit more difficult. There are fewer sex therapists than other kinds of professionals, and they tend to be concentrated in the larger metropolitan areas. There is also great diversity in their training.

You could go to the Yellow Pages and look under Sex Therapists, and possibly find several. However, they are more often listed under their training and licensure headings (i.e., psychologist, psychiatrist, professional counselor, gynecologist, etc.). It should be noted that in most states, anyone can call himself or herself a sex therapist. Typically, there is no separate license for this specialty so it is not a regulated practice. Other sources for referrals include your physician, clergy, or medical and psychological organizations. If you want privacy, you can type in "sex therapist" on the internet.

Unless you have privacy concerns, starting your search with your family physician usually makes sense. This is because your sexual problems could be due to a physical condition or occurring as the result of interactions/side effects of drugs you may be taking. If you do not start with your family physician, the therapist you select should ask at some point for word from your physician that you are not having physical problems that are causing your sexual difficulties.

Your chances of finding a qualified sex therapist increase if you ascertain that the therapist has the appropriate credentials, such as membership in the

American Association of Sex Educators, Counselors, and Therapists (AASECT) or the American Academy of Sexologists. AASECT requires specific training in sexuality areas plus clinical experience in addition to licensure as a psychologist, physician, nurse, social worker or marriage-and-family therapist.

Make one appointment for consultation (not a series of treatments right away). Although sexual therapy is often short (5-20 sessions of very directive and educative sessions), it still involves a relationship. You have to be able to trust this professional in order to do the "homework" and follow directions. Homework assignments may involve reading books about sexuality, touching exercises designed to reduce performance stress during sex, and practicing better communication skills about sex.

In the initial consultation, or even over the phone, you may wish to ask questions about the professional's educational background, whether he or she is involved in professional education or training, and his or her approach to therapy. You may wish to discuss what happens during the course of therapy and what time commitment is needed. Also discuss whether the professional has had experience in the particular treatment suggested for you, and about the fee structure. Health insurance may cover sexual therapy; check with your company. Discuss also if there may be limiting factors (e.g., certain therapists only work with people who are in committed relationships).

WARNING: Do not fantasize about having sex sessions with the therapist, or with a surrogate. Such behavior is an ethical violation on the therapist's part.

Q: Can I make any assumptions about her sex life?

A: The best answer is: NO!! She may have been wild and crazy before, but now she may have changed her ways. Or maybe she always saw sex as a necessary evil. Perhaps she has been searching for greater sexual fulfillment and hopes to find it in a relationship with you. In any case, don't make assumptions about her sexual history or experiences. Talking about your sexual histories is often a difficult topic, but as your relationship develops, it is very important to address, especially in an era of life-threatening STDs. Furthermore, it can lead to a greater understanding of sexual needs and experiences and thus contribute to greater sexual satisfaction.

Q: Sometimes, I find myself wondering, "Can I love just one woman the rest of my life?"

A: Maybe you are the kind of guy who says "I want a little vanilla, a little strawberry every once in a while! Men are just that way!" If this is where you are, maybe a committed relationship is not for you. Let the woman know that is not what you want, and see if she is open to a mutual non-commitment. Or is it that you want her to be committed to you, while you keep your own options open. Many men fantasize about such an arrangement because a mutual non-commitment scares them. They prefer the safety of having the out while the woman is locked in to a steady man. You may know that's not fair for the partner, but may try to pursue it anyway. We can give you lots of stories about where that's likely to end up.

And if a non-committed relationship is what you decide on, be thinking about the risks of STDs. Your risk of developing an STD becomes much greater in non-committed relationships since both you and she may have multiple partners. And remember, some of these STDs are forever, and so barrier methods are best used.

Q: Okay, now I'm stymied! What do I do about sex?

Slow down a bit. We're still into looking at dating. Just dating, with the possibility of finding someone to have a meaningful relationship with. We want you to keep your options open, and at the same time to increase the chances of maintaining a safe, rewarding, sexually satisfying relationship.

Q: So, what about sex?—I'm not into becoming a "Touchy—Feely Sensitive New-Age Guy"!

A: Until a suitable relationship occurs, many guys choose masturbation as an acceptable and non-risky form of sex. Note that our society gives mixed messages about masturbation. Some of the old beliefs are expressed in the form of worries and jokes, such as developing hairy palms, going blind, etc. None of these problems result from masturbation. Nor will a man's strength be sapped—your high school football coach probably forbade sex before the big game because he knew that the athletes should have stayed home and gone to bed early in order to do their best the next day. If your coach was "with it," he would have known that sex relaxes you (and thus would make you do better in the big game)—and should rather have forbade the staying up later and drinking which often accompanied the sex.

A short word about masturbation is in order here. In their numerous research studies of human sexuality, Masters and Johnson observed subjects while masturbating as well as when engaging in sex. They found that the orgasms reached through masturbation were the strongest of all those obtained through various types of sexual activity, and the pleasure obtained from masturbation was the most intense. Why is this, you may ask? Well, you know just the way you want the stimulation, what kind, how much and exactly where.

Q: Okay, you convinced me. Now tell me why I should date after hearing all this?

A: The reason people don't just stay at home and masturbate for their sexual activity is that there is something about sharing the experience with another person. As a professor once said, "you just don't meet interesting people that way." So even though masturbation may be more intense sexually, think of it as a "way-station" on the road to your goal of meeting someone. The person who stays at the "way station" too long may have problems or may fear relating to others.

"Last night I discovered a new form of oral contraception. I asked a girl to go to bed with me, and she said no."
—Woody Allen

CHAPTER 13

"Women need a reason to have sex—men just need a place."
—Billy Crystal

PENIS-VAGINA STUFF

In this chapter, we talk about sexuality. You may or may not already know some of this information. From our experience, correct sexual information does not replace incorrect information; it just sits nearby in an adjacent brain cell. Misinformation coexists with correct information, confusing things. Just because you were married and were sexual with your wife, doesn't mean you're prepared sexually for the dating scene. Also, for young people, the major sources of sexual information such as peers—even parents—are usually not the ones who impart correct information, while the ones who impart correct sex information (such as textbooks and doctors) are few and far between. Even having a "good college education" does not guarantee having had good sources of sex information.

> A school teacher is working on a unit of sex education, and asks her class about how many positions of intercourse there are. Johnnie raises his hand, Susie raises hers, and in the back of the room, Sammy waves his hand back and forth, gesticulating wildly while shouting out "teacher, teacher, I know." So the teacher

first asks Johnnie, who answers "three." Susie's turn is next, and she answers that she knows four different positions. Sammy, now waving his hand violently in large waves, accompanied by assorted noises, quickly replies "teacher, teacher, I know...98!!". The teacher, quite startled, goes back to Johnnie and asks him to name one position he knows, whereupon Johnnie replies "the missionary position." "Teacher, teacher" interrupts Sammy, "Now I know 99!"

We assume that anybody in our culture who would know 98 different positions would of course know the missionary position; apparently not, in Sammy's case.

George and Caroline, a college-educated couple and not exactly newly weds, came into the college counseling center. They were requesting help because they were unable to conceive. The young interviewer, obviously wanting to help alleviate the couple's distress, went over the details of whether and when they were sleeping together. Assured that they most certainly were sleeping together, the counselor went on to more technical details about how to maximize the timing to facilitate conception. But then a lingering doubt came back to him. Once again he asked about their sleeping arrangements and their lovemaking activities. He discovered that when they reported sleeping together, that's exactly what they were doing together—sleeping—but they had no inkling of what went where.

Please use this chapter as affirmation of some of what you already know about human sexuality, as well as an opportunity to discover something new or to think about things a bit differently. We will focus primarily on those topics relating to the divorced guy who is re-entering the dating and sexual scene, and possibly considering marriage. It is not meant to be a comprehensive text.

Q: I've met a woman I'm really excited about—maybe too excited. Whenever we try to be intimate, I climax before I'm ready. Is there any way to prevent this?

A: This problem may be more common than you think. Not that it's trivia, but the situation can usually be improved. Some of the adjustment is mental; some is physical.

For the mental part, you need to know that this sort of problem is more commonly found in younger men who have higher sexual drives, but have sexual release less often. Thus, they go through what Masters and Johnson call "the sexual cycle" quite rapidly.[1]

Masters and Johnson did extensive studies of the sexual cycle in humans and found that males go through a predictable set of stages. Starting with the *resting* phase, in which the genitals are flaccid (limp), there is a change whenever the sensory system indicates stimulation. This could be the sight of an attractive female, the smell of her perfume, her touch, or the sound of her voice. At this point, the male then enters the *excitatory* phase, in which two things occur: an increase in blood flow toward the genitals, called *vasocongestion*, and an increase in muscle tension, called *myotonia*. Now, if she turns the street corner, or if your attention is distracted by a college test, a cold shower, or your mother's voice, there is a return to the resting phase as the reverse of muscle tension and blood flow occurs. Otherwise, if stimulation continues, then after the *excitatory* phase there occurs the *plateau* phase. This, like the geographic term, means a "flat plain." During this phase, there are no outward changes in the size and shape of the genitals. They remain fully engorged with blood, as the venous system has a little set of valves, allowing less blood to leave the penis than enters it through the arteries. This leads to the filling of blood (erection) much like a household sponge fills with water when you put it under the water tap. This plateau phase is necessary to reach the next phase, which is that of *orgasm*. At orgasm, there is a maximum of both vasocongestion and myotonia, and suddenly both are released in a quick, and very pleasurable, burst. At this point, both vasocongestion and myotonia lessen and the genitals return to their resting state during this *resolution* phase.

Now, in the younger male who has not recently had sex or who is receiving intense stimulation, this cycle of excitement, plateau, orgasm, and resolution may occur quickly, or at least, quicker than the male would like. It has been commonly termed, *"Premature Ejaculation,"* which is actually a misnomer. There is no "prematurity"; things are happening just as they should, but before the man would like. Cross-cultural results show that expectations vary across cultures as to how long sex should last. Some cultures think intercourse should be done quickly and rarely. Our culture admires the male who can "last all night," although virtually none do. The person who has an erection for hours is atypical. Even with preparations such as Viagra, the makers warn against the male having an erection longer than three to four hours.

Probably a better term is the one adopted by many sex therapists: *"Fast Ejaculation."* The arousal cycle is done correctly, just too fast. Now in the younger male, having a second sexual episode subsequent to the first often easily solves this problem. This second cycle usually is slower, and if both partners can avoid negative thoughts, it can be totally enjoyable. But if the male is worried about what his partner thinks about his first episode, and there is no communication between the two persons, it can become a problem. The nervous system, which controls the sexual system, is sensitive to thoughts of threat, anger, worry, fear. Such feelings lead to the nervous system literally reacting as if there were a very real threat, resulting in a flaccid penis rather than an erect penis.

Other scenarios which can lead to Fast Ejaculation are those in which there is intense stimulation: having intercourse in which there may be imminent danger of discovery (such as in the back seat of a car in "lovers' lane," or at her parents' house) or when there is a time-clock involved (as with a prostitute, who is usually not too interested in you lasting all night). Even for those of you who have had years of marital sex in the "proper" locations, a change of partner and scene can lead to an increase in excitement, and an issue with fast ejaculation. After all, sexual behavior is learned. Fortunately, such behaviors can be unlearned.

In addition to the "second episode" method mentioned above to help correct fast ejaculation, Masters and Johnson also used a "squeeze technique" to help slow things down, so that the male could learn to keep an erection without necessarily proceeding pell-mell to orgasm. There is a certain confidence obtaining an erection and maintaining it, or bringing it back by increasing stimulation after squeezing (lightly now!) on either side of the glans (or tip) to suppress stimulation for a while.

There are medications purported to help the fast ejaculator but they are of doubtful value. Other techniques involve "dulling" the sensation by the use of a condom (rubber), or even a combination of a rubber with dulling ointment, but since a large part of the ejaculation process is mental, this mental excitement may still result in a quick response to sexual stimulation.

It may also help to insert the erect penis into the vagina without immediately rushing to completion, stopping to rest and just enjoy the feelings of "containment" obtained by being inside. Then, when there is an urge to start movements, to go ahead. Sometimes, men may want to try ten thrusts and then rest again, once more experiencing the feelings of containment.

> *Pete was embarrassed to tell us about his problem with "premature ejaculation" (i.e., fast ejaculation). Although he had tried various ways to slow his ejaculation, his new wife remained irritated—even furious—with him. She believed that the ideal sexual experience was simultaneous orgasm. For her, anything other than this perfect synchronicity of climax was inferior, indicating that he did not love her. She viewed his fast ejaculations as evidence of selfishness and insisted that he gain control over them. This served to only increase his sexual pressure, resulting in him being very anxious about the sexual experience and avoiding it altogether as he could not measure up to her standards.*

It's helpful to note that in the 1960s, when marriage counselors discovered that the female was capable of orgasm as was the male, —indeed, even more so—they reasoned that for each partner to have maximal enjoyment, the ideal would be for them to have this extremely pleasant rush as close together as possible. Simultaneous orgasms were considered the height of earthly pleasure. Soon, marriage manuals of the decade began emphasizing simultaneous orgasm as the goal of marital sexuality. However, when mental pressure is applied such that one or both partners "worry" about timing, this "scrutiny" takes away from the enjoyment of "just letting go" and moves the couple further away from orgasm rather than closer. We now know that it is more likely to lead to pleasure if one person just lets go and then pleasures the partner, reversing the timing of the partners the next time.

Q: I'm at the other end of the spectrum. Whenever I get excited, I lose my erection, whether I'm next to her or inside. This is upsetting! What's going on?

A: This condition, called *Erectile Dysfunction* (ED), has been made famous by advertisements in the mass media, complete with product endorsement by famous people. The problem is more often found among older men, although males of any age can have an occasional bout of ED. Remember that the penis (and sexual system) is not under voluntary control. Magazines like Playboy have featured stories ever so often about males who had complete penis control, and jokes abound about men who can "will" an erection. Folks, it just don't happen! The nervous system must be relaxed. If there is the slightest bit of anxiety, worry, anger, or especially depression, then preservation of the organism takes precedence over sexual excitation. In other words, if a guy was feeling sexy while the saber-toothed tigers were prowling, he probably did not make it long enough to leave any progeny. Again, sexual activity occurs in the arena of safety and security, when both partners are relaxed.

Q: I have erectile difficulties, and so I've started having a drink or two to calm down and lower my anxiety. Makes things more exciting! Nothing wrong with that is there?

A: Big mistake! Remember: although many guys believe alcohol is a stimulant that can be used to "make things happen," it is really a depressant. It's just that the brain reacts to alcohol at different speeds. Initially, the first parts of the brain affected by alcohol are the frontal lobes, which control your inhibitions. By depressing your inhibitions, alcohol may give you the impression that it is a stimulant, loosening you up and making you more sociable, energized and sexy. But alcohol is a depressant. With more drinks, alcohol starts to affect the sensory and motor areas of the brain, located in the middle and back parts of the brain, as well as the centers of the brain controlling sexual functioning, leading to an inability to have an erection. As the old saying goes, "You can't drown your troubles in alcohol." In fact, alcohol irrigates, rather than drowns, problems.

Some men have physical conditions such as diabetes, sleep disorders, and overweight conditions which will cause erectile difficulties. Should you think you have one of them, please see your doctor. And get a regular checkup. Often, a loss of weight, or treatment of the sleep disorder or diabetes can lead to a resumption of potency. Your doctor will know best.

Today, more than ever, men are being prescribed medications that may affect their sexual functioning. The pharmacist is often most helpful in knowing the reactions of these medications. You may notice a third window at the pharmacy: besides the usual "Drop-Off" and "Pick-Up" prescriptions, there is a "Pharmacist Consultation" window. He or she may have more time to discuss this issue with you than your physician.

Erectile dysfunction problems often occur when a guy is taking psychotropic medication (e.g., antidepressants). Many guys have been surprised, when visiting their counselor or psychotherapist, by the series of questions about the medication prescribed by their physician—questions that connect the erectile difficulty with specific medications. Their prescribing physician or psychiatrist hadn't told them about this problem. Unfortunately, men often decide to forego the psychotropic med in order to regain their potency, when the medication may have been crucial for other reasons. Again, consult your doctor or pharmacist. Just because one medication negatively affects your erectile abilities does not mean that all will. Your doctor may substitute another medication, just as he would for any other negative side effect, such as weight gain, dry mouth, etc. You may have to tolerate some minor side effects when taking the medication, but perhaps not one that leads to foregoing sex.

Q: I'm not like either of those other two guys. Even well after my divorce, I just don't care about sex. I can't get turned on. Will that change?

Masters and Johnsons's research on the sexual cycle has been important, but it is not the only game in town as far as the research on sexuality. Helen Singer Kaplan emphasized a stage prior to the excitement phase, called the *desire phase*.[2] Persons with low or absent desire just don't get the initial push to enter the excitement phase, and are content for things to remain just as they are. The lack of desire has been found more often in women, but exists in men, too. Women often have *desire phase problems* when there has been a traumatic history of rape or other violence (emotional or physical) which leads them to distance themselves from others and from their feelings as well.

Desire phase problems can be difficult to treat. Most people with low desire don't come into the sex therapist's office; they just don't see it as a problem. Two people with *desire phase* problems may be happily married, not viewing sex as a big part of their marriage. However, a problem occurs when one person desires closeness and sex, and the other does not. Sometimes, a partner will come in for treatment just to please the other partner who desires sex. The task of the sex therapist is to re-create (or sometimes even create) sexual scenarios that can start the excitatory phase percolating. Some behavioral connections have to be unlearned, and some have to be learned. The sessions usually involve both a diagnostic portion and a treatment portion.

A comment, now, about sex therapy: Masters and Johnson popularized their method, which involved the couple flying to St. Louis (where Masters and Johnson did their research and treatment), staying in a hotel, and going to the hospital offices for an intensive week of couple treatment, which included homework at night. Other sex therapists have developed their own methods of treatment, which differed in length of time and intensity.

Sound expensive? With hotel costs, airline tickets and food, and the therapy fees, the total can be intimidating. Unfortunately, the health insurance companies usually see this type of treatment as "voluntary" (i.e., not medically necessary), just as they view cosmetic plastic surgery and eye surgery to eliminate eyeglasses and therefore don't cover them.

Only a very few insurance plans are beginning to think of the bottom line—that a contented worker is more likely to have fewer absences and thus be more productive.

But before you cast sex therapy aside as economically unfeasible, how many of you would not hesitate to buy the latest automobile with all the gadgets on it—the big gas guzzler, knowing that the moment you drive it past the curb, it is now a "used car" and has lost about $5-8000 in value. Your sex therapy may cost just the same, but should last a lot longer, and be more rewarding.

Q: My problem isn't like any of the above. I can get an erection and "go all night." I can really please the women, but I just don't "come." How can this be?

A: Glad you realized this was a problem, because many men will enjoy having an erection for a long duration. They like the fact that they can please others, and don't see "not coming" as an issue. The problem is that you are not sharing the enjoyment of the release that comes during orgasm with your partner.

In this situation, there appears to be the ability to progress through Masters and Johnson's cycle of Excitement and Plateau, but not enough to send you through to Orgasm. Sometimes it signals a mental "holding back, "almost an unconscious refusal to "let go" during orgasm. While some Freudian therapists may focus on this unconscious element more than other sex therapists and would mention a possible fear of impregnation, they would also see the possibility of fear of involvement, possibly due to an inability to get over past sexual episodes of your ex. You should know that fear of impregnation is a real thing, and just because you do not ejaculate inside her does not negate the risk of impregnation. Men have the Cowper's gland, a small organ inside the penis which secretes an alkaline fluid during the Excitement phase to help lubricate the urethra and prepare for ejaculation. Sperm do not do well in the normal acid environment of the urethra, so the Cowper's glands minimize this problem. You may have noticed a couple of drops of clear-to-whitish fluid appearing at the tip of your penis during excitement. This fluid is the one we're talking about, from the Cowper's gland. However, it also may contain some semen, so those men who practice "withdrawal" (*coitus interruptus*) by removing the penis before ejaculating as a method of birth contro do not remove their risk of a blessed event nine months down the line. One sperm, one egg, one blessed event. That's all it takes!

Women more often have the flip side of this problem, where it is easier for them to let their partner enjoy himself and not reach climax themselves. In addition to the problems mentioned above, our culture still tells women to "let men have their way" while they are not expected to enjoy sex. You may not realize it, but often women's sex education comes about through an unfortunate incident surrounding the start of their periods. And a lot of girls are still told that they will soon be visited by the "curse" of the monthlies! We can't imagine how excited we men would be waiting for a curse to happen to us!

If you are holding back because you fear conception, then maybe talking with your partner about this will help. Use of a condom or other contraceptive technique may allay these fears. Remember, that only a "barrier method" like a condom or a diaphragm for the female is useful to protect against conception plus give protection against venereal disease, should one of you have such. The "pill," although an excellent contraceptive, does not give such protection against venereal disease.

Q: I'm not young, and when I "come," it takes a great deal of time for me to feel sexy again. Same thing when masturbating. What's going on?

A: So far, we have talked mostly about the male cycle. Of course, the big deal with Masters and Johnson's research was showing that, despite the external differences in body equipment, the male and female are more alike than different. The same nervous system is stimulated, reaching the same parts of the brain, in each gender. Both genders go through the stages of Excitement, Plateau, Orgasm and Resolution. There are, however, a few differences between males and females, and your question brings up one those differences. During the Resolution phase, the genital area is proceeding back to the resting state in both genders. In the male, however, there is an additional period of time, called a *"refractory phase,"* during which there is no response to an increase in stimulation, no matter how intense. In young males, Masters and Johnson found this to be short: a matter of 10-20 minutes or so, getting progressively longer as the male ages, to where a male in his 60s may have a *refractory phase* of days before he is interested in, or capable of, a full response cycle.

Females do not have this refractory period, so they are capable of having another orgasm, or orgasms, after their first one.

Since Masters and Johnson published their research, there have been anecdotal stories of young men who have claimed to not have the refractory period and can have another orgasm quickly. The difference, however, is that fewer males than females have the capability of more than one orgasm, and males are not capable of more than two while females have a much more variable capability. Also, with males, the first orgasm is always the more pleasurable, while with females the subsequent orgasm(s) are more pleasurable than the initial.

This information may be helpful to you in understanding what is going on. There may be additional feelings behind your question, however. You may be angry or disappointed that you do not have the capabilities you once had, and you may need to go through a "mourning" period.

If so, then spend a day or so, but not much more, in your mourning. I remember hearing (a while ago) that Jimmy Connors had reached his peak of tennis prowess at age 35 and soon would be retiring. I realized that I was even older than Jimmy Connors and that I would never be a tennis star. I was depressed. I mourned the loss of what might have been. Shortly I broke out of that funk, realizing that I never had wanted to be a tennis star, and thus had never placed myself in a situation where I could even be close to being one. Taking longer to get sexually excited again is just one of the side effects of aging as you channel yourself along life's chosen direction. Some doors open, while some close.

Q: Can we talk about differences between women? My wife was not the greatest sexually, and I'm worried that the new woman I've started to see may be more demanding.

A: Even if you were perfectly matched with your partner, there may be differences in daily sexual desire between you. You, no doubt, are familiar with the female's 28-day menstrual cycle, and you probably know that there are changes in sexual desire during that cycle. Most, but not all, females reach a peak in desire shortly before ovulation (thus helping in procreation). Some females have the peak of desire during other parts of the cycle. Males, previously thought to be relatively "consistent" in their desire, have now been shown to have fluctuations more on a daily basis. For example, many men are more interested in having sex early in the morning. They are rested and their testosterone levels may be at their peak in the morning. Later in the day, they may be physically or emotionally worn out and just wish to go to sleep. Alcohol, heavy eating or staying up late may exacerbate this.

"Thank you for your recent E-mail. I appreciate your concern. However, I am, at this time, completely satisfied with the size of my penis."

Women, on the other hand, may like the security of loving at night, especially if there are children in their home. They may feel better that the kids are asleep and will not be barging in like they might in the morning. Also, the demands of motherhood, of getting the family up and out of bed, preparing breakfast, and shipping them off to school, may make the mornings a time for increased tension. She may fear the children just would not understand what the locked door is all about.

Does your concern about this new woman's demands relate to a worry that you may not be able to satisfy her; that at some time, you may not climax or may be impotent, and you may risk losing her? Most women who care about the man they are with will take such episodes in stride. They do not expect to have orgasms every time. They will spend extra time during lovemaking, or indicate to their man that they just desire cuddling and closeness. At that point, it's up to the man to follow their lead. It is guaranteed that at some time in your life, you will be too tired, too emotionally drained, too distracted, or too full of food or drink, and as a result have an erection problem. Don't worry. Don't get angry. Don't compound the problem with drugs or drinks. Enjoy the closeness, and look forward to the next sexual occasion.

Q: My new sexual relationship is great! Will it continue?

A: You may be having a "honeymoon period" in your relationship with your new partner, which may lead to an increase in stimulation and sexual excitement. Right now, you may be responding well to her sexual needs. However, this period may not continue forever, despite your hoping that it will.

By "honeymoon" period we mean a time when everything is permeated by the new and the exciting. Human beings are wired to respond most intensely to new stimuli and new situations. All responses— from the cellular level to the complex psychological—habituate over time with repeated exposure, so that with familiarity comes a decrease in anatomic arousal. So, over time, your "honeymoon" sexual excitement is almost guaranteed to lessen, as your experience together is no longer so new. However, you can counteract the diminished excitement by having more communication about your expectations, needs, wishes, and desires. Consider changing your lovemaking techniques, a little at times. Maybe she is hoping you could use more "little words of love"? Or maybe you can incorporate something from one of your sexual fantasies.

Just because things are great in your sexual relationship now, doesn't mean that they will continue to be that way. This is akin to the young man's thought of marriage guaranteeing an always willing sexual partner. "If I have two dates with my girl on Friday and Saturday, and have two great episodes of sex, then when I marry her and we're together all the time that means sex seven times a week!" Wrong-o! The math just doesn't pan out.

Q: My new woman friend has asked me about my sexual fantasies, and in turn, expressed hers, which sound like rape to me. Is this what she really wants?

A: Many women express a theme in their sexual fantasies of being coerced to have sex. This does not mean, though, that they really want to be raped or to have the men in their life act out this scene. The scenario, when examined more clearly, involves a very dramatic theme of the man being forthright and "overpowering" the woman with his strong statements of desire and his direct manner of approaching her, leaving her "powerless" in his grasp. So we have Rhett Butler carrying Scarlet O'Hara up the stairs in a direct and forceful manner. Miss Scarlet doesn't have to worry about feeling guilty. Rhett knows what he wants and is going to take it. Other such fantasies may occur in women's dreams. Perhaps she imagines or dreams she is rescued by a handsome fireman who climbs the ladder and saves her by carefully flinging her over his broad shoulders in the fireman's carry. He then takes her down to the ground and carefully and tenderly ravishes her. You get the picture.

Q: My ex turned goofy when I did not have sexual interest in her. I'm starting to notice this in the new woman I'm dating. Sometimes I'm interested, and other times I just don't care. What's going on with me?

A: You need to understand that some (or even "most") women develop proprietary rights when they really care about a man. When this happens, they begin to expect that the man will behave like the cultural stereotype: always ready for sex like the 500-pound gorilla. All they have to do is rattle the cage a little, and we're supposed to be geared up. Show a little lace, a little leg, a breast or two and we're supposed to be hopping up and down, eager for sex. Remember our own myths we perpetuated, especially when we were single. We never had enough sex, so we presumed we were always ready for more. When we have a regular partner, we may find out that there are times when we don't desire sex. Women see it as a special kind of rejection, a very personal kind of rejection of their whole being rather than just not wanting to "do it." This may set up uncertainties about not only their value as a sexual partner, but also as a woman, and as a desirable, worthwhile human being. They may express this uncertainty through feelings of depression, the normal reaction to loss. It can also bring up old insecurities, particularly in women who have been sensitized through early experience of divorce between their parents, and/or separation from their father. It's another confirmation of what she feared might happen (i.e., of being rejected). And then we guys wonder: "What's the big deal? All I said was I just wasn't interested right then, or it didn't get hard! That's my problem, not hers."

Although men are generally less likely to have problems with sexual desire, in our clinical practice we often see couples where it is the guy who is the "not tonight, honey" partner. These guys typically blame their wives for their lack of sexual interest. "You need to lose weight," they may say.

> Quite regularly Reginald found a reason for not having sex with his new wife. He was either "tired" or he found some flaw in her body, her wardrobe, or her attitude. She felt terribly rejected and blamed herself for the problem. He insisted that she get some treatment, and was shocked when the therapist told him he needed to go with her to a sex therapist. He stalled, and ended up in our men's group instead. The guys then challenged Reginald—either he didn't have the guts to do marital/sex therapy or he had already decided he wanted to end his second marriage but didn't want it to look like it was his fault. With their support, he took the couples sex therapy route, learning lots about his own sexuality in the process. He had prided himself in his earlier life of being masterful with the women;

what he thought he knew didn't translate well into his second marriage.

In our experience, women whose husbands are not sexually interested usually blame themselves. Since feminine sexuality is so highly prized in our society, it can be very humiliating for the woman who continues to try new ways to encourage her husband's sexual interest to no result except for unremitting frustration. Some men with low sexual desire suffer from a physical problem such as low testosterone, but, more frequently in our experience, the problem is psychologically driven. After ruling out potential physical causes for your lack of desire, you should seek help from a sex therapist if you truly value the relationship.

Q: My new woman likes to make love in total darkness, while I'm more the type to see what's going on. What do we do?

A: Sounds like its time for a little communication.

First, examine how many times this has occurred. Are you both insisting on your own way of loving? If so, maybe you each need to be a little less rigid with your new love. Perhaps, each of you can enlarge your techniques, including the others' desires and fantasies.

Consider having a serious talk with her and mention that your likes are a little different from hers, and you'd like to alternate. Or maybe during lovemaking you can try a little of her way and then suggest yours. You can get an idea of whether she can respond better through talking or doing by what has gone on already. Some women like talking about what's going on or will be going on (including "talking dirty"), while others want silence.

We are talking here about stimulation of various aspects of our nervous systems. Some people are more visual, some more aural (i.e., hearing enticing speech, listening to romantic music), while others are more tactile. Is there a right way, or even a better way? We doubt it. Even if you were to find the perfect way to make love, you probably won't want to continue it aspect for aspect every single time. Variation and surprise are fun. Just think—even if your favorite ice cream were chocolate, after 30 days in a row, you might want to have vanilla, or strawberry!

THE NEW RELATIONSHIP

CHAPTER *14*

"When I meet a man I ask myself, 'Is this the man I want my children to spend their weekends with?'"
—*Rita Rudner*

BECOMING CLOSER

After you have been dating for a while, you may find someone special, someone with whom you want to build more of a relationship. You think you are ready to have the relationship progress further and start looking at the future possibilities. In this chapter, we discuss issues that pop up as you move from the initial post-divorce dating-again-phase to the next post-divorce phase: intimacy.

Q: Although we just met, I think I've found "the one." Am I rushing things?

A: We encourage you to let things develop gradually. Moving quickly into a relationship is usually problematic. If you get too close too fast, the natural feeling is discomfort and a desire to reinstitute the former distance. This is comparable to having another person get into your "personal space," which usually leads to anxiety. The natural reaction is to push that person away. If either one of you moves the relationship too quickly, the other is apt to back away.

Q: What do I do if she has kids?

A: The first thing is to accept the fact that she does have children, or get the heck out. This is not the time to believe that you are the male lion and your new lioness is going to kill the cubs so you can have your way. Although women may vary in their protective instincts for their kids, in general, you should expect that the children will be very important to them. You new love will probably prioritize them over you. Yet, that's a good thing. After all, what kind of woman would she be if she didn't want to take care of her own kids? Probably not one that you will want long-term. Chances are good, too, that if she does not prioritize the kids now, later she probably won't prioritize you either.

Q: When should I meet her kids?

A: A good clue is to follow her lead. It is not a good idea to insist on seeing the kids right away. Women know that new relationships may not last, and children become confused when a man appears in their lives, only to disappear after a few weeks. Women may rightly feel that it is better to wait until it appears that there is the possibility of a longer-term relationship.

It is very tempting to meet and get to know her kids soon after beginning a new relationship. After all, they are very important people in her life, and their actions will affect how and when you two adults will get together. Women are sometimes eager to have the new man in their lives meet the kids. In part, this may be to see how well you do with children. In some cases, it is literally to check out your skills as a father. In some situations we have seen, the mother wants her children to pass judgment on the new man. Does he seem nice? Would you like him?

In spite of the urge to jumpstart a relationship by getting involved with her kids, we would advise caution. When a relationship is new, the focus should be on the couple's compatibility, not on the compatibility with the children. The latter is important, but not until there is more stability in the couple's relationship. In short, it is putting the proverbial cart before the horse.

Furthermore, when you establish a relationship with her kids early on, you may get confused about who you are really dating. Quite often, a man who either misses his children from a divorce or just wants kids of his own becomes enraptured with his girlfriend's children. These men sometimes look past potential problems in the couple relationship while focusing instead on enjoying her little ones.

When dating women with children, a man often becomes the playful "teddy bear" that is frequently missing from the lives of children. This is especially likely to be the case if the kids' father is relatively uninvolved with them. The children may become very fond of you, quite quickly. However, if the relationship progresses into marriage, you should not necessarily expect that they would feel the same fondness towards you as they did when you were dating their mother. All bets are off as everyone readjusts to your permanent presence in the family.

On the other hand, her children may resent your presence and actively work to sabotage your dating relationship with their mother. Many, if not most, children would prefer that their parents would reunite, adding the caveat "only if they could reunite and not fight as they did before."

Another common error that men make when dating is to assume a parental role of her children. Sometimes the situation seems to beg for a strong masculine hand. The mother (your girlfriend) may seem overwhelmed with the responsibilities of being a parent. The children may be misbehaving and seemingly out of control. Your girlfriend may cast eyes on you pleading for your intervention. It can be so tempting to step in and restore order, as you know you can do. Before you get on your white charger, lower your visor, and gallop off to save the princess, however, recognize that this is a trap. Women in this situation tend to initially appreciate your assistance but later resent it. Typically, there will come a time when she will tell you that you are not parenting the right way. She may reassert that she, not you, is the parent of the children and thus holds the final say so. Furthermore, the kids may resent you because you are not their "real" parent. *(See the section on Step-Parenting in Chapter 16 for more thoughts on this subject.)*

Of course, dating relationships often don't last. If the children become acquainted and establish a relationship with each man that

Mama dates, it can create an image of men as undependable, moving in and out of one's life. This is an unhelpful image for young boys to emulate and equally bad for young girls to expect.

Our recommendation is that you should be slow to meet her kids. If your dating relationship progresses to thinking about marriage, then get to know them. Hopefully, you will not rush into such a committed relationship. You will have known her for awhile and feel that the two of you might make the relationship permanent. She, too, will be thinking of you in the same way. Once you have made the couple relationship solid and are considering a future together, you are ready to meet her children. It will be complicated to enlarge upon your couple relationship to include her children, but it is the surest way to make the marriage viable. Since you have already gone through a divorce, you know how painful it can be, and you should do everything possible to avoid a second one.

On a number of occasions we have known men who quickly became involved with "her" children. What could be more natural? This seems especially likely to occur when the biological father of the kids is relatively absent. Bill, who had never had kids of his own, particularly enjoyed "rough housing" with her kids. He could see how overwhelmed she often felt with the demands of the youngsters, so he offered to help with some of the parenting tasks. The kids responded enthusiastically to this playful guy, and, before long, he too was attending all of the kids' various after-school activities. Unfortunately, though, he began to feel obligated, then resentful, about all that he was doing for the children. At the same time, the couple began to have their own issues about their relationship. They did not see eye to eye on a number of important things like money and religion. He felt very stuck. He told us if the relationship ended, he would feel guilty about leaving her in a difficult situation, he would miss her kids, and the children would have another man drop out of their lives. On the other hand, if he stayed, he was unsure if he and his girlfriend were really all that compatible. It was hard to know what was best.

Q: When should she meet my kids?

A: Most of what we have said about meeting her kids is also true about her meeting *your* kids. Go slow to include her in their lives.

Your children may resent your girlfriend's presence, feeling that it would be disloyal to their mother to even be nice to this "new woman." In our experience, children more commonly resent the new woman in Dad's life than the "new man" in their mother's world. This may seem unfair, but it is what we have found to be true.

There are developmental differences in how children respond to their parents' dating relationships. Very young children, babies and toddlers, usually think nothing of new adults coming into their lives. If the new adult is nice to them, they will usually feel fond of the person. Elementary age children and young adolescents may feel confused about the presence of these strangers. They may feel angry at you for introducing these "replacements" for their mother, and may be unkind to your girlfriend as well. Older adolescents and young adults may essentially ignore your new relationship. They may withdraw and retreat more from you and act disinterested in your new partner. Kids of every age frequently feel jealous when their fathers begin to take an interest in another woman, particularly if Dad seems more interested in her than the children. When their father is less available to interact with the kids or when he showers his new love with presents, children may become resentful.

Ex-wives often react when they learn that their former husbands are dating, especially if those relationships become more serious. They frequently find out about Dad's new girlfriend from the kids, so be careful what the kids learn. In turn, Mama may say some tacky things about you and your ladylove to the kids, negatively influencing how the children react to you.

We are not saying that you should keep your dating relationships "top secret." We are saying that you should be discrete. Keep your relationship low-key. For example, don't have your girlfriend spend the night when you have custody of the children.

> ****WARNING****
>
> Failing to heed this advice about girlfriends spending the night may ultimately result in legal actions by an angry ex-wife. We have seen this lead to allegations that the children witnessed sexual interactions between a guy and his girlfriend. Next stop: an emergency hearing about limiting visitation rights.

Q: I want kids. Will it scare her away if I tell her this?

A: Maybe you have been hoping to have kids, either your first child or more children. For some people, this is a "deal breaker." For them, if the partner is unwilling to have children, the relationship will have to end. We have seen couples that really care about each other but cannot come to an agreement about having children. In such a case, we think it is better for the relationship to end rather than to hope that you will be able to persuade your beloved to change her mind. This is certainly not a topic to tackle early in a relationship, but, if it is very important to you, you need to talk about it before the relationship progresses very far. Of course, she may have similar feelings. If she very much wants children, it is essential to clearly communicate your own position about the matter relatively early in the relationship. For example, she may assume that, because you are of a "certain (older) age" and do not have children, that you don't want any. Letting her know directly that you would like kids may lead to a loss of the relationship, but it may also keep you from wasting time on a relationship that would ultimately disappoint you. You can then focus on attracting a different set of women, ones who want to have children.

Q: What about the holidays?

A: After divorce, holidays (e.g., Thanksgiving, Seder, Christmas)—once fun and joyous—can be depressing and lonely. If you were accustomed to spending holidays with your ex-wife's family, it can be especially tough. Some men return to spending holidays with their own family. Others are invited to spend this time with friends and their families, but many men feel uncomfortable about this arrangement. We recommend that you take some invitations to be with others rather than staying home alone eating a TV dinner. Create limits on the time and activities so that you don't feel like you are trapped or overly obligated. Offer to participate in the preparations, cooking, and clean up rather than remaining a passive recipient.

Of course, your girlfriend may invite you to be with her during her family's celebrations. This can be fun, but it can also put pressure on you to move the relationship into a "more serious phase." If she is asking you to come over to participate with her kids in holiday events (e.g., opening Christmas presents) you may wish to decline. It is probably too early to insert yourself into the lives of her children during the holidays. This might imply to them and to her that you will be a permanent presence in their lives, and, at this point, this should not be the message you are sending.

You might wish to put some limits on her holiday plans to reduce expectations and anxieties. For example, you might come for only part of the day rather than the whole experience. It would also be wise to build some time for just you and your girlfriend to interact rather than making the whole experience about her family. Remember, though, that she and her family have their own ways of celebrating these occasions, and she will probably want to follow those traditions. Don't expect her to drop time-honored family events to be with you. Instead, ask how you and she can carve out time to have your own kind of celebrations. These events would not take the place of her family plans, but rather they would be in addition to those arrangements.

Q: What about taking a trip with her?

A: Taking a trip with your new girlfriend will push the relationship forward (unless it destroys the relationship altogether). A trip may be your first opportunity to see how she acts outside of the normal routine. Although you both will probably still be putting your "best foot forward," it is harder to do this during a trip away. There will be more chances for you to see each other at less than your best.

It is probably not a good idea to take a trip with her until you have had a number of good dates. By "good dates" we mean times when you and she have done things together, and you have had fun.

Although not yet at the stage of commitment, you have gone beyond introductions and know each other reasonably well. There have been no obvious warning signs that the relationship cannot develop further. You have some bases of mutual interest, you find each other at least moderately attractive, and there are no glaring incongruities in values.

Early in the relationship, It is better to do a brief trip together, rather than to plan an extended one. We have seen situations where the couple plans their initial trip as a long vacation in a foreign country. While this might be fun if everything goes as planned, things seldom go as planned. Such an ambitious set-up makes failure and disappointment far more likely. Instead, build upon success by gradually having longer and more elaborate trips together.

It is reasonable for both of you to expect that sexuality will be a feature of the trip. In most cases, after all, you will be staying together. If you have not yet been sexual, it is wise to discuss the issue prior to the trip. This can avoid hurt feelings and disappointment. Don't make assumptions about her feelings in this regard. You should talk about the issue of sexuality as openly as the two of you can handle.

Planning a trip together gives a great opportunity for the two of you to practice problem solving. She may want to go to the beach, while you prefer mountain climbing. Making the decision about what you will do on your trip brings up a number of practical issues:

- ❏ Who ultimately makes the decision about where you will go?

- ❏ Can the two of you make compromises?

- ❏ Will she be assertive in expressing her wishes or will she defer to you?

- ❏ Do the two of you have similar tastes? If not, how can you respect the differences between you?

- ❏ How do issues about money play into the decision-making process?

❏ How do you deal with things when there are problems?

Soon after beginning a new promising relationship Jamison planned a spectacular overseas trip with his new love. The prospect of exploring new exotic places with his new girlfriend was very exciting. The trip was necessarily lengthy and included numerous flight and hotel accommodations. As the trip drew near, though, she seemed to be adding more and more complicating conditions to an already complex plan. It felt to him that she was more concerned about the trip than about him. Eventually, the couple elected not to go, disappointing him greatly. They probably would have been better off simply getting away for a weekend.

CHAPTER 15

"There's only one way to have a happy marriage and as soon
as I learn what it is I'll get married again."
—Clint Eastwood

GETTING SERIOUS AGAIN

Most people going through a divorce say that that they will never marry again or that they don't plan to do so. Nonetheless, after a while, most people do get into another serious relationship, and the majority goes on to marry again.[1]

It is understandable, though, why people deny that this will happen. A divorce is typically one of the most painful events in one's life. The last thing a person contemplates then is another relationship. You are too agonizingly aware of how the last one worked out. However, it is human nature to want to intimately connect with another person. Despite the difficulties in actually making this kind of connection, most of us really want the security and fulfillment of a long-term committed relationship. Here are some things to think about as you contemplate getting serious—again.

Q: What baggage am I bringing into the relationship?

A: By "baggage" we assume you are referring to the psychological "luggage" we all carry with us throughout our lives. It includes your history, your children, your families of origin (parents, siblings, and other relatives), your ex-wife (or wives), and your physical possessions. We would also be remiss, as psychologists, if we did not include in this arena your "psychological possessions": your jobs and job identities, your hopes and fears, as well as traumatic (and happy) past experiences. Note, however, that we usually do not consider happy events in life as baggage. Baggage is what loads us down. This baggage may or may not be visible, but everyone has it.

Some of us travel lightly through life—others of us take everything along with us until our suitcases are bursting. We may even buy more sturdy suitcases with wheels on them so we can carry more "stuff." We may have had incidents of hurting ourselves (back injuries) if we attempt to carry such a suitcase when the baggage handler "gorilla" at the airport knocked off the wheel. Sometimes we insist on a larger house or apartment than we would otherwise need because we have to store our "stuff" from our job, hobby, or past.

Our psychological baggage likewise loads us down needlessly. How many times does a reaction from times past impinge on you, and stop you from doing what you want, because you have to watch out for your "stuff."

We likewise may have concerns about the other person's "stuff", their baggage. One reason why married people have affairs is that they get so bogged down with their own and their spouse's baggage that they cannot enjoy the relationship any more. They may then make the mistake of assuming that they can have an affair with a person without such baggage. You can carry on an affair for a while, disregarding the other person's baggage, but eventually reality begins to set in. Some people just keep moving, on to other people and other affairs, never getting deep enough to have more than a superficial relationship, primarily a sexual one.

Baggage can take many forms. Marc told himself that his girlfriend's history of sexual abuse in childhood would not be a problem in his relationship with her. After all, those events happened many years before he even met her. Although she had initially been sexually open and quite willing in the relationship, over time she seemed to be avoiding sex more and more. She claimed that she was either too tired or that he was not approaching her in the right way. When he finally persuaded her to go with him to therapy about the matter, it became evident that their sexual life together had begun to remind her of the abuse that she sustained in childhood. Not surprisingly, then, she began to withdraw from him, much to his dismay.

Q: When am I ready for a committed relationship?

A: We usually recommend to men that after divorce they wait two years before getting into another committed relationship. Unfortunately, no man has yet heeded this piece of advice; however, we have had many return clients who wished that they had.

The major reason that people prematurely commit to a relationship is to avoid the pain associated with the loss of divorce. It is quite natural to want to avoid pain. Almost everybody will use aspirin to quell a headache, for example. However, the pain you experience from divorce is part of the recovery process. It makes you reevaluate the relationship, its history, the mistakes you have made, and what it means for your life. Most importantly, it can help you avoid making similar mistakes in the future.

Not only do we want to get over the pain from divorce, but also we want it to happen quickly! After all, we are a country of fast food restaurants and short-term profit taking. We tend to opt for convenience over long-term solutions. Similarly, we want to recover quickly from divorce. For many men, this means entering into a new committed relationship almost before the ink is dry on their divorce decree.

You are not ready to engage in another committed relationship soon after divorce. You may think that you are ready, but you are not. Perhaps you have attended a funeral and asked the bereaved how he or she was doing with the loss of their loved one. In most cases, the bereaved person probably answered "fine." Six months later if you asked the same question of that person, he or she will probably tell you, "I'm doing a lot better than I was at the funeral." If you have lost a loved one to death, you know that there is an extended recovery period. The way you felt at the time of the burial is usually quite different than how you feel at six months, a year, and two years. Divorce, in many ways, is similar to experiencing a death. It is one of the most major losses you will ever have, even if you ultimately marry again. We humans need time to recover from these major losses.

When beginning a new relationship soon after divorce men often say things like, "The marriage really ended a long time before we divorced" or "We were separated for six months before we divorced." These kinds of comments are intended to make it seem as if they are well over their ended marriage and ready to start a new relationship. In our opinion, though, marriage is not over till it is over. Until that judge signs the final decree there is still the possibility of reconciliation (Some people even reconcile after divorce!). If the marriage is not truly over, you can't really begin to recover from it. Again, as in death, you can begin to mourn for a loved one before their passing, but you can't finish until they have actually died.

We are *not* saying that you should remain a hermit or a celibate monk. However, we are cautioning you against getting into a committed relationship before you are truly ready to do so. We are all familiar with the term "rebound relationship." The term is well known because it is a common problem caused when people jump too quickly into a new relationship. The stakes are high. Second marriages are far more likely to end in divorce than first marriages![2] Don't rush into a new committed relationship only to get to experience your second divorce.

One way to keep from getting too committed too quickly is to date more than one woman. That will usually put a governor on how fast a relationship will develop. Of course, some men (and women) will be uncomfortable with this idea, feeling that it is being disloyal to do so. If you are uncomfortable with dating more than one person at a time, we would encourage you to at least tell a new girlfriend that you are not in a position yet to be in a committed relationship. This leaves the possibility that you might become ready in the future, but you are not yet there. We advocate openness with your dating partners about what you are doing and why you are doing it. If they object to this kind of openness, consider this a warning sign of problems that would occur with this woman.

Q: How do I know if I am over my divorce?

A: A lot of times people think they are over something before they really are. Sometimes, we desperately want to be over a failed relationship, so we fool ourselves into thinking that it is true. Try this informal True/False questionnaire:

- ❏ I can think of my ex-wife without feeling a great deal of emotion (anger or sadness).

- ❏ Looking back at my marriage, I realize that both of us made mistakes.

- ❏ I can value the good things in my marriage even though it ended in divorce.

- ❏ I can honestly say that I wish the best for my ex-wife.

- ❏ The good qualities of my wife are clear to me.

- ❏ I have no desire to cause harm in any way to my ex-wife.

- ❏ My ex-wife cannot provoke me into anger regarding child support or visitation.

- ❏ If my ex-wife remarries, I will hope for her success in the new relationship.

- ❏ I do not speak ill of my ex-wife to the children.

- ❏ My ex-wife and I can both attend our children's functions (e.g., sporting events, school presentations) without significant discomfort.

If you can answer True to all of these, then perhaps you are ready emotionally to tackle a new relationship. Your goal should be to look at your marriage and subsequent divorce as chapters in a book, not as the entire book.

Q: How can I avoid making a mistake?

A: Of course, there is no way to guarantee that you will not make a mistake, but if you have been following us so far, then you know much of the answer to this question. Probably, the most risky thing to do is to get into a new committed relationship quickly on the heels of a divorce or while still married. There are also some research findings[3] that indicate you are more likely to go through a divorce if you marry a woman who:

- ❏ *Is younger than eighteen.* (Despite the allure, this has "danger" written all over it.)

- ❏ *Has a low level of education.* (She has essentially not completed growing up.)

- ❏ *Comes from a single parent home.* (She may be less familiar with what it takes to make marriage work.)

- ❏ *Has been raped.* (This may interfere with her sexual adjustment.)

- ❏ *Suffers from severe anxiety.* (Any mental disorder complicates marriage.)

- ❏ *Had a child before marriage or early in the marriage.* (You want to make sure that you are marrying because of her, not because of a baby.)

- ❏ *Lived with you before marriage.* (Living together does *not* reduce the likelihood of divorce.)

Nonetheless, no one can confidently predict what will happen with *your* relationship, but if you have several of the risk factors we have been discussing (e.g., you are less than a year after your divorce, she is significantly younger than you, she comes from a very different background) you increase the likelihood that the new relationship will end in another divorce. As Stanley (2000) notes, for many guys the seeds of their eventual divorce are there before they even say "I do."[4]

Q: What about the former men in her life?

A: Most likely, she, too, has had previous relationships. Some men, as well as some women, have great difficulty with feelings of jealousy about those previous relationships. We do not live in a Victorian age. Most women will have had previous relationships and former lovers. You must accept that this is virtually always the case. Take heart!! You're not really in competition with them since she already left those relationships. If she really preferred them, she would never have left the relationship. She may still have a place in her heart for them; that doesn't mean she's not giving you her heart.

"Trust me, David, he meant nothing—it was just a training marriag

Q: When is she ready for a committed relationship?

A: As with you, your new girlfriend may not be ready for a new relationship. However, most of us think we are ready before we really are ready. It is a good idea to consider these issues in estimating her readiness for a new relationship (notice the parallels to you being ready for a new relationship!):

❏ How long has her last relationship been over?

❏ How much anger does she retain at her ex?

❏ Can she think of her ex without feeling a great deal of emotion (anger or sadness)?

❏ Does she acknowledge that she made mistakes in her previous relationships? And can she see what they were?

❏ Does she value the good things in her previous relationship even though it ended?

❏ Does she harbor ill will to her ex?

❏ Can she tell you anything good about her ex?

❏ Does she speak ill of her ex to the children.

❏ Does she have a functional parenting relationship with her ex?

❏ Has she learned to be comfortable with being alone (i.e., Is she desperate not to be alone?).

❏ Is she in financial trouble?

❏ Is she seeking help in parenting her children because she can't do it alone?

Q: When is age difference a problem?

A: Age differences often pose problems in relationships. Unfortunately, many of these issues do not emerge until well after the relationship has begun. If you are interested in just dating a few times, age differences are not very important, but if you are thinking of a longer-term relationship, age differences can be very significant.

Many men would prefer to date a younger woman, but how young is too young? Rather than thinking about a specific number of years of difference, we would encourage you to look at developmental differences. The differences between a 20 year-old and a 30 year-old are vast, but the 10-year difference between a 30 and 40 year-old are not so large.

If the two of you are in very different places developmentally, eventually the relationship is likely to become strained if not untenable. For example, imagine that you have children who are adolescents or are fully-grown. You may not be interested in having more children. If your new girlfriend is over 30, without children, and hearing the biological clock ticking, she may greatly desire children soon. Similarly, how will your new girlfriend fit in among your friends? Maybe they will admire your new "arm candy," but will she be able to converse with your peers? Likewise, how comfortable will you be with her at family functions, with your children, and with your colleagues?

Another common developmental issue concerns career. If your girlfriend is young and beginning her career, while you are a seasoned veteran, she may look up to you. However, as she progresses in her career, the relationship between you may become more difficult as she no longer wants to be "junior" to you. Many relationships like this eventually end with disappointment for both parties.

Age differences can also be quite important with regard to health and retirement. If you are expecting to retire much sooner than she, you may have trouble later in your relationship. Perhaps, you will want to travel just at the point where she is trying to excel in her career. If you are older than she, the age difference might imply also that she will have to take care of you in your older age. We are not saying that you should not date someone of a different age, but we do recommend that you consider these potential issues before getting too far along in a new relationship.

Q: Should we just live together?

A: One way that people attempt to avoid some of the complications of marriage is simply to live together. Some people have compared this to "test-driving a new car." Unfortunately, that analogy only goes so far. You will learn more about your potential mate if you live with her, but the relationship is not identical to marriage. A key feature of marriage is that it is intended to be a life-long commitment. While living together is more of a commitment than mere dating, it is much less of a committed or permanent relationship than marriage.

The ability to walk out of a "live-in" relationship is both the strength and the weakness of this arrangement. There are relatively few strings attached when you are living together, but this also creates a certain amount of tension about how much you can truly count on the other person. More importantly, there is always a lingering question about whether or not the relationship will become permanent.

Of course, some people regard a marriage certificate as just another piece of paper, not reflecting the couple's feelings for each other. So what's the difference? We would argue that a marriage certificate is much more than a piece of paper. It represents a formal commitment—a public statement that the two people are "in this thing together."

If you do decide to live with someone, don't expect the relationship to look or feel like a marriage. It will be significantly different in numerous ways. For example, there is no joint property—your assets remain separate. Neither of you gets the benefits of sharing such things as health insurance, retirement accounts, tax breaks. Secondly, there will need to be agreements about financial responsibilities. Who will pay the rent, the utilities? Furthermore, you will have to come to an understanding about other areas of responsibility that affect each other. How will the two of you manage parenting? Will you share caretaking of the children? Who will be responsible for the various home maintenance tasks: cleaning, household repair, and lawn care? In whose home will you reside? If you live in her home, will you feel like a guest rather than a partner? If she lives in your home, where will she put her possessions? What if she wants to replace your favorite old chair? Where can you hang your collection of military heralds? In marriage, because the relationship is expected to be permanent, couples usually can work these issues out more easily, but if you do not know if the relationship will last over time, you are much more reluctant to give up valued possessions or to change your habits. Couples who live together frequently struggle around these issues. Of course, married couples can have some of the same conflicts, but the expected permanence of the relationship enables people to compromise more in the expectation that, in the long run, you will get more of what *you* want.

Unfortunately, the notion that it is best to first live together before marrying has not proven true. According to data from the Center for Disease Control only about 58% of cohabitation (living together) relationships result in marriage after three years. More importantly, the divorce rate for these couples approximates or exceeds that of other married couples.[5] Couples who marry after living together tend to have the same problems as other married couples. Ironically, these couples often marry hoping that the act of marriage will diminish the problems in their relationship. Living together simply provides no protection from the difficulties of marriage. Essentially, while marriage and living together may seem similar in some ways, they are very different kinds of relationships.

We are not saying that you shouldn't consider living together. You will certainly learn a lot about the other person (and maybe about yourself) by living with her. Don't expect, though, for it to be a panacea for all the problems of marriage. The problems people have in marriage also tend to develop in living-together relationships. These difficulties usually have to do with problem-solving, accepting the other person as he/she is, sharing a joint vision, and resolving conflict. These themes are equally important in every relationship. The major difference between living together and marriage, though, is that it is much easier to leave the former.

If you do decide to live with someone, pay special attention to complaints that she makes which sound strangely familiar (i.e., your ex-wife had the same complaint about you). If this happens to you, chances are good that the complaint is legitimate, and you need to take a close look at yourself about this problem.

Q: What about her pet? I love my new girlfriend, but her pet drives me up the wall.

A: Pets, in a way, are just like children. They are baggage, and you must consider them to be such. Often women (and some men, too) find that their pet has become a substitute child. Some men who would not ever consider parting with their own pets nonetheless have hostile feelings about hers. Maybe she has a cat, and you're a dog man.

Sometimes, the animal becomes a substitute for a life partner, and when you come on the scene, the pet seems jealous, demanding extra time just when you'd like to be "alone" with her. The pet/vet columns of the newspaper often feature articles dealing with pets that howl, scratch and tear up furniture, or poop on the carpet at such times.

If you cannot see your new love and her pet as a package deal, then maybe you should head on into the sunset, or at least into another woman's arms.

> *Tim and Janet came to us after repeated arguments about her dogs and cats. When they first got together he didn't much care for the animals, but he tolerated them. After all, he reasoned, how far could he push her regarding the matter? Now that they were moving in together, though, he began to assert his opinion. "If we are going to live together," he stammered, "the pets have to be outdoors—at least the dogs!" "And I don't want the house smelling like cat urine," he added. His new love was incensed. "If you objected to Fido and Fifi why didn't you say something in the beginning?" she responded. It is best to get this issue on the table early on.*

Q: What about my religious beliefs? I thought marriage was sacred.

A: Many people struggle with the idea of divorce because it conflicts with deeply held religious or moral beliefs. You may have held your marital commitment sacred, and yet you find yourself divorced. We certainly do not expect you to dismiss your values. Moreover, family members may want you to abide with the tenets of their beliefs about such matters. Some parents with strongly-held religious convictions cannot abide with their child's decision to remarry, feeling that it is a mortal sin. We think that ultimately only you can decide if it is acceptable to begin a new intimate relationship. You may wish to consult with your clergy, rabbi, or other religious leader to help you in making this sort of decision.

Similarly, you may feel that living together outside of marriage is sinful or morally repugnant. If so, be careful not to use this as an excuse to move into marriage too rapidly.

Q: How do I deal with my family about my new relationship?

A: Some men struggle with what to tell their family about a new relationship. Most people aren't surprised that you are dating again, but the prospect of a committed or permanent relationship can raise issues within the family.

Understandably, one of your family's concerns will be that you not get hurt again. They may have specific fears such as:

❑ Will you marry someone who will be a good mother to your children?

❑ Will you marry the same kind of person as before?

❑ Are you going through a "mid-life crisis"?

❑ Will this new woman take you away from your family of origin?

Your family's concerns may be legitimate. Don't dismiss them out-of-hand. Consider these issues realistically. Don't be blinded by love. If any of their concerns are true, you may want to rethink your position. You might even try to engage your family in an honest dialogue about their reactions to your new relationship. They may be reluctant to be candid with you, but asking their opinions is the surest way to know what they are thinking. Of course, you get the only vote in whether or not to proceed in the relationship, but it is wise for you to consult with other people who care about you.

Similarly, you might want to talk with your trusted friends about your developing relationship. Again, they may be reluctant to say anything that might hurt their friendship with you, but they may be in a better position than you to evaluate your readiness for a new relationship. In fact, friends may be even clearer than your family about your readiness for a new love. Unfortunately, it is common for friends to tell us after a divorce or breakup that they knew the relationship/ marriage could never work. Try to find out their opinions ahead of time.

Q: What about her family's feelings about the relationship?

A: Her parents (and by extension her larger family), of course, will be worried more about their daughter than about you. They may have seen her last marriage end in divorce and worry about it happening again. They may wonder if you can sustain a good relationship since you have been divorced already. They may have already lost a son-in-law that they liked. In short, they are likely to be cautious in forming a relationship with you, not knowing if you will be around for the long run. They will probably be slow to include you as one of the family. Accept this as normal and allow them time to know and trust you. Win them over by consistently showing them that you are a good guy.

Q: Now that we're serious, how do we get her kids and my kids together?

A: If you and your girlfriend become serious about "tying the knot," then introduce her to the kids and let them begin a relationship.

In an ideal world, everyone will just get along. Remember the old sitcoms about "her kids, his kids, and their kids." In those shows, as in real life, the children frequently squabble. Kids aren't obligated to make favorable impressions, and thus they are more likely to act up in just the situation where you want them to be on their best behavior. At some point, of course, you would want to have the children meet each other, but there is no point in doing so unless the relationship is going to be permanent or you and she will be living together.

When and if one of the situations above is about to occur, then have the children meet each other. It is probably best to begin on "neutral ground" rather than having one set of kids visit the other kids' home turf. Take the kids on a relatively short-term outing such as a picnic or trip to the zoo to give them opportunities to interact around a theme that generally is of interest to them. Later interactions could become longer, and they can spend more time with each other.

The kids, for their part, will immediately know "something is up" and will begin wondering if you are about to marry her. Of course, if you are following our advice, the answer is "yes" (or at least that you are about to move in together). Usually, children are not very happy about this eventuality, but sometimes they will see it as a positive event, more for you than for themselves.

You certainly should *not* expect that:

❑ The children will be happy for you.

❑ The kids will be fond of their new "friends."

❑ Your children will be well behaved so as to make a favorable impression on your girlfriend.

❑ Her children will regard you as a trustworthy adult in their lives.

❑ Her children's initial reactions to you will remain unchanged throughout the length of your relationship to her.

❑ Your ex-wife won't care about the new woman in your life.

❑ Your ex-wife will approve of the parenting style of your girlfriend.

If your kids and her kids don't get along, don't panic. Over time, the situation may greatly improve. There is no rule that says they have to like each other, much less love each other. Don't be angry with your kids if they complain about your girlfriend or her kids. If you feel, though, that they have some legitimate complaints, then take those up privately with your girlfriend. This is a good test of how well the two of you can work through problems if the relationship were to become more permanent. On the other hand, be open to her feedback about your children. Although you may think you have perfectly well-adjusted little angels, she may have different ideas.

Many new relationships break up over the issue of accepting the other person's children. It is difficult to balance supporting your partner's suggestions and criticisms of your kids with continuing your role as the primary advocate for your children. You neither want to give up your special relationship with your kids nor ignore the concerns of your girlfriend. One thing, for sure: don't turn over the parenting to her. It is a recipe for disaster because it gives the children a ready tool to cause problems between her and you, and they often would like to cause exactly that. No matter how busy you are, create time for you to interact with your children without the presence of your girlfriend or her kids. This is the best way to both preserve and enhance your relationship with them as well as to limit their conflict with your girlfriend.

Q: How do I tell the ex about my new love? Or do I?

A: This is a tricky one. Learning that an ex is going to marry again is often a hard realization. Any illusions that either of you held that you might get back together...some day... are clearly dashed by this new development. The news of a new romance sometimes results in renewed "guerrilla warfare." She might become more demanding and irritable, especially if she fears that you will be lavishing more of your attention and money on the new wife's children.

As always, we are advocates of honesty. It is better in our estimation that she learns about the relationship from you than from others. Most of us want to hear such news directly from the source, not "second hand." It can be particularly problematic if your ex learns about the relationship from the children. This puts the children in an awkward position. They may want to feel happy for you, but to do so will probably feel like they are being unfair to Mom. It is not good for the kids to be the keeper of this "secret."

Ideally, you should tell your ex-wife about your new relationship after you have become engaged to marry. It is not necessary and is usually inappropriate to tell your ex about girlfriends that you may have had. When your relationship becomes a more committed one, though, particularly when you will be living with someone new or will be re-marrying, then it is generally best to inform your ex. To our minds, this is essential when there are children involved. After all, there will now be a new adult in the kids' lives. In addition to the psychological impact of this information, your change in status may also affect terms of the divorce such as custody, child support, and alimony. If you have no children, informing your ex-wife of your new status is less imperative. Nonetheless, we believe that it is still good form.

Q: Her ex wants to meet with me. What do I do?

A: Step one is, of course, to talk to her about it. That may seem self-evident to you, but some guys hesitate to tell her figuring that:

❏ Her knowledge that you will be talking to her ex will just upset her and/or

❏ Maybe her ex has some big secret to tell me about her so I have to hide that knowledge.

No matter how reasonable it seems to keep this contact secret, it's a bad idea. Consult with her about why she thinks he wants to meet with you. If you want to meet with him, be prepared to explain this to her. If she objects to such a meeting, you can at least talk about what she fears will happen. After this discussion, you can make your decision. The conversation with her is probably more informative than whatever her ex will tell you.

He may have some "dirt" on her that you might want to know, but you must acknowledge that he is hardly an unbiased source of information. If you do meet with him, begin by informing him that you will discuss his comments with her. At least you will get more than one perspective on the matter.

It is also possible that he is "checking you out." This may be particularly true if you are going to be living with his children. He may want to know the person who will be participating in the raising of the kids. It may be possible for the two of you to become collaborative partners in "fathering." Often, the two men will get along better with each other than the exes do. If you can work with him, it may improve the situation for the children, especially if their parents were fighting before you came on the scene. You may become a moderating force to reduce conflict between your girlfriend and her ex.

CHAPTER 16

"Marriage is a great institution, but I'm not ready for an institution yet."

—Mae West

RE-MARRIAGE

We will now provide a few pointers for you when you are marrying again, whether it is for a second, third, or whatever time. Although every new marriage has some predictable challenges, couples face unique issues when one or both have been married before.

Q: What are the chances that I will remarry?

A: Within two years of divorce, 80% of men remarry. Within five years of divorce, 75% of women have remarried. Perhaps even more surprising is the finding that within only one year of divorce 50% of men have remarried! In short, the chances are very good that you will remarry.[1] This is true even if at the time of divorce you thought, "I'll never do that (marry) again!"

The combination of longer life spans for women and the premium our society puts on physical attractiveness are major reasons that fewer women than men remarry, women are slower to remarry, and men generally marry younger women.

Q: Marriage is supposed to be joyful, right?

A: When most of us think of marriage, we think of a happy occasion, two people coming together because of the love they share for each other. What could be better? Yet, when you marry for a second time, there is invariably a somewhat different atmosphere. Second (or third) marriages have an element of loss built into them. Either there has been a divorce, or there has been a death. The specter of the loss infuses the marriage, reminding the couple that marriages end. After all, *every* marriage ends in either death or divorce. If children were born of the previous marriage, they are reminded—and hence will remind you—of the family that is no more, of the parents that are now permanently separated. Any vestiges of hope the children had that Mom and Dad would get back together are now shattered.

Q: My ex-wife and I are getting back together. We're talking about getting married again. What would you advise?

A: First of all, a few things to think about:

- ❏ You have already been unhappy enough in this relationship to divorce once.

- ❏ The statistics show that second (and third) marriages are more likely to divorce than first marriages.

- ❏ Don't let either your passion for each other or your hurt propel you quickly into renewing your marriage. Go slowly.

- ❏ Don't jump back into living together.

- ❏ Forgo telling friends, family, or your children that you are getting back together until you are sure that you are.

- ❏ Don't let sexual attraction do your thinking for you.

- ❏ Avoid getting back together "for the kids." It usually will not last.

- ❏ Get clear about why your first marriage failed.

- ❏ Enter into joint counseling before you go too far with your plans.

- ❏ Think about how you will deal with other relationships that the two of you have had during the period of your divorce.

- ❏ Consider how the children will react to the two of you resuming your lives together.

❏ Remember that you will probably have friends who will think that it is a bad idea for the two of you to get back together.

Q: What kind of wedding do I/we want?

A: Welcome to the first real crisis in your relationship!

Q: Speaking of weddings, I'm not sure what to do. I had a huge wedding my first go-around. What do I do now?

A: Here are some of our premises about the matter:

❏ The wedding ceremony *is* important—if not to you, then to her.

❏ Your success/difficulty in working through this issue is an indicator of how you two will deal with other issues in the marriage.

❏ Disappointments about the wedding and the honeymoon are often the subject of subsequent continuing arguments later in the marriage.

❏ A person's memories of the wedding are a good predictor of whether the marriage will last. This appears to be particularly the case for husbands.[2]

❏ Planning a wedding has every element needed to make it a big problem: symbolism, involvement of the in-laws, budgetary constraints, and fantasies.

Long white bridal gowns, bridesmaids dressed in organdy, children scattering rose petals—fantasy images of weddings. Maybe that is not what you had in mind, especially if you were married before and already had the traditional ceremony. However, if your bride-to-be has not had that experience, she may desire the big event. Or maybe her first wedding was a humble event, and she always regretted it. Perhaps she will be happy with a small, private wedding, but more than one marriage has started on shaky ground because she wanted one kind of wedding, and he insisted on another. Although she may concede on the point now, wives often bring it up later as a major disappointment. In short, if you (or she) begin the marriage with a sour taste in your mouth, you are likely to end the marriage in the same way.

The details of wedding ceremonies and their associated events (e.g., honeymoons, receptions) are symbolically important as you begin a new marriage. Obviously, there is no right way to get married, but every choice that you make in this regard has significance for both you and her, as well as to both of your families. For example, if you decide to have a private wedding without family members present, what will the impact be on your future relationships with your two families?

> *Steven and Crystal had a "destination wedding," an elaborate affair at a resort located in an exotic location. Complicated to arrange, for sure, and definitely not cheap. Crystal had always fantasized about the wedding she had never had. The couple paid the travel costs for the immediate family members, but it was an expensive proposition. Other guests had to travel a long way and pay for most of the costs of the accommodations. A number of family members and friends could not attend the ceremony because of the distances and expenses involved. Only a few of the couple's most cherished relations witnessed the unusual and spectacular ceremony. From the beginning, the couple felt somewhat isolated and unsupported. Later, they both complained that their marriage had not been fully accepted by their families. Yet, the nature of the wedding ceremony contributed to that very feeling.*

In general, women seem to focus more on the details of the ceremony than do men, especially when dealing with the first marriage. Even when there has been a prior marriage, they may have unfulfilled fantasies or aspirations of an ideal type of wedding. Similarly, some men have strong opinions about the ceremony or other events associated with practical matters such as expense or location, although a few men also may have dreams of the "perfect wedding."

Too frequently, men are reluctant to express their wants or fears about the wedding, resulting in ongoing resentments. The antidote is for each of you to be clear about what will important for both in the wedding plans.

We have seen guys who left the planning all up to the woman, but then they were shocked by the cost. (Divorce is sometimes less expensive than the wedding ceremony!) This became the seed of continuing discord in the marriage as the men suspected their new wives of being irresponsible with money. This is not the time to hold back on your opinions and needs. To do so courts future disaster as you look back ruefully about what you didn't say. It is equally important to sensitively listen to what she wants and needs. Preferences about weddings tend to be emotionally driven. Consequently you fight about the issues long after the rice has been swept up.

We have also seen women who began their marriages with the belief that they were not valued by their new husbands because of his insistence on making the ceremony more simple. We frequently hear comments like, "When he married his first wife, the wedding was a big deal, but with me it was an afterthought."

Once again, we would emphasize the importance of open discussion between the two of you to prevent problems in this area. The specifics of the wedding tend to be well remembered. If she is going to be disappointed that you did not marry in a church, for example, now is the time to get that resolved. If you deeply desire a wedding on your grandfather's farm, it is important for you to be clear about the matters that concern you. Quite often, your initial concerns will be completely different from hers, but further conversation may uncover not-so-dissimilar concerns.

Q: What are typical wedding issues I should be aware of for my second marriage?

A: Here is list of some of the more common issues that arise about weddings (especially for couples where one or both have been married previously):

❑ Who will pay for what?

In our society, the tradition is for the bride's family to pay for the wedding and the groom to pay for the honeymoon. These traditions are not always followed, but they are a beginning place for dialogues about how the couple will proceed in the matter. These traditions arose, though, when people got married once—literally for better or worse. Now when divorce and remarriage are common, what are the "new rules" for paying for the wedding? You could ask Ms. Manners for some ideas, but our experience is that there are no generally agreed upon ways to handle this thorny issue. Couples have to hash out how they will handle the matter.

This issue can raise anxiety for all parties. Her family may fear being expected to pay, but they may be reluctant to address the issue directly. On the other hand, if your bride expects you to pay for everything, you may resent her assumption.

Many couples elect to split these costs in some fashion, sometimes without any parental contribution. If you are going to pay for part or all of the wedding, this is a great time to practice the skills of setting a budget and making joint financial decisions. Don't wait until after marriage to learn if you can master these critical marital skills. If each of you is going pay for part of the wedding, have a frank discussion about how much each of you will pay. For example, is each of you contributing equal amounts or does the person who earns more money contribute more? The difficult issues of money, bills, and budgeting do not become simpler after you say "I do." Start your marriage on the right foot by openly communicating about money matters and by making the decisions jointly rather than unilaterally.

❏ Will it be a religious or civil ceremony?

The religious beliefs of both of you and your families may immediately be put to the test, especially if you disagree on this area. The goal here is to prevent resentments later on in the marriage. The ultimate decision should be one that each of you will support. There should not be recriminations about the choice later.

❏ Where will we have the ceremony?

Maybe she has always dreamed of a big church wedding, but you have already done that. Or maybe she envisioned a romantic ceremony on the beach, but who will pay for all the travel costs? Religious, cultural, and personal expectations may all affect this decision.

❏ Will the kids be involved in the ceremony?

Couples often want to involve the children, especially young ones, in the wedding in some way. However, your (or her) children may choose to act up at the wedding.

❑ Who will be invited to the wedding?

This is always an issue for couples, but it takes on new complications in second marriages because of such factors as disapproving relatives and friends who also knew the ex-spouse.

❑ What about the ring?

Is the ring you bought her inferior to the one you gave your first wife? What happened to the ring (or stone in the ring) you gave your ex-wife? Will you both wear rings?

❑ What about the honeymoon?

She may be hoping for an exotic get-away, but you may feel that it would take you away from work for too long. Furthermore, who would watch the kids?

Q: Maybe we should just elope?

A: After the previous discussion, you may be ready to just elope and avoid the whole mess. We are skeptical, though, that the avoidance of the ceremony will save you from "the grease" or keep you from "getting fried." It may well communicate to her that you are not willing to "invest" in her, either publicly or financially. She may voice, "Are you ashamed of me?" Of course, you will probably save money in the short run, but if she winds up disappointed, it may not be worth it.

Elopement has traditionally been the choice of couples when the parents disagreed with the union. In this kind of elopement, at least the couple begins the marriage with an "us against the world" mentality. That can actually help, especially in the beginning because it pulls the couple into a closer alliance, leaning more on each other. However, if elopement is contemplated as a "cost-saving measure," it probably will have a negative impact.

We think there is value in having a public ceremony and involving family members. Public ceremony signifies both to the families and to the couple that there has been a major change in relationships and priorities. More private marriage arrangements often lack the public statement. Yes, it is more complicated to have others attend, but it does not necessarily have to be more expensive. You can still have a simple wedding and invite key family members. Asking them to attend is like sending out a proclamation to all of the important people in your "kingdom." The main point is that it communicates to all parties that there is a new, permanent, and very significant commitment. It also encourages the families to recognize the new reality.

Q: Should we include the children in our wedding ceremony?

A: It has become fashionable to include his/her children in the ceremonies when parents marry again. There is merit to this idea. It indicates that you are creating a new family and that the children are part of that new creation. Sometimes, special vows are written that include commitments to the children as well as to the spouse. Rings or other similar gifts may be given to the children to commemorate the occasion and the new relationships. These are all nice ideas, and we commend them to you. However, they do not mean that the children are going to embrace the new arrangement. After all, most people exchange rings, make vows, and have a solemn ceremony when they marry, but sometimes they break those vows.

We would recommend that you and your intended have a long talk about how—and whether—to include your children in the ceremony. If you fear that your kids will act up or cause a scene, they probably will. Don't count on them being well behaved. Anticipate how they might act up and plan accordingly. Avoid starting the marriage having to make up for children misbehaving on your "special day."

Sara and Steve took great pains to include the children in their wedding ceremony. They carefully planned a role for each of their respective children. The affair seemed to go off without a hitch. After the ceremony, though, the couple was surprised to find some colorful comments in their wedding registration book, courtesy of the unhappy children.

Q: What kind of rings should we get?

A: As we briefly touched on previously, rings can be a major source of controversy in any wedding. Maybe she wants the "big rock" to show off to her friends, or maybe you want her to have it. It's probably not worth it, though, if you are going to put yourself in debt to the jewelry store to buy it for her. Nor is it worth it if she is going to be "in debt" to you because you resent how much it cost. Better to get something a little more humble than to risk either of those outcomes. Perhaps for yourself you prefer a simple ring, or maybe you don't want to wear a ring at all. On the other hand, you not wearing a ring sometimes makes the new bride feel that you are not all that serious about the marriage. Your best bet is to discuss these issues openly and honestly with her. If you can't talk about the issue of the wedding rings effectively, you are surely not going to be able to talk about later issues with any greater success. Talking about this subject is actually a great way to practice having dialogue about sensitive issues, a critical skill for a successful marriage.

Q: What if my grown kids don't like her?

A: Even your "adult children" may resent or actively dislike your new woman. We have seen this even among 35 year-old "children." In our experience, many people have a hard time seeing Dad with another woman, regardless of the circumstances. This often simply reflects your offspring's affection and loyalty for their mother. Of course, it is less likely to be a problem if you didn't divorce (or bury) Mom last month and introduce them to your new girlfriend this month. If your children feel that you haven't waited an "appropriate" amount of time before engaging in a new romantic relationship, they are far more likely to be angry with you and her.

Another factor will be their assessment of the appropriateness of your choice. If you are marrying someone only marginally older than them, they are more likely to troubled by your decision. After all, how they will relate to their new stepmother whom they view as more of a peer? Often their feelings about this matter are mainly directed at your new wife. Welcome to the family, honey?! She may be a wonderful person, but they just can't see it. They might get over it in time, but don't count on it. Often, their hard feelings towards her (and you) persist, and they may view whatever efforts you might make to repair this rupture with a jaundiced eye. This does not mean that you should let your kids pass judgment over whom you should marry, but it does mean that you should anticipate it might be an area of difficulty.

We would recommend that before you get too far in your plans for marriage you meet privately with your kids and talk with them about your new relationship. Ask them about their feelings regarding your dating and now having a serious, new relationship. How do they feel about the prospect of you marrying again? How do they feel about your new woman? Don't indicate to them that they have veto power, but rather let them know that their opinions are important to you. It is like when you first planned to get married and (hopefully you did this) went home to tell your parents about it. You hoped that they would approve of your choice of a bride. You sought their blessing, but even if they didn't give it, it was still your call as to whether or not to marry. With the parents' blessing, though, a marriage starts off on a much better footing. Similarly, you should seek your kids' "blessing" without giving them the right to decide for you.

You should also indicate to the kids what you expect from them. For example, even if they don't like your fiancée, you should ask that they be respectful and kind to her and that any anger they have about this be directed more appropriately at you. As you probably learned long ago, it is OK for kids and parents to be angry at each other if at the end of the day they still maintain that bond of love. Finally, reassure them that you will always care for them. This is especially important if you will have more children with your new wife or her children will be living in the home with you.

Arnold, a man in his early 30's, came to see us soon after his father began dating a woman who herself was in her 30's. Arnold felt that his father had begun dating too soon after the parents' divorce, and objected vociferously to his father's choice of girlfriend. The son felt that his father choosing to date such a young woman was not only inappropriate, but also insulting to his ex-wife, Arnold's mother. It seemed to Arnold that his father had simply discarded an older woman and replaced her with a newer model. Eventually, the father not only married the new woman but also had two more children by her. This added insult to injury from the son's point of view. Arnold broke off his relationship with his father and had nothing to do with either his new "step-mother" (a woman of his age) nor his stepsiblings. Was this an overreaction on Arnold's part? Maybe. Arnold knew he did not hold veto power over his father's relationship, but he couldn't get over how his father handled it. The result was a permanent rift between the father and son, which has impacted most of Arnold's adult life.

Q: What about the honeymoon?

A: It is interesting to see how many people forgo the traditional honeymoon. The honeymoon was invented to give the couple an initial period of privacy and relaxation away from the rest of the world, affording them the opportunity to really get to know each other and to form initial bonds. Today, though, most couples have already known each other for quite a while before the marriage. Indeed, many of them have been living together before marriage, so what is the point of having such a getaway? Why not wait to take a celebratory trip until it is more convenient or less expensive? We again remind you that there are no correct answers to these questions, but our goal is to help you consider the matter from new angles.

Couples who do not have a honeymoon sometimes regret it later. The woman, in particular, may complain that not enough was done to mark the special nature of the occasion. You are more likely to hear this kind of complaint if you have been a workaholic ever since the wedding day. Your new wife wants to know that you are going to prioritize her over your job, just as you are hoping she is going to put you ahead of her job or other aspects of her life (e.g., her parents). Furthermore, the honeymoon symbolizes the major transition in your lives that marriage entails, and it can be a major respite for the couple from the stress of the wedding plans and events. In general, we would encourage you to plan some sort of honeymoon together. You may wish to keep the costs down or to limit the length of time that you will be gone, but be sure that you are not communicating to her that she is not as important as your last wife or as your job.

Q: I don't think her family (parents, siblings, children) cares much for me. What can I do about that?

A: Earlier, we discussed how to handle things if your family, especially your children, don't like the idea of you getting married again. Now, in this scenario, we are looking at the marriage from the other end—her family's reaction to you.

Among the biggest mistakes to be made here is trying overly hard to fix the situation. It is quite natural for her family to be unsure about you, especially if this is not her first marriage either. If she was married before, the family may have been fond of their former son-in-law. They may even have been opposed to the divorce, wishing the couple would have stayed together. Then along comes you. You may seem to be an interloper, a "Johnny-come-lately." Even if her family agreed with the need for a divorce from her previous husband, they are likely to view you with skepticism. After all, her previous marriage didn't work out. This may lead them to be more guarded in their response to you.

Over time, you may be able to win their approval. The best thing you can do is to treat your wife with the love and care she deserves. If her family sees you doing that with consistency, they will become more accepting of the marriage and more positive about you. Ultimately, though, you don't have to please all of them, but you must be able to please your wife. So the worst thing you can do is to make enemies of her family. Don't expect, though, that she should intercede on your behalf with her family. It's your job to establish a relationship with them. It would be nice if you and her family "hit it off," but it is more realistic to aim for politeness and cordiality. Treat her family with friendliness and respect no matter how they treat you. In so doing, her only complaints about misbehavior would lie with her family, not with you.

Q: My ex-wife and I often struggled around money issues. How can I keep this from happening in my new marriage?

A: This is a good example of the type of issue that is different in a first marriage than in a later marriage. If a couple marries at a young age (e.g., in their twenties), they typically do not have much income or, for that matter, much in the way of bills. These young couples usually share a joint bank account and pool their financial resources.

When a couple marries later in life, the situation is often much more complex. There may be, for example, considerable debt that was acquired before the new partner came into the picture. Furthermore, the two persons may have been accustomed to managing their own bank accounts without the influence or participation of a second party. Frequently, these couples do better by maintaining individual accounts and each contributing to a third account to pay for shared expenses. The contribution by each party to this third account does not have to be equal, but it should reflect a sense of fairness. For example, if one of you makes twice as much as the other that person should contribute more to the joint "pot." At some point, it probably makes sense for the partners to be signatories on each other's account, but this is not essential in the beginning of the marriage. To insist on this early in the marriage potentially creates a difficult challenge to the level of trust. Trust cannot be assumed, but rather it must be earned over time and through experience, particularly true when it comes to money.

There must be a continuing dialogue between the two of you about how to deal with financial issues. Unfortunately, many couples avoid dealing with money because it is anxiety provoking to do so. You may vainly hope that she will deal with money matters in the same way as you would. Of course, your wife may be expecting the same thing, which invariably leads to conflict. We would recommend that a newly-married couple have regular joint financial meetings, at least twice a month. In these meetings, the couple should discuss financial concerns and plans, review bank statements, and jointly pay the bills.

Q: She wants kids. What if I'm not so sure?

A: Lots of guys get scared when the woman starts talking about having kids soon after they first get hitched. Hopefully, you talked about this issue long before you got married, but the tempo and the tenor of this conversation often change after marriage. This is particularly likely to happen if she never had kids and now wants them or she is feeling the biological clock ticking.

Of course, you may want kids, too. Even so, you might want to wait until at least the rice from the ceremony sprouts, while she might be hoping to conceive on her wedding night. Many men agree to the idea of kids "in theory," but when she is pushing to get pregnant as soon as possible, they may begin to rethink the whole idea. If you become reluctant, she is apt to react negatively, seeing it as a betrayal (i.e., "But you promised!"). We have seen a number of women in this situation who bluntly say that they would never have married the man if he was not ready and willing to have a child.

Perhaps you already have other children, and you don't want any more. Or you may have decided you just don't want children. These are certainly acceptable decisions, but if you have indicated that you will have a child with her and now renege, you are likely to have read this book a second time. Often, the issue of whether or not to have kids breaks up marriages.

You may be more successful asking her to delay getting pregnant until after you have been married for a time. Even asking for such a delay, though, can create suspicion, anger, and mistrust if she has her heart set on getting pregnant right away. Clearly, the best course of action is to come to an agreement about this subject long before you walk down the aisle. If you don't, you are taking a dangerous risk with the marriage. Most certainly, don't succumb to the pressure of saying "yes" to having a child unless you are willing to stick by that decision.

Q: She wants kids, but I had a vasectomy. Now what?

A: On several occasions, we have seen men who get married after having had a vasectomy. Typically, these men had decided that they did not want any more children, and they took the prudent step of permanent birth control. However, some of these same guys fall for a woman (often a younger woman) who insists that she can only marry if they will have children. Driving down the freeway we have seen numerous billboards advertising "Vasectomy Reversals," suggesting that this dilemma is common.

Getting a vasectomy in the first place is a major step. Lots of guys faint from the tension at the thought of someone with a knife near their privates. You may get just as nervous thinking about reversing the whole deal. Men often promise to get the reversal, but then they are slow to actually do it. We have seen several couples where failure to reverse the vasectomy became the beginning of the end of the marriage.

As we suggested previously, don't promise something you are not prepared to do. Don't tell her you will reverse the vasectomy unless you are truly ready to do so. To promise this in the heat of passion or in a moment of weakness is a bad idea. You might even think about getting the reversal *before* you marry. That's a better self-test of your willingness to go through with it. She will also see this as a testament of your commitment to her.

Even if you are willing to have a vasectomy reversed, it does not mean it *can* be reversed. The success of the reversal depends upon: a) the method used by the original surgeon to sever the vas deferens (either cutting or burning/cauterizing) and b) the new surgeon's skill in reconnecting the vas. Even with the scientific/medical advances today, reversal surgery should not be considered a "sure shot."

> *Ronaldo promised his young bride that he would reverse his vasectomy soon after their marriage. Yet, once they exchanged wedding vows, he kept putting off the appointment to see his urologist. Somehow, he never got around to having it done. He already had two college-age children, so perhaps he was hesitant to have more kids. In any case, it remained a big disappointment to his wife. Although the marriage continued on for a number of years, she eventually left him, just as her "biological alarm" was going off for the last time (i.e., she was nearing 40).*

Q: What about step-parenting (a.k.a. blended families)?

A: Most children from divorced families will eventually experience living in a step (or blended) family since their parents are likely to remarry. We tend to think of families as being born out of love, youth, and excitement. The advent of children is usually considered a happy time. Step-families, though, are always born of loss from either divorce or death.[4] The children in step-families may feel that they are more of a burden than a source of joy. Furthermore, children often have difficulty accepting a step-parent who, to them, may seem like an interloper. The child frequently feels that it would be disloyal to the biological parent to accept the step-parent.

Being the parent to your biological child is hard enough, but the role of the step-parent is even harder to play. Most of us tend to think that being a step-father is pretty much the same as being a biological father. However, the roles are really quite different. Unfortunately, there are not very many popularly-accepted models of an effective step-father. Can you think of an example from popular movies, television, or books of a successful step-father? Indeed, the step-fathers from popular media are usually either lecherous, evil bad guys, or just nincompoops.

One model you might consider emulating is that of a "good uncle." An effective uncle is a man that you can count on to give sound advice or take you to the ballgame, but he is careful not to overstep his bounds. He is reluctant to give unsolicited guidance, and he doesn't forget that he is not really the parent. He cares about his nephews and nieces, but he knows they don't know him as well as their parents. He doesn't try to supplant or replace the parents, but he provides another, often more objective, adult viewpoint. He sets some limits on behavior, but the uncle knows he is not in charge of discipline. A good uncle can be an inspiration and a mentor, but he is humble in his role, rejoicing in the strengths and successes of the child, less condemning of the child's weaknesses.

Frequently, step-parents are lulled into complacency when entering into a new relationship. The children may have liked you before you moved in with or married their mother. Now, though, they may have a changed attitude, seeing you as more of a threat, especially if you have tried to discipline them. As long as you are just a playmate, you pose little risk. In fact, they may think you are pretty cool since you like to do "guy stuff." Tell them to do their homework, though, and they may turn a cold shoulder. Often there is also an implicit—or sometimes explicit—expectation by the adults that the children will simply accept their new step-parent. If the children do not accept the stepparent, the adults frequently blame each other rather than seeing this is to be expected developmentally.

Second marriage vows.

Complicating the situation is the fact that many women really want the man to take on a parental role. Women often feel overwhelmed with the responsibility and difficulty of being a single parent. These women may anticipate you lessening their burden as a parent and actively encourage you to take on the role of "Dad." This is usually a trap. The kids may not respond well to the idea, and, quite frequently, she herself may have second thoughts about it later. When you parent in a way that is different from hers, she may decide that you were too strict or that you don't understand her children. The kids may point out that you are not the "real" father.

Of course, being a step-mother is not easy either. After all, how many evil stepmothers are in our popular culture? Remember the story of Cinderella? So, if you have children and remarry, remember that your bride will probably have trouble being a stepmother, too.

Q: Where should we live—her house, my house, or our house?

A: Many couples struggle with the housing issue. Often the decision is ultimately made based on economic or practical issues, but psychological issues should also be considered. If you move into her house, will you feel that you are a "second class citizen"? If she moves into yours, where will her furniture go?

When feasible, we believe that it works best to live in a home that is neither yours nor hers. You may love your old home, but hopefully you love your new wife more. Moving into a new place (apartment, townhouse, 3-2-2, mansion, or mobile home) together is an important symbol of starting your lives fresh, leaving past entanglements behind. When this is not possible, the person who is moving in should be made to feel not only welcome, but a co-owner. Rather than making room for her "stuff," make plans with her how to incorporate her possessions into the household.

Q: What about our "stuff"?

A: As adults we all have possessions that are important to us. Some of them have literal value like that autographed basketball jersey. Others have sentimental value like her grandmother's love seat. When couples meld, each person will want to keep their "stuff." Perhaps this sounds trivial. Who really cares about "stuff"? Pay attention here. Everybody cares about *their* stuff, but we all wonder about the *other person's* stuff. Some of us are greater pack rats than others, but all of us have things—whether they are art or memorabilia—that define our lives. Maybe "primitive" societies don't have this problem so much

("Yes, honey, you can keep your wildebeest jawbone") but American families tend to have lots of "stuff." You are likely to encounter the "stuff problem."

Personality, family, cultural, and gender differences come to play in making decisions about what to do with our "stuff." Do we keep her antique Chinese urn in the living room? What about my baseball card collection? Some couples decide to have certain rooms or areas of the house for each person (e.g., you get to put your sports mementos in the den, but she gets to decide about the living room). Other areas (e.g. the kitchen) might be jointly planned. The main thing here is not to decide what your partner should do. Don't persuade her to get rid of her possessions. Let that be her decision. A better plan is to describe the problem and ask for her ideas (e.g., "We've both got master bedroom suites. How do you think we should handle that?"). In addition, don't be overly attached to your own things, particularly those that have little sentimental value for you. Do you really care about your refrigerator? You might suggest the use of a self-storage unit or moving something into the garage or attic; however, for the most part, that means you will never actually see or use it. Probably it is better to have a series of conversations about what to retain and what to take to Goodwill. Just avoid deciding for her; decide about *your own* things.

There are some things, though, that tend to be more problematic. The most common objection is about "the bed." You know, the one in which you and your ex-wife slept? Or the one in which she made love to her last boyfriend. If you are going to buy one new thing to start your new household, it probably should be a bed. Start with clean sheets and a new bed.

Q: She's a career woman. Will she get over that?

A: Maybe you have expected a traditional arrangement where you are the breadwinner, and she will stay home with the kids. However, many women today are also career-oriented. Guys sometimes expect that their wives will be willing to give all that up, especially if he brings in enough income for the family. Such expectations often lead to marital discord. She may have always wished that she could stay home to raise the babies, but she may also aspire to be the CEO of a Fortune

500 company. You can garner a good clue to what she really wants by looking at her history before you. If she has been a hard-charging corporate exec prior to meeting you, that is probably how she will want to be in the future. Maybe she is burned out by the corporate rat race, but you are best off not making that assumption. If she suggests she is ready to be Susie Homemaker, be skeptical. Ask her if she is ready to stay home with the young 'uns and give up the corner office. Lots of women become dissatisfied with this choice even after initially opting for it. It might be possible to forge some middle position where she could try it for a while without committing to it permanently.

Husband Gets Lesson on How to Be Single[5]

When Roslan Ngah took a second wife, he might have wondered if she would get along with his first. It turns out they got on so well they decided to leave him at the same time. Faced with their united stand, the 44-year-old Malaysian Muslim divorced both wives Tuesday in an Islamic Shariah Court held in northeastern Terengganu state, a lawyer said Wednesday. The Star daily quoted Roslan as saying that he was aware his two wives had become close over the years. "They are like good friends but I never imagined that both of them had collectively decided to divorce me," Roslan was quoted him as saying. "I never expected our marriages to end in this manner."

"Yesterday is history, tomorrow is a mystery, and today is a gift; that's why they call it the present."
—*Eleanor Roosevelt*

EPILOGUE

Robert Sternberg, who devoted his entire professional life to researching love in relationships, identified three components to love: Intimacy, Commitment, and Passion. In his *Triangular Theory Of Love*,[1] Consummate Love is that relationship in which all three sides of the triangle are balanced, forming an equilateral triangle. Consummate Love, he said, is the cultural ideal. Many relationships, indeed many marriages, are out of balance or are characterized by one of the three components. Sternberg described eight types of relationships based on these three components:

❑ *Non-love.* None of the three components (Intimacy, Commitment, and Passion) is present.

❑ *Friendship.* Only Intimacy is present.

❑ *Infatuation.* Only Passion is present.

❑ *Empty Love.* Only Commitment is present.

❑ *Romantic Love.* Passion and Intimacy are present.

- ❏ *Fatuous Love.* Passion and Commitment without Intimacy.

- ❏ *Companionate Love.* Intimacy and Commitment, but without Passion.

- ❏ *Consummate Love.* Having all three components: Intimacy, Commitment, and Passion.

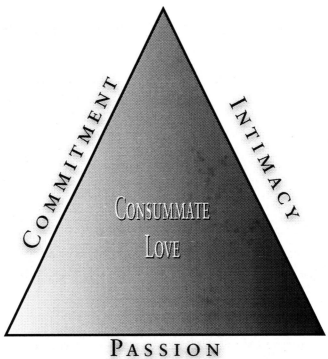

Steinberg's cultural ideal: Consummate Love composed of Intimacy, Cmmitment, & Passion

As marital relationships progress, various components dominate at various stages. Early in a relationship, Passion is high but Intimacy and Commitment are low. Later in the life of a relationship, Commitment is generally the strongest of the three components, followed by Intimacy, and finally by Passion.

As you view your last marriage and your present or future relationships, consider where your relationship falls in terms of Sternberg's categories. It is likely, for example, that in a new relationship you will feel a lot of passion. Passion may fade over time, but this doesn't mean that something is wrong, any more than gray hair signals something being wrong. It is simply a sign of maturation and normal development. Or your relationship may lack Intimacy: you may may still be sexual but you no longer confide in each other and are no longer "best friends." Or you may have grown older together, seeing the grandkids, maintaining your properties, keeping up with family obligations, in which Commitment is high but there little in the way of Passion or Intimacy.

Achieving and maintaining Consummate Love is a "tall order." We would argue, though, that striving to keep *Intimacy*, *Commitment*, and *Passion* in your relationship is a goal worthy of your efforts.

It is our hope you can use the Q&A conversations in this book to prepare yourself to take the steps toward a more fulfilling future. You may have been focusing, though, on simply "getting through" the divorce.

There truly is "more" to life after divorce. While it may take a while to realize this experience for yourself, and to re-orient yourself in your new search, we remind you of the following points as aids in this process:

❑ Clean yourself out of anger.

❑ Prepare yourself to be the person you'd like her to meet.

❑ Get out into settings where she might meet you.

❑ See the process as a learning experience.

❑ Don't be too hard on yourself if you're not a "finished product" on the first date.

❑ Keep your sense of humor throughout.

Remember that you are coping with divorce, what some professionals have labeled as one of the most stress-filled times, short of death of a spouse or a child, that you can experience. Keeping your sense of humor means sometimes distancing yourself from problems rather than letting them get right in your face, and remembering that things "could be worse."

NOTES

CHAPTER 1

[1](p. 17, *divorce statistics*) For one of the most-cited reports of divorce statistics and the longitudinal effects of divorce, see Constance Ahrons' The Good Divorce (1994).

[2](p. 18, *female complaints*). For an elabortion of why women quit complaining but don't change their mind, see J. Gottman & N. Silver's *The Seven Principles for Making Marriage Work* (1999).

[3](p. 20, *dignity and honesty*). See Robin Green's *Divorce: When It's the Only Answer* (2005), p. 45. It's refreshing to find a lawyer emphasizing dignity and respect in the divorce process.

[4](p. 21, *second thoughts*). Despite his own personal struggles, Dr. Phil (McGraw) offers some pretty good, guy-friendly advice on how to reconnect with your partner if you're having second thoughts about leaving, in his *Relationship Rescue* (2000).

[5](p. 23, *marriage counseling*). For more interesting findings on men's perspective on marriage counseling, emotions, and commitment, see Neil Chethik's (2006) *VoiceMale: What Husbands Really Think about their Marriages, their Wives, Sex, Housework, and Commitment.*

CHAPTER 2

[1](p. 43-47, *things to do when you separate*). Used by permission. (From Robin Green's (2005) *Divorce: When It's the Only Answer*, pp. 23-26.

CHAPTER 3

[1](p. 53, *divorce-related emotional problems*). For a closer look at research on children's adjustment to divorce, check out J. Kelly's (2000) *Children's Adjustment in Conflicted Marriages and Divorce: A Decade of Research* for emotional issues; p. Amato's (2000) *The Consequences of Divorce for Adults and Children* and S. McLanahan's (1999) *Father Absence*

and Children's Welfare for financial issues; and R. Emery's (2004) *The Truth about Children and Divorce* for issues related to marital conflict.

[2](p. 54, *psychological hardiness and divorce*). Despite the popular focus on psychological hardiness and divorce, R. Emery (2004) articulates in compelling fashion the profound impact divorce has on children across the board.

[3](p. 55, *parental conflict and damage on kids*). The evidence on the negative impact of parental conflict on children is insurmountable. For exceptionally clear presentations, check out (Amato and Keith, 1991; Cummings and Davies, 1994; Cummings and O'Reilly, 1997; Kelly, 2000; Lamb and Kelly, 2001).

[4](p. 56, *fighting a lot*). If you have any doubt about the devastating role of parental conflict during divorce, take a look at Constance Ahron's highly readable and frequently cited work: with R. Rodgers (1987) *Divorced Families: Meeting the Challenge of Divorce and Remarriage* and (1994) *The Good Divorce: Keeping Your Family Together When Your Marriage Comes Apart.*

Chapter 4

[1](p. 64-65, *example of traditional divorce process*). Modified by permission from Peter Sperling's (2003) *Selecting Your Divorce Lawyer,* pp. 22-27.

[2](p. 66, *free legal representation*). As an example of what's available in Texas for those with minimal resources, check out R. Lipman's (2007) column in the Houston Chronicle, *Divorce Still Possible, Even If Money's Tight.*

[3](pp. 71-71, *how to select an attorney*). Sperling (2003) goes into a lot more detail about selecting an attorney. A good place to start if you're looking for legal representation.

[4](p. 72, *how to talk to partner*). S. Margulies, in *A Man's Guide to A Civilized Divorce* (2004), provides more extensive suggestions —all quite useful—on how to handle the discussion with your wife about divorce.

[5](p. 76-77, *sample budget form*). Sample budget form is adapted with permission from S. Margulies (2004) *A Man's Guide to A Civilized Divorce*, pp. 228-229.

[6](p. 83, *collaborative divorce*). An excellent place to start, if you're interested in collaborative divorce, is J. Brumley's (2004) *Divorce without Disaster*. The book is specific to Texas, but the same principles apply in most states.

[7](p. 86, *counseling for men*). If you're looking for a therapist who is competent to handle men's issues, they should be familiar with some of the following work: F. Rabinowitz and S. Cochran's (2002) *Deepening Psychotherapy with Men*; G. Brooks & G. Good' (2001) *The New Handbook of Psychotherapy and Counseling with Men*; M. Englar-Carlson & M. Stevens' (2006) *In the Room with Men*;.J. Vessey & K. Howard's (1993) *Who Seeks Psychotherapy?* (1993).

[8](p. 86, *men and therapy*). See the same ones?

[9](pp. 87-88, *community property*). For a more detailed look at issues related to community property, see R. Green's (2005) *Divorce: When It's the Only Answer*. Though oriented towards Texas, it's a good, easy-to-read description of the issues.

CHAPTER 5

[1](p. 100, *divorce remedy*). Michelle Weiner-Davis (2001) provides a highly readable account of divorce in today's culture in *The Divorce Remedy*.

[2](p. 104, *divorce ceremony*). Phil and Barb Penningroth (2001) wrote a book chronicling their own divorce ceremony as well as describing ways for other couples to plan such an event, *A Healing Divorce: Transforming the End of Your Relationship with Ritual and Ceremony*. You can also visit their Web site on the topic: http://www.healingdivorce.com. Mary Ann Fergus also described divorce ceremonies in her column in the Houston Chroncle, *A Different Kind of Divorce* [Mary Ann Fergus, A Different Kind of Divorce: As Ex-Spouses Focus on Happy Children "Happily Ever After" is What Happens When a Marriage Ends, Houston Chron., Feb. 10, 2001, Lifestyle, at 1, available at 2002 WL 3240754].

[3](p. 105, *emotional behavior with men and women*). For a fascinating look at male-female differences and similarities in emotional responsivity, see Wester et al.'s (2002) *Sex Differences in Emotion*.

[4](p. 105, *normative male alexythymia*). R. Levant (1995), who has written extensively about men's issues, coined the term "normative male alexythymia" to refer to male difficulty with word search when describing feelings, *Toward the Reconstruction of Masculinity*.

[5](p. 109, *parental alienation syndrome*). "Parent alienation syndrome" was first described by R. Gardner (1998), in *The Parental Alienation Syndrome*.

[6](p. 111, *Darnall's parental alienation syndrome checklist*). The parental alienation syndrome checklist is adapted with permission from Darnall's (1998) *Divorce Casualties: Protecting Your Children from Parental Alienation*.

[7](p. 118, *Texas Family Code*). Most states now post the state family code online, but it's not always easy to locate. For an excellent starting place, see J.R. Hays, E. Sutter, & R. McPherson's (2005) *Texas Law and the Practice of Psychology* or (2006) *Texas Law for the Social Worker*.

CHAPTER 6

[1](p. 119, *collaborative law guidelines*). For more information on collaborative initiatives, see the Collaborative Law Institute's (2006) *The Collaborative Professional's Guide to Developing a Parenting Plan*.

[2](p. 120, *The Good Divorce*). Constance Ahrons (1994), in her classic *The Good Divorce*, describes four styles of parenting relationships post-divorce.

[3](p. 121, *parenting duties and time with kids*). Women still perform more parenting duties than do the men, despite popularization of other ideals. [See Hawkins, Marshall, & Allen (1998), *The Orientation toward Domestic Labor Questionnaire*; A. Hochschild (1997), *The Second Shift*].

CHAPTER 7

[1](p. 141, *first time living alone*). Robin Green (2005), *Divorce: When It's the Only Answer* .

[2](p. 142, *Bobby Bare*). Bobby Bare (1980), "I've never gone to bed with an ugly woman, but I've woke up with a few." *Drunk and Crazy*.

[3](p. 145, *cognitive errors associated with depression*). Adapted from R. Rook (2007), *Cognitive Behavioral Therapy with Long Term Care Patients*, personal communication.

[4](p. 146, *competition where everyone is above average*). G. Keillor (2007), *A Prairie Home Companion*.

[5](p.148, *hobbies*). Find citation for no pastime leads to death, or delete the comment.

[6](p. 153, *male depression*). For more on male depression, see Terence Real *I Don't Want to Talk about It: Overcoming the Secret Legacy of Male Depression* (1997).

[7](p. 154, *women cry*). Radio talk show host Dr. Laura Schlessinger (2006) reinforces the male/female difference in handling depression in *The Proper Care & Feeding of Husbands*.

[8](p. 154, *socialization of depression*). See John Lynch and Christopher Kilmartin's (1999), *The Pain Behind the Mask: Overcoming Masculine Depression*.

CHAPTER 8

[1](p. 160, *drumming*). Two key writers on men's issues, Robert Bly (2004), in *Iron John* and S. Keen (1992), in *Fire in the Belly: On Being a Man* have noted that masculinity seems less valued in modern societies than it has been in native cultures. They advocate men finding ways to celebrate masculinity.

[2](p. 160, *modern masculinity*). Again, an exceptional starting place for those interested in the modern societal notion of masculinity is S. Keen's (1992), *Fire in the Belly: On Being a Man*.

[3](p. 163, *The Bob Newhart Show*). See The Bob Newhart Show (2005), 20th Century Fox.

CHAPTER 10

[1](p. 194-195, *Maslow's Hierarchy of Needs*). Maslow's foundational ideas have been applied, with reliability, across the board for decades. To check out his original presentation on the topic, see A. H. Maslow's (1943), *A theory of human motivation*. **Psychological Review**, 50. 370-396.

[2](p. 199, *examining feelings of sexual inadequacy*). With the advent of the Internet, there is lots of inaccurate trash regarding male sexuality. Some excellent, reliable and well-researche sources on male sexuality are D. Dumas' (1997), *Sons, Lovers, & Fathers: Understanding Male Sexuality*; D. Saul's (1999), *Sex For Life: The Lover's Guide To Male Sexuality*; B. Zilbergeld's (1999), *The New Male Sexuality*.

[3](p. 208, *Mary Ainsworth's attachment theory*). M. Ainsworth (1978), *Patterns on Attachment: A Psychological Study of the Strange Situation.*

[4](p. 213, *dating a married woman*). See research by Lusterman (1998), *Infidelity: A Survival Guide*; A. Spring (1997), *After the Affair: Healing the Pain and Rebuilding Trust When a Partner Has Been Unfaithful.*

CHAPTER 11

[1](p. 219, *personality theorists*). "Lovers, fighters and withdrawers" are based upon the personality theory of Karen Horney, who used the terms "moving toward," "moving agains," and "moving away from."

[2](p. 236, *Jimmy Soul*). Jimmy Soul (1994) "If you wanna be happy the rest of your life, be sure that you marry an ugly wife," *The Best of Jimmy Soul*. Ace Records.

[3](p. 237, *The Moral Animal*). See Robert Wright's (1994) perceptive book *The Moral Animal.*

Chapter 13

[1](p. 257, *sexual cycle*). W. H. Masters and V. E. Johnson (1966), *Human Sexual Response.*

[2](p. 262, *desire Phase*). Helen Singer Kaplan (1974), *The New Sex Therapy.*

Chapter 15

[1](p. 283, *remarriage statistics*). For more information on remarriage statistics, see Center for Disease Control (2002), *Cohabitation, Marriage, Divorce, and Remarriage in the United States*; Margulies (2004), *A Man's Guide to a Civilized Divorce: How to Divorce with Grace, a Little Class, and a Lot of Common Sense*; and also check out www.Divorceinfo.com.

[2](p. 286, *second marriages*). See M. Weiner-Davis (2001), *The Divorce Remedy.*

[3](p. 288, *younger woman*). See Center for Disease Control (2002), *Cohabitation, Marriage, Divorce, and Remarriage in the United States.*

[4](p. 288, *your relationship*). S. Stanley (2000) and his coauthors note that despite statisical probabilities, no one can confidently predict what will happen with YOUR relationship, in *Structural Flaws in the Bridge from Basic Research on Marriage to Interventions for Couples.*

[5](p. 293, *living together*). For compelling review of research on cohabitation, see S. Janus & C. Janus (1993), *The Janus Report on Human Sexuality*; J. Trussel & K. Rao (1987), *Premarital Cohabitation and Marital Stability,* and again, The Center for Disease Control (2002, *Cohabitation, Marriage, Divorce, and Remarriage in the United States.*

CHAPTER 16

[1](p. 301, *remarriage chances*). If you are interested in taking a closer look at remarriage statistics for both men and women, each of the following are excellent places to start, each with a slightly different slant: C. Ahrons & R. Rodgers (1987), *Divorced Families: Meeting the Challenge of Divorce and Remarriage*; M. Margulies (2004), *A Man's Guide to a Civilized Divorce: How to Divorce with Grace, a Little Class, and a Lot of Common Sense*; Center for Disease Control (2002), *National Survey of Family Growth Data Bank.* In general, fewer women than men remarry, women are slower to remary, and men generally marry younger women.

[2](p. 304, *wedding memories*). John Gottman has done interesting research on the role of wedding memories in predicting marital success (see his (1994) *What Predicts Divorce?).*

[4](p. 316, *stepfamily loss*). See J. Bray & J. Kelly's (1998), *Stepfamilies: Love, Marriage, and Parenting in the First Decade.*

[5](p. 322, *double divorce*). Article on double divorce reprinted by permission, Houston Chronicle Publishing Company Division, Hearst Newspapers Partnership, L.p. Houston Chronicle, 04/03/2008, Section: A,Page: 2.Edition: 3 STAR R.O. "THAT'S ODD"

EPILOGUE

[1](p. 323, Robert Sternberg). In his writings from 1986-1988, psychologist Robert Sternberg developed a theory of love, involving three components [*see* R. Sternberg & K. Weis (2006), *The New Psychology of Love].* Termed the Triangular Theory of Love, the vertices (corners) contain the elements of Intimacy, Commitment, and Passion. An equal balance among the three components leads to an equilateral triangle. His term for such a balanced relationship is Consummate Love, the cultural ideal. If only one or two of these elements predominates, the triangle is not equilateral.

ANNOTATED BIBLIOGRAPHY

If you want to know about other men who have experienced divorce, read:

Kaganoff, P. & Spano, S, (1997). *Men on Divorce: The Other Side of the Story.* San Diego, CA: Harvest.

A series of essays by men who describe their own experiences with divorce.

If you think divorce will "destroy" the kids, read:

Ahrons, C. (1994). *The Good Divorce: Keeping Your Family Together When Your Marriage Comes Apart.* New York, NY: HarperPerennial.

Research based, it is a good counterweight to the predictions that divorce is always harmful to children.

If you think that kids generally aren't that negatively affected by divorce, read:

Wallerstein, J. (2000). *The Unexpected Legacy of Divorce: A 25 Year Landmark* Study. Hyperion.

The counterweight to Ahron's book (cited above), psychologist Wallerstein is much more negative about the effects of divorce on kids.

If you want to avoid a custody battle, check out:

Kramer vs. Kramer (1979).

Dustin Hoffman and Meryl Streep give a riveting and realistic portrayal of a couple engaged in a bitter custody battle. Don't repeat their mistakes.

If you want a more positive view of how parents can work together after divorce, check out:

Life as a House

A divorced couple work together to redeem a son who is headed in the wrong direction.

If you want more internet resources on divorce, take a look at:

www.divorcedirectory.com

Provides listings, descriptions, and link to many internet resources on divorce.
AND/OR

Divorcemagazine.com

An on-line magazine with area specific resources.

If you want the kids to read about divorce, we recommend:

Ages 3-7:

Brown, K., & Brown, M. (1986). *Dinosaur's Divorce: A Guide for Changing Families*. Boston, MA: Atlantic Monthly.

Lansky, V. (1999). *It's Not Your Fault, Koko Bear*. Minnetonka, MN: Book Peddlers.

Ransom, J. F. & Finney, K. K. (2000). *I Don't Want to Talk About It*. Washington, D.C.: Magination Press.

Schotter, R. (2002). *Missing Rabbit*. New York, NY: Clarion.
  A good story for children who go "back and forth" between two homes.

Ages 8-12:

Heegaard, M. (1991). *When Mom and Dad Separate*. Minneapolis, MN: Woodland Press.

Rogers, F. (1996). *Let's Talk about It: Divorce*. New York, NY: Putnam.
  Mr. Rogers offers calm, caring advice to children on divorce.)

Ages: 13-18:

Brogan, H., & Maiden, U. (1986). *The Kids' Guide to Divorce*. New York, NY: Fawcett Crest.

If you would like to use a video to explain divorce to kids, we recommend:

Loughhead, S. & McGhee, C. *Lemons 2 Lemonade: How to Handle Life When Things Go Sour Between Mom and Dad*.
  Written and produced by two divorce experts, this entertaining and informative 45-minute program features children and adults talking in child-level language about divorce. A workbook is available to go along with the video.

If you are worried about parental alienation, read:

Gardner, R.A. (1998). *The Parental Alienation Syndrome*, 2nd Ed. Creative Therapeutics.
  His was the first book in the field, and it remains one of the best.

If you are trying to make the marriage work, read:

Gottman, J. & Silver, N. (1999) *The Seven Principles for Making Marriage Work*. New York: Three Rivers Press.
  Research based, it is our favorite book on how to repair a broken marriage.
  AND/OR

McGraw, P. C. (2000). *Relationship Rescue: A Seven-Step Strategy for Reconnecting with Your Partner*. New York: Hyperion.
  A gritty, no-nonsense approach to making your marriage better from TV's Dr. Phil.

If you think you might be depressed, read:

Lynch, J. & Kilmartin, C. (1999). *The Pain Behind the Mask: Overcoming Masculine Depression*. New York: Haworth.
  AND/OR

Real, T. (1997). *I Don't Want to Talk About It: Overcoming the Secret Legacy of Male Depression*. New York: Scribner.
  Two good books to help you understand about male depression.

If you have an anger problem, read:

Hightower, N. (2002). *Anger Busting 101: New ABC's for Angry Men and the Women Who Love Them*. Houston, TX: Bayou Publishing.
Practical, looks at anger as an addictive process.

If you want to see how miserable you can make yourself and your ex, check out:

The War of the Roses.
Michael Douglas and Kathleen Turner make war on each other before, during, and after divorce with deadly consequences.

If you want to understand more about men and masculinity, read:

Keen, S. (1992). *Fire in the Belly: On Being a Man*. New York: Bantam Books.
A classic, it will make you think more about your own life.

If there has been infidelity in your marriage, read:

Lusterman, D. (1998). *Infidelity: A Survival Guide*. Oakland, CA: New Harbinger.
Helpful in recovering from infidelity, regardless of whether or not you stay together.
AND/OR

Spring, J. A. (1997). *After The Affair: Healing the Pain and Rebuilding Trust When a Partner Has Been Unfaithful*. New York: Harper Perennial.
Maybe the best book on the subject, but sometimes criticized for not being tough enough on the unfaithful partner.

If you are currently going through a divorce and you are concerned about the legal process, read:

Margulies, S. (2004). *A Man's Guide to a Civilized Divorce: How to Divorce with Grace, a Little Class, and a Lot of Common Sense*. Emmaus, PA: Rodale.
Written by a divorce mediator, it is very helpful as you go through the actual divorce.
AND/OR

Shenkman, M. & Hamilton, M. (2000). *Divorce Rules for Men: A Man to Man Guide for Managing Your Split and Saving Thousands*. New York: Wiley
More focused on the economic side of divorce.

If you are trying to select a divorce attorney, read:

Sperling, P. (2003) *Selecting Your Divorce Lawyer*. Legal Guide Publishers.
Good tips on what to look for and what to avoid in hiring a family attorney.

If you are trying to avoid going through a divorce, read:

Weiner-Davis, M. (2001). *The Divorce Remedy: The Proven Seven-Step Program for Saving Your Marriage*. New York: Simon and Schuster:
Her "divorce-busting" approach has been widely popularized.

If you are thinking of marrying your ex-wife, look at:

Divorceinfo.com/remarriageeachother
A nice article with provocative ideas. Their general website (Divorceinfo. Com) has useful information about various aspects of divorce.

If you have questions about sexuality, read:

Zilbergeld, B. (1999). *The New Male Sexuality*, Revised ed. New York: Bantam:
The authoritative source about male sexuality.

If you are trying to improve the sexuality in your relationship, read:

Schnarch, D. (1997). *Passionate Marriage: Keeping Love and Intimacy Alive in Committed Relationships*. New York: Owl Books.

Not a how to book, rather it is about integrating emotional and sexual intimacy.

If you are going to be in a blended (step-family), read:

Bray, J. H. & Kelly, J. (1998). *Stepfamilies: Love, Marriage, and Parenting in the First Decade*. New York: Broadway Books.

Based on a 10 year longitudinal study, this book presents research-based tips for success in step-parenting.

REFERENCES

BOOKS

Ahrons, C. (1994). *The Good Divorce: Keeping Your Family Together When Your Marriage Comes Apart*. New York, NY: HarperPerennial.

Ahrons, C. & Rodgers, R. (1987). *Divorced Families: Meeting the Challenge of Divorce and Remarriage*. New York, NY: Norton.

Ainsworth, M.D.S. (1978). *Patterns of Attachment: A Psychological Study of the Strange Situation* (Loose Leaf). Philadelphia, PA: Lawrence Erlbaum.

Amato, P. (2000). *The Consequences of Divorce for Adults and Children*. **Journal of Marriage and Family,** 62, 1269-1287.

Amato, P. & Keith, B. (1991). *Parental Divorce and Well-Being of Children: A Meta-Analysis*. **Psychological Bulletin,** 110 (1), 26-46.

Bare, B. (1980). *I've Never Gone to Bed with an Ugly Woman, But I've Woke Up With a Few*. **Drunk and Crazy**. Raven Records: RVCD-267 (07).

Bly, R. (2004). *Iron John: A Book about Men*. Cambridge, MA: De Capo Press.

Bray, J. H. & Kelly, J. (1998). *Stepfamilies: Love, Marriage, and Parenting in the First Decade*. New York, NY: Broadway Books.

Brogan, H., & Maiden, U. (1986). *The Kids' Guide to Divorce*. New York, NY: Fawcett Crest.

Brooks, G.R. & Good, G.E. (Eds.). (2001). *The New Handbook of Psychotherapy and Counseling with Men: A Comprehensive Guide to Settings, Problems, and Treatment Approaches*. San Francisco, CA: Jossey-Bass.

Brown, K., & Brown, M. (1986). *Dinosaur's Divorce: A Guide for Changing Families*. Boston, MA: Atlantic Monthly.

Brumley, J. P. (2004). *Divorce without Disaster: Collaborative Law in Texas*. Dallas, TX: PSG Books.

Center for Disease Control (2002). *Cohabitation, Marriage, Divorce, and Remarriage in the United States*.

Chethik, N. (2006). *Voicemale: What Husbands Really Think about Their Marriages, Their Wives, Sex, Housework, and Commitment*. New York, NY: Simon & Schuster.

Collaborative Law Institute of Texas (2006). *The Collaborative Professional's Guide to Developing a Parenting Plan*.

Cummings, E.M. & Davies, P. (1994). *Children and Marital Conflict: The Impact of Family Dispute and Resolution*. New York, NY: Guilford.

Cummings, E.M. & O'Reilly, A.W. (1997). *Fathers in Family Context: Effects of Marital Quality on Child Adjustment*. In M.E. Lamb (Ed.), *The Role of the Father in Child Development* (3rd. ed., pp. 49-65, 318-325). New York, NY: John Wiley.

Darnall, D. (1998). *Divorce Casualties: Protecting Your Children from Parental Alienation*. Taylor Trade Publishing.

Dumas, D. (1997). *Sons, Lovers, and Fathers: Understanding Male Sexuality*. Lanham, MD: Jason Aronson.

Emery, R. E. (2004). *The Truth about Children and Divorce*. New York, NY: Penguin Books.

Englar-Carlson, M. & Stevens, M. A. (Eds.) (2006). *In the Room with Men: A Casebook of Therapeutic Change*. Washington, DC: American Psychological Association.

Fergus, M. A., (2002). *A Different Kind of Divorce*. **Houston Chronicle, Sunday, February 10, 2002.** Houston, TX. [Mary Ann Fergus, A Different Kind of Divorce: As Ex-Spouses Focus on Happy Children "Happily Ever After" is What Happens When a Marriage Ends, Houston Chron., Feb. 10, 2001, Lifestyle, at 1, available at 2002 WL 3240754]

Gardner, R.A. (1998). *The Parental Alienation Syndrome*, 2nd. Ed. Cresskill, N.J.: Creative Therapeutics.

Gottman, J. (1994). *What Predicts Divorce?* Hillsdale, NJ: Erlbaum.

Gottman, J. & Silver, N. (1999). *The Seven Principles for Making Marriage Work*. New York, NY: Three Rivers Press.

Green, R. M. (2005). *Divorce: When It's the Only Answer*. Dallas, TX: Ordinary Mortals Guide.

Hays, R.J., Sutter, E., & McPherson, R. (2005). *Texas Law and the Practice of Psychology: A Sourcebook*. Housotn, TX: Bayou Publishing.

Hawkins, A.J., Marshall, C.M., & Allen, S.M. (1998). *The Orientation toward Domestic Labor Questionnaire: Exploring Dual-Earner Wives' Sense of Fairness about Family Work. Journal of Family Psychology*, 12, 244-258.

Heegaard, M. (1991). *When Mom and Dad Separate*. Minneapolis, MN: Woodland Press.

Hightower, N. (2002). *Anger Busting 101: New Abc's for Angry Men and the Women Who Love Them*. Houston, TX: Bayou Publishing.

Hochschild, A. (1997). *The Second Shift*. New York, NY: Avon.

Horney, K. (1964). *Collected Works of Karen Horney*, Vol 1. New York, NY: Norton.

Janus, S. S. & Janus, C. C. (1993). *The Janus Report on Human Sexuality*. New York, NY: Riley.

Kaganoff, P. & Spano, S, (1997). *Men on Divorce: The Other Side of the Story*. San Diego, CA: Harvest.

Kaplan, H. S. (1994).*The New Sex Therapy*. New York, NY: Brunner/Mazel.

Keen, S. (1992). *Fire in the Belly: On Being a Man*. New York, NY: Bantam Press.

Keillor, G. (2007). *A Prairie Home Companion: With Garrison Keillor*. American Public Media.

Kelly, J. (2000). *Children's Adjustment in Conflicted Marriages and Divorce: A Decade of Research*. Journal of the American Academy of Child and Adolescent Psychiatry, 963-973.

Lamb, M.E. & Kelly, J. B., (2001). *Using the Empirical Literature to Guide the Development of Parenting Plans for Young Children: A Rejoinder to Solomon and Biringen*. Family Courts Review, 39 (4), 365-371.

Lansky, V. (1999). *It's Not Your Fault, Koko Bear*. Minnetonka, MN: Book Peddlers.

Levant, R.F. (1995). T*oward the Reconstruction of Masculinity*. In R.F. Levant & W.S. Pollack (Eds.), *A New Psychology of Men* (pp. 229-251). New York, NY: Basic Books.

Lipman, R. (2007). *Divorce Still Possible, Even if Money's Tight*. Houston Chronicle, Monday, December 24, 2007.

Loughhead, S. & McGhee, C. *Lemons 2 Lemonade: How to Handle Life When Things Go Sour Between Mom and Dad*. Available at Lemons2lemonade.com.

Lusterman, D. (1998). *Infidelity: A Survival Guide*. Oakland, CA: New Harbinger.

Lynch, J. & Kilmartin, C. (1999). *The Pain Behind the Mask: Overcoming Masculine Depression*. New York, NY: Haworth.

Maclaine, S. (1975). *The Other Half of the Sky: A China Memoir*. Shirley Maclaine Productions

Margulies, S. (2004). *A Man's Guide to a Civilized Divorce: How to Divorce with Grace, a Little Class, and a Lot of Common Sense*. Emmaus, PA: Rodale.

Maslow, A.H. (1943). *A Theory of Human Motivation*. **Psychological Review**, 50. 370-396.

Masters, W. H. & Johnson, V.E. (1966). *Human Sexual Response*. Boston, MA: Little-Brown.

McGraw, P. C. (2000). *Relationship Rescue: A Seven-Step Strategy for Reconnecting with Your Partner*. New York, NY: Hyperion.

McLanahan, S. S. (1999). *Father Absence and Children's Welfare*. In **Coping with Divorce, Single Parenting, and Re-Marriage: A Risk and Resiliency Perspective**. Hetherington, E. M. ed, Mahway, NJ: Erlbaum.

Penningroth, P., & Penningroth, B. (2001). *A Healing Divorce: Transforming the End of Your Relationship with Ritual and Ceremony*. Author House.

Rabinowitz, F. E. & Cochran, S.V. (2002). *Deepening Psychotherapy with Men*. Washington, D.C: American Psychological Association.

Ransom, J. F. & Finney, K. K. (2000). *I Don't Want to Talk About It*. Washington, DC: Magination Press.

Real, T. (1997). *I Don't Want to Talk About It: Overcoming the Secret Legacy of Male Depression*. New York, NY: Scribner.

Rogers, F. (1996). *Let's Talk about It: Divorce*. New York, NY: Putnam.

Rook, R. (2007). *Cognitive Behavioral Therapy with Long Term Care Patients*. Personal Communication.

Saul, D. (1999). *Sex for Life: The Lover's Guide to Male Sexuality*. Ferndale, WA: Apple.

Schlessinger, L. (2006). *The Proper Care and Feeding of Husbands*. New York, NY: Harper.

Schnarch, D. (1997). *Passionate Marriage: Keeping Love and Intimacy Alive in Committed Relationships*. New York. NY: Owl Books.

Schotter, R. (2002). *Missing Rabbit*. New York, NY: Clarion.

Shenkman, M. & Hamilton, M. (2000). *Divorce Rules for Men: A Man to Man Guide for Managing Your Split and Saving Thousands*. New York, NY: Wiley.

Soul, J. (1994). *If You Wanna Be Happy.* **The Best of Jimmy Soul.** Ace Records.

Sperling, P. (2003) *Selecting Your Divorce Lawyer.* Houston, TX: Legal Guide Publishers.

Spring, J. A. (1997). *After The Affair: Healing The Pain And Rebuilding Trust When A Partner Has Been Unfaithful.* New York, NY: Harper Perennial.

Stanley, S.M., Bradbury, T.N., & Markman, H.J. (2000). *Structural Flaws in the Bridge from Basic Research on Marriage to Interventions for Couples: Illustrations from Gottman, Coan, Carrere, and Swanson (1998).* **Journal of Marriage and the Family,** 62, (1), 256-264.

Sternberg, R. J. & Weis, K. (2006). *The New Psychology of Love.* New Haven, CT: Yale University Press.

Trussel, J. & Rao, K. U. (1987). *Premarital Cohabitation and Marital Stability: A Reassessment of the Canadian Evidence.* **Journal of Marriage and the Family,** 51, 535-544.

Vessey, J.T., & Howard, K.I. (1993). *Who Seeks Psychotherapy?* **Psychotherapy,** 30, 546-553.

Wallerstein, J. S., Lewis, J. M., Blakeslee, & Lewis, J. (2000). *The Unexpected Legacy of Divorce: A 25 Year Landmark Study.* New York, NY: Hyperion.

Wester, S.R., Vogel, D.L., Pressly, P.K., & Heesacker, M. (2002). *Sex Differences in Emotion: A Critical Review of the Literature and Implications for Counseling Psychology.* **The Counseling Psychologist,** 30, 630-652.

Weiner-Davis, M. (1992). *Divorce-Busting.* New York, NY: Summit Books.

Weiner-Davis, M. (2001). *The Divorce Remedy: The Proven Seven-Step Program For Saving Your Marriage.* New York, NY: Simon and Schuster:

Wright, R. (1994). *The Moral Animal: Evolutionary Psychology and Everyday Life.* New York, NY: Vintage

Zilbergeld, B. (1999). *The New Male Sexuality,* Revised ed. New York, NY: Bantam.

Movies

The Bob Newhart Show. (1995). 20th Century Fox Television.

Kramer vs. Kramer. (1979). Sony Studios. *Life as a House.* (2002). New Line Home Video.

The Parent Trap. (1998). Disney.

War of the Roses. (1989). 20th Century Fox.

The Mankind Project. (2007). *The New Warrior Training Adventure.* Malone, N.Y.

WEBSITES

Waking the Passion (2007). Wakingthepassion.com.

Million Man March (2006). Chicago, Ill.

Divorceinfo.com

SOFTWARE

Microsoft. (2007). Microsoft Money.

Intuit. (2007) Quicken.

·

INDEX

ABOUT THE AUTHORS

Sam J. Buser, Ph.D. is past-president of the Texas Psychological Association. He is also a member of the American Psychological Association's Division 51 (Society for the Psychological Study of Men and Masculinity) and has specialized in treating men for more that 15 years. Dr. Buser is an adjunct faculty member of the Counseling Psychology Program at the University of Houston teaching graduate courses in marital and family therapy.

Dr. Buser has appeared on the nationally syndicated Montell Williams Show, and has frequently appeared on local radio and television programs as an expert on a variety of psychological topics. A veteran himself, Dr. Buser previously worked for many years doing family therapy in VA Medical Hospital. He is very familiar with the particular problems and sensibilities of men from all walks of life.

Glenn F. Sternes, Ph.D., is an expert in the field of interpersonal relationships, men's issues and human sexuality. He teaches graduate courses on the subjects and maintains a clinical practice in the Houston Area. He frequently presents at local, state, and national conferences. He has edited college-level texts in human sexuality and marriage and the family, and co-authored the accompanying instructor's and student's manuals. He has served as the book reviewer for the Houston Post. He is a member of the American Psycholocial Association, the Texas Psychological Association, and the Houston Psychological Association, and served on the HPA Board of Trustees.

Please visit Sam and Glenn at www.GuysOnlyGuides.com.

ORDERING INFORMATION

Additional copies of *The Guys-Only Guide to Getting over Divorce and on with Life, Sex, and Relationships* from the publisher. Orders may be placed by phone, by mail, by FAX, or directly on the web. Purchase orders from institutions are welcome.

- ❏ *To order by mail:* Complete this order form and mail it (along with check or credit card information) to Bayou Publishing, 2524 Nottingham, Houston, TX 77005-1412.

- ❏ *To order by phone:* Call (800) 340-2034.

- ❏ *To order by FAX:* Fill out this order form (including credit card information) and fax to (713) 526-4342.

- ❏ *To place a secure online order:* Visit http://www.bayoupublishing.com.

Name: _____

Address: _____

_____

City: _____ ST: ___ Zip: _____

Ph: _____

FAX: _____

E-mail: _____

❏ VISA ❏ MasterCard ❏ American Express ❏ Discover

Charge Card #: _____

Expiration Date: _____

Signature: _____

Please send me ____ copies at $16.95 each _____

Sales Tax 8.25%(Texas residents) _____

plus $4.50 postage and handling *(per order)* _____$4.50

Total $ _____

Bayou Publishing
2524 Nottingham, Suite 150
Houston, TX 77005-1412
Ph: (713) 526-4558/ FAX: (713) 526-4342
Orders: (800) 340-2034
http://www.bayoupublishing.com